M000096797

From: "Conflicting Feelings" By John Newton

Strange and mysterious is my life.
What opposites I feel within!
A stable peace, a constant strife;
The rule of grace, the power of sin:
Too often I am captive led,
Yet daily triumph in my head.

This book is dedicated to:

My husband, LeRoy, and my sons, Matthew and Daniel. To my daughter-in-law, Cheryl and my grandbabies, Maya and Gage: You inspire me to reach for a higher purpose in life. You are my joy.

FAR TOO SIMPLE A WISH

FAR TOO SIMPLE A WISH

By JoAnn Skinner
With Daniel E. Skinner

MILL CITY PRESS

Mill City Press, Inc.
2301 Lucien Way #415
Maitland, FL 32751
407.339.4217
www.millcitypress.net

© 2020 by JoAnn Skinner

All rights reserved solely by the author. The author guarantees all contents are original and do not infringe upon the legal rights of any other person or work. No part of this book may be reproduced in any form without the permission of the author. The views expressed in this book are not necessarily those of the publisher.

Printed in the United States of America.

Paperback ISBN-13: 978-1-6312-9580-5
E-Book ISBN-13: 978-1-6312-9581-2
Library of Congress Control Number: 2020910363

TABLE OF CONTENTS

TRUTH: THE GREAT STABILIZER

The greatest obstacle I've had to overcome thus far in my life is the hatred I felt for my mother. There, I said it. I'm not proud to admit that the woman who gave birth to me was the very person I feared and despised growing up. She wasn't my only heartache, just my constant. I also had to contend with an alcoholic father. I was too young to envision what life had in store for me and too inept to defend myself from my mother. Nothing could stop her rage-driven beatings and incessant belittling from piling one on top of the other until my childhood played out. By the time I turned seventeen, Mom's cruel and erratic behavior erupted into a full-blown nervous breakdown that manifested into mental illness. This, in turn, spilled into my adult life and altered my perception of my true self. I became obsessed by an irrational fear that I, too, could easily lose my mind just as Mom did.

Until I could come to terms with the inner conflict between my heart and head, my perception of Mom and my life would continue to collide and torment me. *How do you escape from a painful past?* I somehow had to find a way to fix our broken relationship, even if it meant living with Mom's one-sided bias. I knew not to put all the blame on Mom for it seldom is solely one person's fault, so I made my mission to be one of truth. *The truth according to JoAnn, that is.*

Something good had to emerge from our relationship or else my life would evolve into a never-ending, whining, miserable pity party spiraling downward. I struggled for the courage needed to sift through all the painful episodes that kept me bogged down with sadness. Though I hadn't mastered my insecurities, I was determined the cycle of abuse I experienced would not be rekindled through me. I wonder, *"Is truth the great stabilizer in life or merely an illusion to comfort my own flawed insight?"*

I can't gloss over or deny what happened to me. I've seen and heard things growing up I wish I could erase from my mind–hurtful things I will never forget. But I have also been blessed with common sense and reason, so in an attempt to connect with my parents' lives, I first needed to understand the conditions in which they were raised. I realize there isn't an instruction book for any of us to read on how to raise a happy (I can't say perfect-one doesn't exist) family, but I know we all could use one. I wished my parents had had such a book. They seemed to earnestly try to do right by us, though somewhere along the way, their lives took copious wrong turns as their view of life became woefully distorted.

By choosing to embrace my parents' shortcomings in an honest manner, I hoped all the dissension that I had bottled up would subside. If I could resurrect some good from my upbringing, only then would I feel justified in spilling my guts and exposing my family's dirty laundry. Mom often said, "Don't let people fool you; they've all got dirty laundry."

The idea of writing had always been in the back of my mind. I heard writing could be therapeutic for defusing pain so I began jotting down my memories so I wouldn't forget them, only I wasn't very disciplined. I didn't have a clear grasp of my true intent due to my lack of self-esteem, *whatever the hell that is*; however, my inner voice kept nagging me to keep writing.

Why did I feel compelled to write down such personal and hurtful secrets? Was it to convey to the world how malicious Mother was to my siblings and me? Was I trying to get even for all the pain she inflicted on me or simply wanting to move on from it all? God knows I couldn't stand up for myself growing up. Could this be my way of finally being heard? I felt obligated to publicly denounce my parents and apologize for their shameful conduct. And by doing so, I received validation and acceptance from people that could not possibly understand the insanity that went on in my life.

It's a shared belief that learning about other people's experiences can help you cope. I tried to stay on track by reading self-help books and memoirs. I was amazed how my life and opinions mirrored other writers. I felt connected emotionally even though we all had endured different layers of abuse; some not as hurtful and some more so. By sorting out my feelings and working through my pain, maybe the shadowed sadness would diminish. Learning how to forgive and move forward seems to be the common thread that most people struggle with. *Come on, JoAnn, try. What makes you think your narrative is any less important than any other person's story? Stop believing that other people are better than you are. Quit seeing yourself as damaged.*

I mustered up the courage and enrolled in a writing course offered at the local college. I wasn't comfortable tackling "my battles with Mom" or "Dad's liquor woes" just yet so I chose to write about my dad's father. My thoughts flowed with ease in spite of the fact I hardly knew anything about him. As I read my story out loud, the class responded with "Ahh." My teacher, Mrs. Estes, notated on my paper that I had wonderful ideas, and thanks to her, a seed of confidence was planted. However,

I worked full-time and had put my project on hold for so long that I misplaced most of my notes. Life had its way of spinning past, allowing little time for personal projects. Sorting through all the emotional crap was much harder than I anticipated. I leaned on the excuse of being a terrible speller and no college education, but the truth was, family episodes were still unfolding with no end in sight.

After Mom and Dad died, there was nothing more standing in my way, just the daunting task of sorting out all the drama. I rationalized, what harm could their be in writing down my thoughts, even if I never did anything but lay them in a desk drawer. If writing is a true form of therapy, it could just be my salvation. I needed validation in my life and writing was the only way I knew how to level the playing field. I naively convinced myself it had become vogue to keep a journal. But I realized that if I wrote down my secrets, I couldn't take them back. Once you see your words in black and white, reality sets in. I had to keep reminding myself this doesn't have to be a painful process, just an honest one. Much to my surprise, the process proved extremely painful as well as liberating.

Life's journey leaves many scars, and most of my scars are remnants of how I was treated by my mother throughout my formative years. I may not be correct on some of the dates or have the events in proper sequence, especially in the darkest period. Still, above all else, I must be true to myself. I wrote as I remembered things, not from my siblings' recollection but from my own. The time has come; like my Dad always said, "Shit, or get off the pot."

ROOTS RUN FAR AND DEEP: MOM & DAD'S EARLY YEARS

Mom, named Charlotte Sarah Madaline Alamia, was born and raised in New York City in 1929. Regrettably, I don't know much about Mom's side of the family. She chose to keep most of her memories to herself. Mom never spoke an unkind word about her mother. What little she shared convinced me she dearly loved her. But each memory ended in deep sorrow as Mom recounted all the abuse her mother endured in their home. Her mother, Carlotta Levy, came from England in the early 1900's. She became widowed at a young age so I never knew if Levy was her maiden or married name. She needed to support herself and her son, Willie, so she worked as a housekeeper for my grandfather, Salvatore Alamia. Carlotta and Salvatore later married and four children were added to their family; two boys and two girls.

On the other hand, Mom never stopped obsessing about how much she detested her father, a Sicilian immigrant, malicious and unapproachable to say the least. Growing up, her father revered his sons and displayed disdain for his daughters. He controlled his wife through intimidation and a deplorable temper that he shamefully brought to bear upon his family. Mom said her mother tried to keep the peace by deftly concealing things she knew would send him into a rage while unconvincingly making excuses for his behavior. Mom perceived her mother as weak for not standing up for herself or her children. This left Mom feeling betrayed. But that's just the way it was in the twenties and thirties; a woman stood by her husband and accepted her fate while the children came second.

At the age of fifteen, Mom's life would take a dramatic turn. Her father kicked her out of his house with a denouncing roar, "You're nothing but a goddamn whore. Time you were on your own, so don't expect even a nickel from me." She had no choice but to drop out of school and move in with her older sister, Kay, brother-in-law, and their baby in New Haven, Connecticut.

Within several weeks of Mom's leaving home, their mother was admitted into the hospital and died four days later. She was in her early fifties but suffered from diabetes, high blood pressure, obesity, and heart problems. Their father didn't call Mom or Kay to tell them their mother had fallen ill, therefore they never got a chance to reconcile any grievances or say their final goodbyes.

Trying to make sense of her mother's sudden death provoked a tremendous amount of confusion and anger within Mom. Though Mom was raised Catholic, she wasn't as devout as her mother. Mom questioned many of the Church's beliefs and struggled with *why* God would take her devoted mother (the good one) so suddenly from this earth and leave her callous father (the son of a bitch), that had caused most of the misery in their lives. Her father's failure to disclose their mother's illness would be the last malicious act Mom endured from him. She truly hated him.

Mom felt like an intruder in her sister's home, but until she could get on her feet, she was at Kay's mercy. Each viewed life differently. I assumed their ten-year age difference, personalities, and Mom's appetite for wanting to go out and enjoy herself played a role in their tiffs. She described Kay as penny-pinching, bossy, and curt, yet she was one of the few people Mom expressed a sincere love for. They all struggled to make ends meet, so Mom decided it was time she made her own way. She got a job in a factory making various gadgets for the war and rented a room at the YWCA. Mom said the first two weeks were surreal. Until she received her first pay check, she could only afford one jar of peanut butter, reducing each meal to one tablespoon for breakfast and one tablespoon for dinner. How shameful to be kicked out of your home, with no choice except to move to a new city, and forced to support herself, all the while, grieving the loss of her mother at such a pivotal time in her life. *Could the immense trauma from the many changes have been the birth of Mom's mental illness?*

I studied an old photograph of Mom's parents hoping to feel a connection between our heritage but sadly, my curiosity came too late. I felt only a void. The fact that Mom never displayed her parents' picture in our home or shared more about her family was an enigma. Mom had a photograph book of black and white snapshots of her brother Sal, and girlfriends with herself, however, the pictures weren't dated nor were many of the people identified. Only their fashions and the scenery chronicled their existence. Most of the pictures were taken around the time she was living on her own and dating Dad. The camera captured in some of the snapshots Mom's beautiful smile that revealed glimpses of a happier life; even if it only lasted for a brief time. I would occasionally catch Mom looking through her album, but regrettably she tucked it away and set it apart from her present life. Mom detached herself from the people around her and she wouldn't divulge her true self.

On a rare occasion in the summer of '75, I learned a little about Mom's family when her older brother, Tony, who lived in California, came to visit us. He explained the reason why Grandpa came to America and his narrative astonished me. Mom barely spoke about her father's life except to say that he came from Sicily at the turn of the century and had a malicious temperament and a bitter attitude towards everyone. Since she painted my grandfather as such a monster, I had no desire to know him. I'm sorry to say, my uncle did not mention anything about my grandmother. She died so young, perhaps no one had the chance to really know her.

Here is a quick down and dirty scenario of Uncle Tony's version, and even though it was quite an eye opener, it would be the only time I heard the story. I have no way of verifying the events and due to the passing of years I have probably done an injustice to the truth-but this is all I had to unlock Mom's family secrets.

As his story went, Salvatore lived in Carini, Sicily in the early 1900's with his parents and only sibling, an older sister whose name was never spoken. Uncle Tony painted the picture of my great grandparents being wealthy. They owned a large amount of land and an enormous villa with tall marble columns on the front and scattered cottages in the back for the workers. They exported figs and lemons to the United States, however, my younger sister, Kathy, recalls olives as the exported product. This is what I mean; too much time had passed for accurate details to be confirmed, plus everyone involved is deceased. As the story goes, Grandpa's sister earned the title "Madam" of a bordello in their village. She brought dishonor to the family while inflicting shame upon her brother. Salvatore left his birthplace for America and arrived at Ellis Island in July, 1911, at the age of nineteen.

It was only after Mom's death that I learned Uncle Tony attempted for many years to find out what became of their father's home in Sicily. Up until his own death, Uncle Tony tried to track down records of the villa but kept running into obstacles. The most he could uncover through rumor was that the villa had been taken over by Mussolini's regime during World War II. With records lost, memories silenced, and relations deceased there wasn't a way to validate the truth, creating an enigma with more questions than answers. If there could be any new information to surface, it had already been buried by the passing of time. What a fascinating story to an outsider, but for the ones involved, it only held heartache. That may explain why Grandpa was bitter and displayed no compassion toward his own family.

I hardly knew anything about Dad's parents except that they were originally from Orangeburg, South Carolina. How they met, or why they settled in Augusta, Georgia was never talked about.

My memories of my Dad's father are few. I knew him as a quiet man who had worked at a mill and enjoyed hunting, but farming was their lean on source of existence. I overheard that in Granddad's younger days he and several other relatives dabbled in bootlegging moonshine.

Granddad over time relied on a wooden cane for support. I saw it as an extended part of his right arm that he would shake at anyone who crossed him. He wore a dingy gray fedora that kept part of his face hidden, and the exposed part was three days past a shave. I would find Granddad sitting under a huge chinaberry tree, grumbling about crops and the weather with the other family men, or barking orders to my grandma. He'd bellow, "Old woman, get movin' with my supper," or "Old woman, bring me my ale." Atlantic Ale was his brand of choice. He wasn't cruel, just demanding. Grandma didn't fret over his testy disposition or his indifference toward her. They had been married for over sixty years, long past the time of harboring hurt feelings. Sadly, I never witnessed either one of them showing affection towards each other; that would be considered foolishness. In their own routine, they connected.

Grandma lost several babies at birth but managed to raise five healthy boys and three girls. She worked hard in the cotton fields and canned vegetables from their garden which helped them get through many difficult times. She was a good cook, but it had to be a challenge to feed their large family. I recall Grandma's stern ways, but always kept a twinkle in her eye for all of her offspring, especially the young'uns that she lovingly nicknamed Pootie.

Grandma's only vice was dipping snuff. I'd find her on the back porch in her rocker, digging into her raggedy apron pocket for her can of Tops. With each craving, she'd unscrew the top, dip two fingers deep into the can and drew a heaping size full of the fine golden powder managing not to spill a speck. She then packed it against the inside of her cheek and waited for the flavor to release. Taking her gnarled hands, she unceremoniously began weaving her long kinky salt and pepper hair into one extensive braid. Next, she'd twist it into a bun, pin it to the back of her head, lean forward, and effortlessly spew a stream of brown juice at the spit can close to her chair. She almost always hit her mark. She'd end her satisfying ritual by wiping her mouth with the corner of her apron and whisper, "Do ya' wanna' try a little pinch, Pootie?" Its sweet earthy aroma mixed with a hint of cinnamon, orange, and exotic spices spiked my curiosity, but I was much too timid. "No Ma'am" was all I could utter before jumping off the porch to find something to explore.

Mom heard rumors that Grandma didn't have a father and that naturally gave cause for whispers back then. I've since learned that my grandma was part Pee Dee Indian; native to South Carolina. That explained her skin tone and high cheek bones. Dad never mentioned his ancestry, and the people who could shed any light are all deceased except for Aunt Jean, the last living sibling who is knowledgeable about our family tree. I approached her once with questions about Grandma, but I seemed to anger her for just asking. She curtly remarked, "I can't understand why everyone wants to dig up what went before." Just like with Mom's life, what one perceives as an interesting and colorful past, another views as too painful to share. Perhaps their wounds still bleed. But they're my family too, and finding out these tidbits about my relatives late in my life put me in a fevered pitch to trace my roots.

I made one last attempt to contact one of Dad's cousins, hoping he could shed some light on our relatives. Buford said, "If you'd called sooner, my cousin could've told you about em', but she since died." He shared what he knew but I realized we held two different versions that had been neglected by waning memories and indifference. I'm not the only person disconnected with their past. I think about orphans and the millions of families that were displaced or destroyed by natural disasters and wars. The truth is, none of us are here by our divine order, but only through past generations that have no control for their time and place on Earth. For whatever reasons people came together proved they did the best they knew how to, just by trying to survive. It took all their resources, whether it was Dad's people living off the land in the South or Mom's people crossing the Atlantic to carve out a new life in America. How they lived and whom ever they found comfort with should not be picked apart.

After talking to Buford, I realized most facts were forever lost. The sting of not knowing ended. Perhaps it was the heightened concealment that intrigued me, but they are dead and I'm here. As big as Dad's family was and as many family gatherings we attended, it would've been an honor to have learned of my lineage. Their lives should have been celebrated and their struggles acknowledged. I can only dance around the footprints that my relatives left behind.

Just because Dad grew up in the South didn't mean he led a charmed life as is sometimes perceived in Southern lore. He had his own woes to shoulder. Dad was a man of few words and hardly talked about his young days. The little bit he'd share left me with a feeling of sadness for him. I recall how vividly he described their poverty and what it felt like to go to bed with an empty stomach. Each time he recounted his childhood, he emphasized how hard his parents worked while doing their best to raise a large family, and make it through the aftermath of the Great Depression. He seemed grateful for what he had, though he realized it was a meager existence.

Dad shared with me once about how much he wanted a red wagon for Christmas. Each year, he'd ask for a wagon and when he turned thirteen, his wish finally came true. As he brought to light this part of his uneven childhood, he shook his head in a downward motion recounting his feeling of disappointment. That was all he said about the subject. The wagon had come too late. He must have felt slighted by life. Dad wasn't about to accept poverty for his future. So his survival instincts kicked in at an early age, and he developed a strong work ethic as well as a healthy dose of stubbornness, and a quick temper.

As a young boy, Dad had looked after himself by helping the farmer who lived down the road. Dad recounted, "A many a time I had nothin' to eat the entire day; unless you count a potato I dug straight from the field; just wipe off the dirt, sprinkle on some salt, eat it, then get back workin.'"

Dad believed a man was only as good as his word and he used the example of the time that farmer failed to keep his word. Dad was about thirteen when he began going to the downtown movie house that was about fifteen or so miles away. Each Saturday they featured an afternoon matinee filled with excitement and adventure for ten cents admission. Dad reflectively described how wrapped up he had become in the Western sequels. They kept him on the edge of his seat by creating an ending involving the fate of the hero, *the cliffhanger*. It enticed him back the following week to witness the hero emerge from the previous peril only to once again be caught up in a different yet equally harrowing scenario. This gave Dad something to look forward to, and he was determined not to miss a single episode. One Saturday, the farmer asked Dad for help in the fields; Dad reluctantly agreed, but only if they could be back in time for him to make the matinee. Well, they didn't make it back in time causing Dad to miss an episode. The farmer didn't intentionally mislead Dad; after all, his crops held more importance than a picture show. Dad allowed his stubborn pride to get the best of him and he never helped the farmer again.

After my grandparents died, I went with Dad to his parents' home for one last look. Inside their shed were shelves filled from top to bottom with jars of fruits and vegetables all canned by Grandma. I asked Dad why she continued to preserve so much food if she was the only one left at home. He affirmed, "If you had lived through The Depression, you'd make damn sure never to be without food again." I couldn't respond; his blunt vivid affirmation put all their struggles into perspective.

I pondered on my grandparents' simple life and I'd never known them to stray far from their home. Perhaps they simply had no desire to travel. Most of their family lived close by. Since I loved the beach, I wondered if they had ever experienced an ocean trip. Dad recounted the time his brother, Robert, drove them to Tybee Island, Georgia. I hoped that a fair share of happiness had been woven throughout their lives because all I recalled was two worn out, hard-working souls with duty, pride, and ailments as their only reward.

PRELUDE TO CIVIL WAR

I n 1946, Dad was drafted into the Navy and stationed in New Haven, Connecticut. Dad had never strayed far from his Georgia home until he received his draft notice. He was the typical handsome sailor out on the town. I can just imagine how the world exploded all around him, and he, with not an ounce of self-control. Dad was a true "good old Southern boy" who loved to flirt, smoke, drink, and have a good time. I bet he took advantage (too excess) of every liberty the big city had to offer.

It was in this very city in 1947, that Patrick Herbert Hoover and Charlotte Alamia met at a skating rink. Mom described Dad as drop dead gorgeous; a real "lady's man. Mom chuckled, "Pat (that's what Mom called him) was drunk, and off his feet more than he was on them!" He utilized his wavy brown hair, sparkling blue eyes, and his crisp, white Navy uniform to his advantage. Asserting his Southern charm, he bummed a pack of Pall Mall cigarettes to break the ice. Ironically, that's when she fell for the drunken rookie sailor.

They had an ongoing tease about who chased whom. When Mom told her rendition of their courtship, she donned a sheepish smile and a rosy shade of embarrassment. Dad would smirk, shake his head, but never disclosed his version of what first attracted him to Mom. Maybe, it was her petite frame, long jet-black hair, big brown eyes and olive skin. Could it possibly have been her feisty personality?

Mom was nineteen and Dad told her he was twenty-one, however she later found out he lied about his age and that he was actually nineteen; both being born in 1929. Adding insult to injury, she was older, by five weeks. While Dad was finishing his hitch in the Navy, Mom moved to Augusta, Georgia, with nothing more than two cotton dresses, a change of underwear, and her insecurity tightly tucked in her suitcase. Mom must have loved him deeply to make such an enormous leap into marriage. So began a new chapter in Mom's life that she frequently referred to as her *hell on earth*. Their whirlwind courtship was a mistake from the beginning, but it was *the everything in-between* that went wrong in their lives.

Mom couldn't acclimate to her new surroundings. It was a culture shock to say the least. Her opinionated views of the South hindered her ability to accept Southern ways, especially her new in-laws with their foreign language-a.k.a. Southern drawl. In fact, Mom didn't know much about Dad or his family, and he didn't know much about her as well. *Had they both made a hasty misguided mistake?*

She viewed all Southerners as hillbillies and perceived Dad's family as treating her different because she was a Yankee. Perhaps Dad been sweet on a hometown girl before being drafted and, if so, would she be waiting for his return? Was his family whispering behind her back, questioning their sudden romance? Had this Yankee gal tricked him into marriage? Was it even his child? Mom and Dad married on the first of February, 1947, and my sister, Rosemary Frances Hoover, bounced into the world, five pounds, two ounces, on the fifth of November, exactly nine months and four days after they officially said, "I do." Well, let's just say they all had fingers, and even Southerners can count. Mom affirmed to anyone in shouting distance that Rosemary was born premature. As far as Mom was concerned this should silence for good their lewd suspicions and wagging tongues about her trapping Pat.

I only heard Mom's version of each upsetting incident that happened to her when the "Damn Yankee" moved down South. *Holy shit, the North was invading the South once more.*

Everything from the climate, food, and living conditions disagreed with Mom. Southern heat and humidity are brutal even for those who've lived down South their entire lives. Morning sickness made her ill to her stomach while southern cuisine compounded to her nauseated misery. Fried chicken, fried fish, fatback, gravy, turnip greens, butter beans (all swimming in grease), mashed potatoes, homemade biscuits, cornbread, grits, macaroni and cheese, (all smothered in butter), sausage, eggs, bacon, and buttermilk were enough to make any person's stomach churn. It was a culture shock, to say the least.

They rented a three room house that was located right down the hill from Mom's in-laws. Mom callously referred to her new home as a *damn shack.* Mom, in her delicate condition, had to carry water from the well to her house several times a day. And if being introduced to an one-hole outhouse wasn't humiliating enough, it had to be shared with the entire clan. All Mom's misery spilled over onto Dad as she often threw in his face, "Just because my family lives in an apartment; we at least have indoor plumbing." But truth be known, there was only one bathroom located in the apartment's hallway that had to be shared with all the tenants that lived on the same floor. She never made the connection that they were equally as poor, just in a different environment. If Mom was going to split hairs, then she had to concede that at least Dad's parents owned their home and land; her dad had always rented on the third floor. The higher your apartment floor, the cheaper the rent. It wasn't until the early seventies that Dad's parents had indoor plumbing installed.

Mom never bit her tongue when it came to feelings of hostility towards her mother-in-law. Each morning, Grandma would let herself into their house unannounced and begin nosing around. When it came to privacy, my grandma proved to be a thorn in Mom's side. In the South, that's considered *being neighborly* and knowing Grandma, I'm sure she tried to make Mom feel like part of the family. She may have pitied her daughter-in-law as she generously tried to share her skills of cooking and raising *young'uns*. But Mom with her insecurity and jealousy, rejected her mother-in-law's hospitable hand. I can only imagine how different Mom's life could have been if she'd allowed Grandma to fill the void that was left by her mother, but that would never be. Perhaps Mom resented Dad for sending home money to help his mother while he was still enlisted. Or could their discord stem from whether Dad had betrayed Mom's trust by confiding in his mother about their early marriage woes? *Aren't everyone's in-laws enemies in disguise? Why else would their relationship turn sour so soon?*

Mom's rendition of the day she and her mother-in-law got into a horrendous fight grew more venomous with each recollection. Armed only with her temper and vulgar insults, Mom forewarned her, "Keep your goddamn nose out of our business, stop telling me how to raise my kid, and keep your goddamn ass at home unless you are invited." Mom's disrespect for Dad's mother didn't sit well with him and a quarrel rapidly heated. Mom, with no one on her side and nowhere to turn crossed the line by selfishly demanding Dad must choose between his hillbilly family or her and baby Rose. Dad would never turn his back on his parents, not even his sacred marriage vows would sway Dad from the loyalty he held for his mother.

The verbal fight intensified when Mom yelled out to Grandma, "I'll drag your damn big ass off your goddamn porch by your long kinky braid, and beat the shit out of you." The contention and the vulgar insults escalated to the point that Mom picked up a brick, threw it at her mother-in-law, and it cut her nose. Dad pushed Mom down and began to choke her. I don't know who stopped the fight but Mom, feeling trapped, called the police, and had Dad arrested. What a heartsick way to begin a new life. *Had this been the first time Dad witnessed Mom's mental illness emerge?*

It was apparent Mom disliked Dad's family early on, so a tug of war began in her mind over Dad's loyalty. Dad's family called him Herbert, but in the first of many defensive plays, Mom promptly established her hold by calling him Pat. Mom's feelings for Grandma never waned. As the years passed, the best Mom could do was tolerate her. Did my parents love each other in an immature yet self-centered way? Even if true, neither one of them could see that if things didn't change, their future together would run bleak.

Sadly, Mom's new life was nothing like she hoped it would be, and admittedly, she regretted she had traded one miserable dilemma for another. *Was she homesick?* It was no secret that Charlotte hated the South. Why didn't she move back North? Had Mom shared with her family her predicament and how miserable and trapped she felt? Why didn't Dad cut his losses and divorce her before any more of his life was consumed in misery?

To say the least, their marriage was explosive from the beginning. Times were tough enough for a newly married couple with an infant to care for, only to be burdened fifteen months later with my arrival, JoAnn Hoover. A second child unquestionably compounded their problems. They were poor and unhappy with two children in tow.

ALL IS
REVEALED VIA DEATH

You would be amazed at what gets uncovered through various means after someone's death. Relatives and old friends will intuitively indulge you with more than you bargained for by breathing new life into old pictures, distorted facts, and long kept family secrets that end with, "Oh honey, I'm sorry, you hadn't heard, I thought you knew." Or, "I had no idea someone hadn't told you. So much happened so long ago." When they called to check on how you were doing, were they being sincere or merely meddling? I wondered how many knew and exactly what they were really privy to. Either way they'd inadvertently supply you with another fragment of the puzzle. One piece here, then another piece, and soon the picture comes into focus. Putting the puzzle together after everyone involved has died is a hollow victory. Death randomly masks pitfalls and secrets from even the closest ones, and the answers to the *reasons why* are buried with their bones. You will never know the sum of someone's feelings, loves, dreams, regrets, or shame. We are born alone; will die alone, but in-between, we should live in a constant desire to be better, achieve more, learn and exhibit compassion for our loved ones; all in the hopes of making a difference on this earth. The answer to my parents fifty plus years of misery had just been dumped into my lap via death.

I began the process of settling their estate when, hidden deep within a desk drawer, I ran across their birth certificates and marriage license amid all their other legal documents. For years, their documents rested untouched until the inevitable brought to light their sad but indisputable secret that shrouded their stormy marriage. *It took my breath away.*

I hadn't thought to look over any of their legal papers before now. Why should I? When Dad died, his death certificate was the only record I needed to conduct his affairs. Everything else was Mom's personal business and I didn't have the right to pry. However, this one authentic sheet of paper was all that unified Charlotte and Herbert to their dreams and sorrows. I hungered for any nibble of information concerning their lives, but I realized the more I revealed, the less I had known about them. It felt as if I had uncovered a treasure chest rich in truth. The good news is, through this enlightenment, I invoked a connection with them on a different level. Any newfound knowledge would keep them vivid in my mind and heart. *I'm not ready to let go of them just yet. I just can't.*

For fifty-three years, they had celebrated their wedding anniversary on February first of each year. But when I examined their marriage certificate, the date May 4th, 1947 had been typed in the marriage block. This legal document had a three-month, three-day discrepancy from Mom and Dad's unwavering verbal date. In reality their marriage date had long been concealed in a vow of silent deceit making the shame of Mom's pregnancy the only foundation for starting a life together. Could this be the root of their lifelong unhappy marriage that trapped them both?

Most years, their anniversary was celebrated at a Chinese restaurant then having cake and ice cream at their house. Since their anniversary was February 1ˢᵗ and my birthday is February 2ⁿᵈ. I'd tease them about the two dates. Dad would roll his eyes and Mom would blush and plead, "JoAnn, don't spread lies; someone might believe you!" How ironic, they kept this secret just between themselves and none of us ever caught on.

In my feebleness to digest their scandalous secret, I tried to place myself in both of their shoes. Their lives began out of step with complications that could not be rectified. It was Jesse, Mom's friend, who also lived at the YWCA that filled me in on the crucial details that gave their marriage validation. You see, it wasn't just the disgrace of Mom getting pregnant that they had to deal with. Mom feared she would lose Dad and worried about how she could take care of a baby by herself. It devastated Mom to know Dad resented marrying her, even in her condition. Mom became hysterical to the point of breaking. Jesse had become Mom's confidant and encouraged her to track down Dad's commanding officer, and speak to him about her predicament. Soon after, Dad was ordered (forced) to do the right thing; his duty was to marry Mom and take care of his child. The military expected men to own up to their mistakes and accept responsibility for their actions, so with one swift command, an outsider had altered their future.

Had Mom confided in her family about her dilemma or was she too ashamed to ask for help? Maybe they figured she made her bed; she must lie in it. But regardless of whether she told or not, she must have contemplated the shameful, sobering reality that her father's perception of her had come true. Perhaps the echo of her father's voice replayed in her head: "You're nothing but a goddamn whore." How else would a nineteen year old, unwed, pregnant woman in the forties be perceived? Did she think she wasn't worthy of a better life?

Dad must have felt ambushed for being forced to marry a damn Yankee that he barely knew and had never intended to spend the rest of his life with. Deep inside, Dad had to concede that his impulsive behavior had ruined his fate. His freedom had been pulled right out from under him, leaving him feeling angry and trapped. So began their sullied life of shame and secrecy that released a smoldering bitterness toward each other. This would ultimately consume them both, collectively sucking in their five children, relatives, friends, and anyone else who crossed their path. There are countless casualties spit out during wartime; my parents were no exception.

I shared with my siblings my bittersweet findings. We were all stunned. Who can keep a secret for over fifty years? How could we not have known? Not that what happened to them was any different from thousands of others during times of war, or peace for that matter, but the fact they kept it a secret their entire lives, and took it to their graves blew us away. I honestly respected their discretion; their union was their business, not ours.

Rosemary, whom I call Rose, told me she always sensed a feeling from Dad that she wasn't wanted. But I never picked up on his disregard of her. I was too busy wondering why Mom hated me. Inversely, Rose never witnessed the slight I felt either. We both felt unloved at an early age and that in some way, it was my/her fault for their unhappiness. That was the unfair reality we lived in because our parents chose to live a lie. Their burden became the essence of their lives that induced a ripple effect that they passed on to us. I wish they could have gotten past their one misstep and moved on to have a better life for themselves as well as their children. *But that is far too simple a wish.*

HANG ON: MARRIAGE IS A ROLLER COASTER RIDE

After the Navy, The Charleston & Western Carolina Railroad hired Dad as a trainman. The job provided decent pay and good benefits, with only one drawback. Dad was subject to layoffs at any time if business slacked off with no recourse except to wait to be called back when business picked up. The realization was one he dreaded, but since the older men held seniority, Dad knew until he built up time with the company, he remained the low man on the totem pole. To insure job security, Dad joined the Union for the Brotherhood of Railroad Trainmen, but this, too, had a downside. The Union could implement a strike at will and Dad had no choice but to honor his allegiance. There was never a convenient time *to be on strike* and not knowing how long negotiations would take proved worrisome. Every lost work-day meant lost wages. Dad was very conscientious about his credit and did everything possible not to let his bills fall past due. If Dad owed anyone money, it became his priority to pay them back. Dad's motto, "You keep your needs and your wants separate." He was proud that way.

Railroad work was physically demanding and dangerous. After Dad died, I uncovered nine accidental death and dismemberment policies. Insurance was cheap, especially for the amount of coverage needed in case of an unforeseen accident. Not being able to support your family in case you were laid up for any length of time or were maimed or killed while on the job was a constant worry for every railroad man.

Even as young as four years old I didn't see Mom trying to make Dad's life easier. Providing for his family was a huge responsibility, yet Mom showed him little support. It was customary for Dad to be away from home for a week at a time. The day Dad's train was scheduled to arrive, Mom would call the dispatcher and get an estimated time of arrival. The operative word is *estimated*. When Dad arrived an hour or more past the estimated time, Mom had already worked herself into a tizzy, allowing unfounded "what ifs" to entertain her mind. "What in the hell is holding him up? Had he stopped for a drink or detoured past an old girlfriend's house? Did he drop by to see his mother first? Where in the hell is he?"

The moment Dad got his foot in the door, Rose and I would run giggling to greet him, but Mom did not. She seldom mustered up any interest to ask about his trip or showed him any affection. He barely got his satchel down when Mom, with folded arms shot him a glaring stare; a deliberate message that she wasn't about to believe any excuse he had to offer. She demanded to know, "Why in the hell are you so god-damn late coming home? I'm one step ahead of you, Pat. I called and the dispatcher told me what time the train was scheduled to pull into the station." She hadn't taken into consideration that he had to fill out his reports and pack up his gear before heading home.

Dad attempted to justify, "Damn, Charlotte, the train got held up just outside of town. You know each train's time is iffy." Dad's explanation made sense to me, why not to her? She grew relentless in her continuous allegations of him running around, making her suspicions impossible to trust him. Dad must have dreaded the drive home, knowing each time he'd be walking into a firestorm, with nothing to look forward to, not even a hot meal after his hard week at work. She could have fed us kids early and waited to eat with him, but she didn't. His only constant from his wife would be a cold, dried-out plate of food that had been sitting on the stove for hours. He always ate alone.

Maybe my eyes were deceiving me or I only heard half of what was said. I couldn't possibly comprehend the complexity of their relationship since everything I had witnessed filtered through my young, impressionable mind that sided with the one that appeared wounded.

Mom never backed down from a fight. She knew how to push his buttons and by doing so, gave him the perfect excuse to storm out and land at the local bar. Dad grumbled, "Your mother is damned and determined to always have the last word." At a very young age, I saw how my parents treated each other, and I had a clear opinion of which one kept things stirred up and which one didn't try. I know it was a long time ago, *but I remember.*

One night, Dad took Rose and me to the corner grocer and allowed us to pick out a toy. We both chose a yo-yo with sparkling rhinestones across one side. When we arrived home, Mom was furious and that prompted another fight. "What possessed you to buy all this needless shit that we can't afford?" Mom called the storekeeper and demanded, "Come get all this goddamn shit you sold Pat. Why in the hell did you sell it to him knowing he's drunk? We can't afford it!" The storekeeper took everything back except for our yo-yos. Rose and I hid under the bed until he left so we got to keep them. Was she fighting over money or his drinking and driving? She certainly had reason to be mad at him, but whatever started the fight paled in comparison to the events that were set in motion for later that evening. Dad stormed out.

Several hours later, the doorbell rang. Mom opened the door as a policeman identified himself. He informed Mom that Dad had been in a wreck and, yes, he was drunk. He explained the car had rolled three times, but by the grace of God, Dad's only injury was a deep laceration across his upper left arm. If he hadn't been drinking, he would have died instantly. The booze kept his body limber enough to withstand the force of the wreck. I remember being fearful of the policeman, ashamed of Dad's drunken recklessness, and terrified of Mom's wrath. Just like riding a roller-coaster, their volatile relationship would climb, twist, then quickly plunge up and down again and again.

Dad loved the outdoors, though in his married years, he never seemed to have the time to devote much of himself to the things that gave him pleasure like hunting and fishing. He ran on a combination of adrenaline and obligation and seemed to be a month behind in living. I pitied Dad.

He managed to plant a garden that produced an abundance of tomatoes and vegetables. This gave him a sense of pride to be able to provide for his family. The garden served as Dad's recreation, therapy, and religion all rolled into one. I enjoyed gardening as much as he did and helped him all I could. No one gave him the time of day when it came to helping with the garden. He'd grumble, "They scatter like bugs when there's weedin' or pickin' to do; scared a little work might kill em'." True to his nature, Dad generously shared his vegetables with family and neighbors, He'd say, "I'd rather give it away, than watch it rot."

This, too, annoyed Mom. It never occurred to her that sharing is one of the pleasures of gardening. For someone who disliked the outdoors and never gave a helping hand throughout the process of planting, watering, weeding, or harvesting, what made her so controlling? Why couldn't she be grateful knowing the garden helped feed us? How simple it would have been if she enjoyed some of the things he enjoyed, or to be fair, vice versa. Eventually, his gardening went by the wayside.

Dad also enjoyed raising bird dogs, quail, and rabbits. Mom didn't grasp that the outdoors was an inherent part of Southern life. Her ongoing gripe; he never spent time with her or his kids. When Dad went hunting or fishing and came home empty handed, he caught hell as soon as he walked through the door. It was either he lied about whom he was really with, or she questioned if he actually went at all. Everything Dad tried to do spawned conflict, while Mom suffocated him with her constant nagging, fault-finding, and distrust. Arguments were constantly simmering on the verge of boiling over, with Dad losing the fight each time. He quit trying to appease her and he gave up each hobby, one by one, and replaced them with a new one, *boozing*.

As hard as Mom tried, she couldn't keep tabs on Dad. She grew more furious and paranoid with every hour he stayed away. If he took time to drop by his parents before making it home from work, there was hell to pay. The respect Dad held for his parents never wavered, but had his loyalty been woven out of duty? No matter, he helped them every chance he could. Mom never realized that no amount of bitching would create a wedge between Dad and his folks; it wasn't going to happen.

Mom would make Rose or me call his parents to see if Dad was over at their house. Granny insisted either, "Pootie, we haven't seen him," or "Sugar pie, he just left." If the latter were the case, he'd be walking through the door within ten minutes. If my grandparents hadn't seen him, then we'd go down the list of railroad (drinking) buddies and local bars he was known to frequent. If we found him, we were made to say, "Mom said you gotta' come home Daddy, right now!" If they said he wasn't there but Mom felt they were lying, she conveyed a different humiliating message, "I know Pat is there. You tell him to get his ass home to his family!" I imagined a lighthouse keeper beaming a search light from the top of our house, guiding Dad on the right path so he could find his way back home.

Dad's whereabouts were a tossup with a 50/50 shot of his being where he originally told Mom he would be. Plenty of times, Mom learned Dad had played poker with his rowdy buddies in the back room down at the corner gas station. How pathetic to watch a grown man sneak around and lie about where he was going every time he left the house. Had Mom's intuition been right all along? Had Dad been off with a woman? Was Mom right not to trust him, or did her accusations push him to stray? Mom attempted to control his every move; that in turn left him feeling hen-pecked. He was suffocating under her constant scrutiny.

The maddest Mom got was when Dad came home carrying two gallons of moonshine swaying and boasting that he wanted to join the Ku Klux Klan. It seemed many of the railroad men and a few of Dad's kinfolk had already joined, and he was chomping at the bit to be a Klan member. But Mom put her foot down. That was the last I heard about the KKK. It was time for Dad to face his responsibilities. Mom tried to hold on to her man with endless demands and ultimatums, but Dad was wild as a buck, and bolted every chance he got.

WISHING WELLS, OUTHOUSES, AND HELL: MY CHILDHOOD

The outcome of a child's life is sometimes measured by an old saying that describes which viewpoint is taken; (a question I frequently asked myself) *were you raised up or drug up?* There is a vast distinction in the two and it all depends on your own definition of family and how you grew along the way. As to the consequences that follow, they are yours alone. Raised having a mentally ill mother and an alcoholic father certainly wasn't the best environment to be in. As a child, I perceived wishing wells, Grandma's outhouse, and hell all to have the same immeasurable depth contained in a pitch-black, bottomless hole with only one outcome that petrified me.

Rose took the path of fantasy to escape and I took the path of logic to endure. Cartoons and fairy tales annoyed the hell out of me. If there was such a thing as a Prince Charming, I never met one, at least not in my natural world nor had I known anyone who ever encountered one. As for the proverbial wishing well or a rainbow's pot of gold, this proved nonexistent as well. I thought what nonsense, sane people believing in ridiculous fairy tales. Grandma's dark, musty, smelly, paper deprived, spider-infested, one hole outhouse, and hell were more of a reality; and I was equally afraid of descending into both. My journey through childhood and adolescence for the most part was cheerless, hurtful, and unstable without a clear outlook. *I alone had to find my way.*

Day-to-day living as a child was uneventful with little influence from the outside world. I knew very little about the dynamics within my friend's home, but I sensed an air of confidence about them that mine lacked. They seemed happy-go-lucky with not a care in the world. Unlike me, they didn't seem afraid of their mothers. I began to detect something was different between how we lived. I had the foresight not to invite friends into my house. I never knew what to expect. What if my parents were at odds with each other again?

Growing up in the fifties, all you needed to create fun was to use your imagination and energy, and the day took care of itself. I kept myself entertained with my favorite activity, paper dolls. I consumed endless hours cutting out and placing tattered outfits over their shabby little bent, cardboard bodies. I liked playing board games with my siblings, but we could never coax Mom into joining us. All she wanted was to smoke and be left alone.

Mom showed no interest for the outdoors, however, she eagerly sent us out to play with the neighborhood kids. We enjoyed the sunshine and the customary games of jump rope, hopscotch, street skating, bike riding, and getting squirted with the garden hose. This gave Mom a little peace and quiet from her rowdy brood.

Periodically, while playing with the neighborhood kids, a fight would erupt and we would run home crying to Mom that a kid hit us or called us a name. Mom would phone their mother and enlighten her on what good-for-nothing brats she raised, and if she didn't control her kids and keep them out of our yard, she would come to their house and slap the *living shit* out of her. I never understood exactly what *living shit* meant. One word led to another, as Mom threatened to mop up the streets with her. She never backed down from a fight with anyone, especially when it involved defending her kids. Mom could hold her own with that New York scrapping way of hers. She was determined those backwoods Southern bitches weren't going to let their brats run all over us. Hell, Mom could wound anyone with her wide-eyed glares and her loud, sharp tongue peppered with accusations, threats, and endless vulgarities.

Mom made quite a few enemies in the neighborhood. Many times, the police were called to settle an argument and, as usual, I would hide in my bedroom closet, shaking with fear as my mind conjured up all the "what ifs." What if the neighbors turn the tables on Mom and slap the living shit out of her as well? What if the police haul Mom to jail; what will happen to us? What'll Dad do when he finds out? How could I face the kids at school the next day? I will forever be branded as the girl with the psycho witch for a mother.

Then, as if she had used up all her strength on the fight, she would break down sobbing. It was always "Poor Charlotte" that was put-upon. The irony of it all was she believed she was doing her best to protect us from the neighborhood bullies. We denied starting the fights but ultimately, we were punished and forbidden to play with them until the dust settled. Kids get over fights more quickly than adults do.

Typically, Dad was away at work when the fights broke out so we had to re-live each battle through Mom's eyes as she described word for word to him what had transpired. Time and again, I was humiliated and terrified by Mom's fiery temper. Dad appeared to be outdone by Mom's actions and inability to get along with people, but there was nothing he could do about her.

We kids repeatedly fought amongst ourselves and at times, a fight would turn vicious as we mimicked Mom's actions. Each time Mom had to break up one of our fights, her disposition was equally as intense as it was with the neighbors' kids. We quickly learned that it would be safer if we settled our own fights through bribery. The sibling that was in the wrong would have a change of heart and beg their sibling for forgiveness, or if it was a scuffle, the wounded kid would execute the last lick in lieu of telling Mom. If that strategy failed, you were labeled a tattle-tale and shunned until the incident blew over. This led to countless days of me playing alone. I kept myself occupied on rainy days with coloring books or my Tiny Tears doll. I had a knack for taking care of my doll because that would naturally be my destiny, to be a mother. I instinctively knew not to whip my doll or call her ugly names, even if she wasn't real.

The fifties introduced a new medium for families to pass the time, television, although children's educational shows were limited. I watched Captain Kangaroo religiously but I thought most of the skits were ridiculous. Kindergarten wasn't mandatory; our education began when we entered the first grade, so I learned my A B C's from Rose.

I grew up in a modest home with few amenities but we never went hungry. I understood early on that we were more fortunate than others. We were clean children and had decent outfits for school, even if some were hand-me-downs given to us by a church lady. Some were out of style, yet in good condition. I wouldn't tell Mom when the kids made fun of my clothes. I was afraid she would cause a scene. I got a pair of black and white oxfords at the beginning of each school year but fore-warned that I better take care of them. They were the only shoes I'd get until the start of the next school year. I polished them every Sunday night while perched in front of the TV watching Ed Sullivan.

Most men in the fifties were the breadwinners of the family, and Dad was no different. Supporting a family of five consumed most of his time, but I do recall one time when I was about six, Dad took me fishing. The pond was covered in enormous lily pads in bloom. I was unbelievably content, just me and Dad fishing on a beautiful summer morning. Suddenly, the flat-bottom boat got stuck on a log. I was afraid we'd never get free, or worse, tip over and drown. But Dad's strong, reassuring voice told me everything would be okay, and sure enough, it was. One stinking outing alone with Dad in a lifetime is all I remember. *Damn, Dad, not very much to hold on to.*

At a very young age, good manners were instilled in us by our parents. Strangers would compliment them on how well-mannered their children acted in public. We addressed grownups with ma'am or sir, and you better not forget to say please and thank you. You did as you were told with no questions asked: speak only when spoken to, and never talk back. We were also taught to show respect to people of authority, especially policeman, teachers, and elders. These were fundamental rules to live by. My parents expected no less from us. If I stepped out of line, Dad was quick to put me in my place, "We're your parents, and you're gonna' mind us." Obedience may build character but strict rules create a downside by infusing angst and feelings of little self-worth.

I became fearful of all adults. I viewed them as being larger than life and indisputable. Added to the equation was Dad's audacious presence and Mom's quick temper. When he spoke in his deep, authoritative voice, I obeyed. When she glared at me with those dark brown eyes, I froze. In actuality, I wasn't allowed to stand up for myself. I expected a father figure to give me a nod that it was okay to speak. I also feared any person could just as easily backhand me the way Mom did. If I made a verbal jest like, "Ah gee," Mom would slap me across my face for being disrespectful to her. It made no difference where I was or who was around: friends, relatives or strangers. I recall the ghastly looks that people gave Mom after she would strike and demoralize me in front of them, but no one came to my rescue; that would be interfering and it just wasn't done in the fifties. That was Mom's way of keeping her kids, callously referred to as her *hellions*, in line. *Doesn't everyone throw a few vulgarities and punches when they get frustrated and things don't go their way?*

It was practically written in stone that each one of us would graduate from high school with no variation in the rule. It was also understood that summer school wouldn't be an option, especially since it cost to attend. Dad reasoned, "If you haven't learned it in nine months, how in the hell can ya grasp *any smarts* in six weeks?" A high school education meant everything to my parents because neither one of them were able to graduate. Dad's stumbling block was poverty and Mom's was her hard hearted father. The absence of an education in their lives was part of their entrapment and part of the problem. They believed that getting a diploma would be the magic blue print for a successful future, but they didn't think beyond high school so neither did I. We all graduated from high school except for the youngest sibling, but she later earned her GED. I viewed every girl's fate (specifically mine) would be to graduate high school, marry, have many babies, and (hopefully) live happily ever after. *Isn't that the natural order of life?*

Dad had little tolerance for waste and nonsense spending. For example, when the ice cream truck rolled into our neighborhood, we would beg Dad for money to buy an ice cream. As he fiddled through his deep, blue jean pockets for loose change, he echoed his steadfast rule, "Don't be wastin' my money on none of that colored water (popsicle);

just buy ice cream." That was fine by me; I agreed with Dad; colored water is a rip-off.

It had to be hard for Mom, day in and day out, not having any help with five children in tow. But she did have help-us kids. I was six when I began using a steep stool so I could reach the sink to wash dishes. If I missed a spot on a dish, Mom yelled, "You better not do a half-ass job or I'll make you rewash them all." God help me if I accidentally broke a dish; a hard slap to the face was inevitable along with her degrading reprimand, "Watch what you're doing you clumsy little shit." Saturday was cleaning day. Rose and I took turns with all the chores. We hung the clothes out to dry, folded, and then put away. I watched Tarzan and American Bandstand on TV while I ironed mounds of clothes. Rose fixed breakfast and cleaned the kitchen. We swept the house, dusted furniture, and made beds while Mom sat on the sofa smoking one cigarette after the other and barking orders, "Sweep under the table; you missed a spot; get busy. Stop dragging your damn feet, and fix me a cup of tea. Pay attention before you break something. Don't make me get up from here!"

As soon as we were tall enough to see over the stove, our duties were expanded to cooking. We made a simple breakfast from canned biscuits, toast, or scrambled eggs. Lunch consisted of sandwiches or a can of soup. As we got older and Mom grew further withdrawn, we were saddled with all the chores.

One task we didn't do was yard work. Dad did that on his day off. He also kept the car in working order and paid the bills. It had to be daunting after working long hours to come home and not even have the front door close behind him before one of us was screaming that something in the house had broken and needed his immediate attention.

Mom was out of control more times than I care to confess. My first memory of her unstable behavior was around the age of three. I vividly recall lying in my crib with Mother standing over me, holding my legs up by my ankles with one hand, and slapping my bare bottom with her other hand, threatening, "You better do as you're damn told; now say your prayers!" While trying to squirm out of her clasp, I screamed and kept begging her to stop. It was a simple child's prayer, "Now I lay me down to sleep, I pray the Lord my soul..." *Had I been sassy, or having a childish tantrum by refusing to say my prayers? Or, in that moment of fear, had I simply forgotten the words?* For whatever reason, my actions that night sent her into a rage, and I was too young to understand why with no way to defend myself.

In our house, there was no such thing as an accident. We were punished verbally and physically for any mistakes made. I remember one time when I was about four years old, I had to pee. The problem was we only had one bathroom. Mom needed to go as well. So, while I waited my turn, I just couldn't hold it any longer. I involuntarily peed my pants. What a bizarre image etched in my mind; Mom sitting on the commode glaring back at me with those dark, cold eyes promising, "You're getting a whippin' as soon as I'm done. You should be ashamed of yourself for wetting your pants; you filthy little pig." I stood in the dark hallway, immobilized and shaking from fear, knowing if I ran, I would track pee through the house, making matters worse, and yet I wanted to run away from her before she could get off the commode. Well, I got a beating that day and there were many incidents prompting verbal abuse, beatings, face slaps, and hair pulls that were interwoven through out my adolescence. The absurdity in being abused by a loved one is, when their rage ends, you simultaneously believe everything is your fault while feeling a primal need to be comforted by the very person who wounded you.

Mom's nerves stayed on edge, and so any little thing we did triggered a swift consequence. One of her frequent punishments was to be banished to a corner. You couldn't talk, just stand with your nose pressed where the two walls met and waited until she decided when your punishment would end. From a child's point of view, time is exaggerated, so it seemed that I stood for hours. How much longer do I have to stand here? Did she forget about me? If I call out to her, I'll upset her more and she will make me stay longer. The longer I stay, the longer she has peace and quiet and doesn't have to deal with me...*or I with her.* While waiting for Mom to grant permission for my punishment to be over, I'd sometimes take it upon myself to sit down, then fall asleep on the floor. Dad came home early one day and found me in the corner. He let Mom know he didn't think that was a suitable punishment for a child, but his opinion carried no merit.

I found a picture of Rose and myself when we were four and five years old standing side by side, at attention, like obedient little soldiers. When Mom dressed us alike, we could pass as twins. Rose was fifteen months older, but I was the same height as she. Mom would bark, "Stand up straight, stop squirming, and smile, or I'll come over their and slap the shit out of you," We did as we were told. *Wild Indians, shit asses, and dirty little ragamuffins* were Mom's terms of endearment for us.

Rose and I were playing outdoors on a summer day when bumblebees wouldn't stop buzzing all around us. We were hot, thirsty, and frightened. I banged on the screen door and begged for Mom to let us in, but she wouldn't unlock the door. We seemed to grate on her nerves. She was forever smoking, shaking, and crying. *Why had she turned her back on us?* Dad would never lock us out of our own house.

Another time, when I was about four, I stepped into a pile of ashes that I thought were cold, not realizing that hot embers were still smoldering underneath. I severely burned the bottom of my foot. Dad swept me up and rushed me to a doctor. I was taken care of by Mom but any pampering was nil. The accident was my fault. I stayed silent, fearing Mom would remember she hadn't punished me for my carelessness.

When we developed the typical childhood illnesses, we weren't neglected. We received the customary medical attention in Mom's dutiful manner. I was five when Mom caught me crying in the bathroom. "What in the hell is wrong with you?" She felt my head with the back of her hand and realized I had a high fever. I reluctantly confessed that my ears and throat hurt so badly that I could barely swallow. Instead of being hugged and reassured that everything would be all right, I was sent to bed with a deep feeling that my illness was somehow my fault. Soon after, I had my tonsils removed. It was Mom's duty to take care of me after the operation, and she did, but again, she was void of any nurturing.

Looking back, a child's first swing set should be pure bliss and I couldn't wait to run outside and swing up to the sky. But first, Mom had to braid my hair and that's when my excitement evaporated. Exploiting her prickly temper, she repeatedly gave my hair a hard yank and my head a whack with the hairbrush and vowed, "If you don't stop your damn fidgeting, I'll make you stay in the rest of the day." Mom had a way of spoiling any morsel of joy. While Dad was putting the swing set together; he had no idea how I was being berated. *Isn't that how a five-year-old acts? Why was I punished for showing my excitement to play? Maybe I was unruly and deserved all those whippings and tongue-lashings.*

Mom's behavior, as malicious as it was, seemed customary to us because that was all we were exposed to. Only when I started elementary school did I realize that something was terribly off balance with the family I was born into. I would visit playmates and see how their mothers acted towards them: enthusiastic smiles, sharing a quick hug and kiss, or lending an attentive ear to hear about their day. I never wanted to go back to my house. I thought to myself so many times, *why wasn't I born to another family?* I never felt safe yet that was all I desired. I would sometimes spend the night with a girlfriend. She didn't have a mother; I never asked why. But even with one parent, her life seemed more balanced than mine. I never heard her and her father argue, just a gentle return of affection between the two of them. *Wow, it seems so simple to have a stable existence.*

We weren't so poor that we didn't have toys; however, we received them only on birthdays and Christmas, so I was excited when someone gave me a unclothed baby doll. I immediately assembled a dismal ensemble from various colored scraps of cloth. I cut out armholes, sewed on matching buttons, and I made a carrying case out of a shoebox. It developed into my adaptation of the 1950's store-bought Madame Alexander doll with wardrobe and steam trunk. I loved playing with her, but I came home from school one day and learned that Mom had thrown the doll, box, and all the clothes in the trash. She glared and made her intentions clear, "Serves you right. I'm sick of telling you to pick your goddamn shit off the floor." She was right; once again, I had forgotten to pick up after myself, but this is typical behavior for a young child. The rage she unleashed was disproportionate to my blunder. Years later, after leaving home, I realized she hadn't saved anything that belonged to us, not a single toy or keepsake from our childhood, just some random photos. I assumed since she didn't have any mementos from her childhood, she didn't think it was important for us to have any as well. But childhood keepsakes and photos help define who you are, giving you a calming sense of belonging.

I was around eight years old and decided to ride my bicycle around the block. In fairness, Mom warned me not to leave the front street, but I didn't listen and around the block I flew. Just as I approached a wide curve, I skidded on a patch of sand and fell onto the asphalt. The inside of my left ankle got chewed up pretty bad. With blood gushing, and my thoughts spinning, I limped home using my bike as support. I had to hide this mess I created, knowing that if she found out, I would get a beating for disobeying her. I could hear her voice as I had so many times before, "What in the hell did you do now? See what happens? It serves you right. Maybe next time you'll mind me and stop acting like a goddamn wild Indian." I quietly went into the bathroom and cleaned my wound. I wished Mom could help me and tell me it would be alright, but I was more afraid of her wrath than my leg getting infected and rotting off. I sucked up my tears and dealt with my bloody ankle without help. I did my best to avoid her for a couple of days and she never even noticed. It was a rational tradeoff; I forfeited any medical attention, but I didn't get punished, berated, or slapped. I learned early how to silence my emotions and take care of my own needs.

One hot summer day while riding down the highway, Mom threw her cigarette butt out the window. I'd learned that Smokey the Bear urged everyone; "Only you can prevent forest fires." It hadn't rained in a while. I feared her cigarette would catch the woods on fire. I should've known better than to test my viewpoint with Mom. She barked, "You better sit back and shut the hell up before I knock your goddamn teeth down your throat." *I guess she thought I was sassing again.* I couldn't suggest anything without being demoralized. As young as I was, I lost respect for her that day for belittling me and for her blatant disregard for Smokey.

I became a quick study on what actions pushed Mom's buttons that would send her into a rage. I kept a standoffish attitude towards her as my intuition prompted me to conform to the way she wanted me to act. I rehearsed my every move around her, and I tried to anticipate that what I said was what she wanted to hear. When I showed hurt feelings, I was told to stop pouting. Each time I cried, I was ridiculed and called a crybaby. If I got the giggles, I was told to stop acting silly. When I played hard, I was labeled a dirty ragamuffin. If I asked the wrong question, I was called stupid. Each time something scared me, I was never consoled and titled scaredy-cat. If I acted curious, I was warned to stop being so nosy. If I forgot to wash behind my ears, I was scolded for being a filthy little pig. I was demoralized if I forgot my manners. Each of Mom's pessimistic findings chipped away at my existence until my confidence weakened to apathy. She never showed an ounce of patience or empathy, in fact, compassion was non-existent with her. Mom treated us like unwanted orphans. Why couldn't she realize? *To receive love, you first must give love.*

Dad wasn't much better. "Children are to be seen and not heard," was his motto. He wasn't in tune with his children's feelings; his duty was to financially take care of us and keep us safe. Even Dad, in a joking manner, made fun of me, but his teasing still hurt. If Dad caught me crying over a sad movie like Old Yeller, he would call me a crybaby. He didn't have a clue how sensitive little girls were. Not knowing why, I felt ashamed for crying in front of him, so I would hide my face and blink away any tears. Many times, I would will myself not to cry.

A visit to Grandma's house should have been a happy warm experience; instead it was reduced to a disappointing day. Grandma would ask, "Wanna' piece of cake, Pootie?" But Dad, in his deep commanding voice, decided for me, "No, she don't need it." No more words would be spoken, that was that. But I wanted a piece of Grandma's cake. *What child wouldn't? He didn't even ask me!* I never had the luxury of having my desires heard.

At Grandma's house, if we acted rowdy or disobeyed, by the third warning Dad was breaking a switch off the chinaberry tree. He kept his word; I straightened up fast. My aunts used a different tone when they spoke to my cousins. They never seemed to mind the squeals made in play-their children didn't grate on their nerves. Why did we act so unruly? Maybe we were hellions and we deserved what we got.

I didn't participate in school activities until the third grade when auditions were held for a Christmas play; a reenactment of Jesus' birth. I tried out for the role of Mary but wasn't chosen. Instead, the ones that didn't get picked were given a part in the chorus. The teacher confirmed, "You each give life to the play by creating a bridge between story and song." The girls dressed in white blouses and navy blue skirts with big red bows made by the PTA mothers. The boys wore red ties, white shirts, and navy blue pants. The stage held a magical ambiance. As the lights lowered between scenes, and the dark purple velvet curtain flowed open, I'd get goose bumps. I was elated to be singing all the traditional Christmas carols. I'm not a good singer, but I had a loud voice and I knew all the words by heart. Dad had to work and Mom stayed home with my siblings, which left no one to cheer me on, but I was thrilled to be a part of something. I savored a little of the applause for myself.

Not to be redundant, but we were poor. We didn't have central air conditioning so we kept the windows open, letting one large window fan keep us cool. So needless to say, when Mom went into a rage, the neighbors got an ear full. Mom lost her temper and began screaming and beating me. I don't remember what I did that day (*though I must have deserved it*). I ran outside to the side porch sobbing to the point of choking on my snot and tears. My entire body shook. Our next-door neighbor, Maybelline, tiptoed over, and I knew by the worried look on her face that she had overheard Mom's caustic rant. She whispered,

"Oh, honey, are you all right? Can I help you?" I thought, *"Oh God no, please go away. You can't stop her."* I hung my head in shame and timidly retreated to the corner of the porch like a wounded puppy that needed to lick its wounds and tried to subdue my tears. I became frantic knowing that if Mom saw her coming to my rescue, I would be in more trouble. Damn, the neighbors heard her. I'm glad; now they know what a hateful witch she really is. What if they phone the police or tell Dad? If I'm as bad as Mom says I am, they might put me in a juvenile home. It was abnormal to be terrified at such a young defenseless age, but I was incessantly fearful with nowhere to run or anyone to turn to. I wanted to jump into Maybelline's arms and beg her to take me away from all the madness. I knew her home was safe. I never heard any yelling coming from her house. I envied how she doted on her two daughters.

Again, I became curious about the way other people lived and compared everyone's life to mine. I viewed people's lives through a pair of imaginary *rose-colored glasses.* And the more their homes appeared perfect, the more mine fell short.

Weird, I never knew how any of my siblings felt about Mom. We remained isolated in our own web of fear. *We were so young; what did we know?* Occasionally, we exchanged a mutual, "I hate her" to each other if we had a tempestuous day, but we never intruded on each other's space, shared our inner pain, denounced Mom's behavior, or comforted the wounded one; consequently, we failed each other.

Saying, "I hate her" under my breath gave me the power to release my anger, but my quandary remained. I equally felt an enormous amount of shame and confusion because there had to be something wrong with me to hate my own mother. *Would I be damned to hell for thinking that way?* Still, something had to be wrong with her to curse and mistreat her kids. She could do and say anything she pleased to us, and we couldn't do anything about our situation except endure.

Among Mom's numerous punishments, the one I dreaded most was being put on restriction, and she knew it. I tried to avoid her wrath by not speaking unless spoken to, not sass, use manners, clean my side of the bedroom, and do my chores without being told. Hopefully, I could stay out of her path and she'd focus on one of the others. Each time Mom punished one of my siblings, I felt pity for them but grateful it wasn't me. They must have deserved it; according to Mom, we all did. As hard as I tried, I could never please her. It took all my cunning ability to stay under Mom's radar. When I got whipped, called stupid, or told what a good-for-nothing I was, I realized it wasn't as much about my behavior as it was about her frame of mind. *Damn, just leave me alone. I hate you so much.*

Another sure way to steer clear of punishment was to have a good report card. Mom never gave a helping hand with homework unless you count her roar coming through the walls each night, "Stop all that god-damn racket; your homework better be done." At the end of six weeks when report cards came out, I prayed I had passed. Any failing grade guaranteed a tongue lashing on how stupid you were as well as getting placed on restriction until a passing grade showed on the next report card. By no means was I smart, but I never failed. The thought of being confined to the house kept me motivated. Rose did not think like me. She sassed constantly, wouldn't clean her side of our room, and failed some of her subjects. She stayed on restriction more times than not. My heart ached for her, but I couldn't rescue her. How could I when I stayed too absorbed in trying to save myself?

Nighttime brought no comfort. At each day's end, Mom ordered, "Time to get to bed, and you better go to sleep." I played hard and had tired myself out, so I usually fell right to sleep. Rose and I shared a bed and we sometimes got the giggles, only to have Mom bellow, "You two, shut the hell up; don't make me come in there." We knew we better settle down fast. Mom never read us a bed time story, or tucked us in bed, and good night kisses were nonexistent. We were out of her hair every night by 8:30 P.M. Her motherly obligations had been met. She could now enjoy the rest of the night in peace.

I longed to be a part of something, so at nine, I joined the Girl Scouts. I felt guilty knowing they had to buy my uniform. I hoped to earn a merit badge in art. For my first project I molded Mom an ashtray out of a block of clay. It warped into a lop-sided, lumpy, putrid grey-greenish, unrecognizable heap. My endeavor failed. Without encouragement, my mood teetered from insecurity to inept. With no recognizable talents developing and nothing challenging my curiosity, I simply floundered through youth. *Nothing held my interest.*

CHARLOTTE'S FLYING SOLO

I assumed I might be adopted because of the distance I felt between us, but that notion was short-lived. I repeatedly overheard Mom telling her friends the distressing tale of getting pregnant again, six months after Rose's birth, and how her labor with me was long and agonizing. Rose was five and I was four when Kathy was born. Rick arrived three years later, then Gail four years later and the last born. We were now a family of seven.

Lucky for parents in the fifties, heads turned the other way if they were observed striking their kids in public. No one dared to stick their nose in other people's business. People presumed the brat had misbehaved and surely had it coming. What degree of discipline a child endured, whether it was a pop, spanking, or a beating depended on the child's actions. A fine line defined the three, and what punishment was administered was at the parents' discretion. That's just the way it was. But abuse begets abuse. Child Protective Services would intervene only in extreme cases, so unless you made a trip to the hospital with a broken bone or a concussion, no one got blamed for child abuse. There was no sparing the rod in the fifties, especially in our house.

It was no secret poor Charlotte had a temper-after all she was flying solo. It had to be tiresome raising five brats while dealing with an unfaithful alcoholic husband who wasn't around to give her any support. Most of the time Mom acted like a drill sergeant, barking orders and expelling malicious threats for the simplest request. Her verbal scolding carried as much sting as her backhand. Her stance was black and white and she executed all punishment with total justification and no compromise. If Mom smacked you, then realized after the fact she hit the wrong child, she would coldly remark, "Stop that damn crying; you had it coming. That's for things I didn't catch you doing." If you persisted in taking up for yourself and said you didn't do it, she accused you of lying; you did not escape punishment. Mom processed every incident negatively; therefore, it wasn't in her character to say she was sorry or admit she made a mistake. Remorse was never shown.

Mom lacked the motherly instincts and skills to take her children into her arms with hugs and kisses and assurances that everything would be all right. *But isn't mothering a natural instinct that flows unconditionally to protect and nurture your own flesh and blood?* She couldn't share what she never experienced. She leaned on the premise of being a damn good wife who didn't drink, hang out in bars, or whore around. She held fast to her conviction that her only vices were swearing and smoking.

Mom stayed on edge, allowing her temper get the better of her. She had a knack for blindsiding you with a sharp blow to the head using whatever object she could reach. Many instances the wooden broom got the job done. It created welts on your head that throbbed for days making it painful to comb your hair. Each time the bump throbbed, you were reminded of her anger. Degrading and smacking her kids around became a recurring response to most situations; that's all Mom knew. She could throw a nasty punch that you never saw coming. She believed her hellions deserved each face slap, every belt beating, and verbal humiliation, making her style of punishment the rock-solid formula for molding obedient kids. It was only by God's grace that none of us landed in the emergency room.

Mom kept a long, wide leather belt (turned weapon) down the side of the sofa where she sat. She purposely bent it in half for maximum thickness. Thank God, the buckle was missing. I hate to think of the bruises it would have created. If you misbehaved, she could grab it and plant three licks on you before you had a chance to take cover. It didn't matter where the belt landed, your back, arms, legs, *wherever,* and you were guaranteed to have stinging welts for hours. I finally had enough of the belt, so I threw it in the outside garbage can. *Never to be used again.*

Mom looked everywhere for her belt. In her low, unnerving voice she questioned, "Have you seen my belt?" With all of the fabricated concern and spontaneous persuasion I could muster I replied, "No Ma'am; haven't seen it." She persisted, "If I ever find out who took it…" Well, she never did. I lied to save myself as well as my siblings, and I wasn't one bit remorseful. Fear of a belt beating had a stronger hold on me than any mortal sin of telling a lie. I didn't confide in my siblings that I had disposed of her weapon. I was afraid they might turn on me in a weak moment, or use my secret over my head like a get-out-of-jail-free card. But I was sure of one thing, my siblings had to be grateful to the brave soul for their heroic deed.

Mom's methods for keeping her brats in line grew effortless. It was a controlled hysteria fused with a dose of satisfaction in every punishment she handed down. One of her spontaneous acts of chastisement would be to grab a fist full of my long brown hair and turn it into a makeshift torture device. My head bobbed like a yo-yo between her fist and the floor, her fist and a wall, or her fist and the brick fireplace as she reiterated, *"I'm tired of your sassy mouth, or I'm tired of you not minding me, you stupid, good for nothing little shit ass."* I instinctively stiffened my neck and let it act as a shock absorber between her fist and the upcoming target.

There were beatings for not remembering how to tie my shoes, spilling milk, breaking something, not minding, fighting with my siblings, and on and on. The list was as long as her arm that snatched me up whenever the mood struck her. Believe me, anything would set her off and someone had to pay for her misery. My mind stayed in a *why* mode and I dared not look her in her eyes. She perceived each glimpse as a imagined defiance. Mom demanded, "What in the hell are you staring at? Don't give me that dirty look. Wipe that goddamn smirk off your damn face before I slap it off." Stay still JoAnn. Keep your mouth shut.

I tried to cope with Mom's temperament by rationalizing her burden of taking care of five children and trying to hold her marriage together. Were her kids all tugging for attention too much to handle? But the truth is, Mom had a dark side that she couldn't control. You never knew when she would fly off the handle. Had her callous spiteful nature played a part in her downfall? She stayed at odds with most people, especially Dad, and her kids caught the brunt of her frustrations. *Were we being punished for every time Dad upset her? How can a mother cause harm to her children?* We couldn't have been that wicked to warrant the magnitude of punishment she inflicted on us. Did she ever turn to God for strength or forgiveness? She was raised Catholic after all.

Each slap to my face formed a red mark on my cheek in the shape of Mom's palm, with a lingering sting that I wouldn't soon forget. I stayed hidden until the mark vanished. Every slap landed indiscriminately, my cheek or the back of my head, but it was the slaps to the ear that were the most painful. I learned how to protect myself by throwing my arms in a crossed position over my head and cowering down until her screaming and beating rampage ended. Many times I was left crying and shaking to the point of getting physically ill. After being knocked around and shamed, she would eject an added layer of humiliation, demanding, "Get the hell out of my sight; you make me sick." She never realized she made me sick too: sick with hate and fear, and I didn't want to be anywhere near her either, but I had nowhere to go. Mom's salty language and glaring eyes matched pure evil that held an unremitting reminder that she was in control. You better not ever forget it. I realized that even if I was right, expressing my opinion about anything would have only one outcome; it made her more furious. I stood trapped face to face with her as I endured each rage. Don't cause trouble and don't let your guard down.

As I got older, the physical brutality escalated; still getting slapped regularly in the face. I had my share of split, bloody, bruised, and swollen lips; with Mom vowing, "I'll give you another fat lip if you don't shut the hell up and get out of my goddamn sight." Mom's absurdity was haunting, "Do you want me to give you another busted lip?" My thoughts were, *"Hell no, who would? Who in their right mind wanted more of the same? Are you crazy?* It usually took a day or so for the swelling to disappear. Dodging my school friends became my shameful secret. Naturally, I lied about what happened. *Damn, I hate her so much."* Of course, I kept this to myself as I cowered back to my room and hid until she calmed down. It became a test of wills. If I could hold back my tears, I could declare victory, *in my mind.* I became quite a pro at keeping my mouth shut and not crying after each conflict. Don't you dare cry; her ranting will eventually end. She recited her acrimony so often that I finally became insensitive to her threats and my only reaction was to give a cold glare back at her. There must be a clandestine award for the child that can hold back the most tears, and if so, I would be the winner. Each beating, face slapping, and hair-pulling incident would be accompanied by her heartless, degrading remark that ended in, *"I wish the hell I never had you."* Her malicious catch phrases still impose a veiled sting that I can't seem to shake, even after her death.

If Mom had deviated from her customary disposition, for instance by saying she was sorry for losing her temper or even telling me she loved me; I probably wouldn't have felt so detached from her. But her actions were so heartless and one sided, while never counterbalancing with any form of affection, that I believed she honestly hated me. She never validated my need for approval. I didn't have a voice of my own, making her cruelty the only constant interaction in our relationship that unified us as mother and daughter. I'd stop myself short of wishing Mom dead, honest. What if my sinful thought came to pass; that alone would seal my fate; damning me straight to hell. I couldn't bear that magnitude of hatred or guilt on my conscience. I mentally battled with myself not to embrace Mom's ideology.

Dad caught Mom screaming at me about a chore she felt I wasn't doing correctly. With a stern retort Dad interrupted, "Stop your damn yelling, Charlotte. You can't expect her to learn if she's never taught." This incidence formed a fallacy in her mind that I was Dad's favorite child and she threw it in my face every time I crossed her. Her coldness towards me manifested into deep resentment; I became her enemy. Just because I obeyed Dad, didn't mean I received different treatment or had been shown any special attention. I simply stayed out of trouble more than the others.

I wonder if Dad had an inkling how violent Mom was to us growing up or if he knew how often we were beat and punished? Did it ever cross his mind we had more bruises and busted lips than normal? When Dad was home, she knew better than to hit us in front of him. Maybe we acted better when he was around. After Mom's death, I found a letter she had written to Dad, though I don't know if she actually presented him with her ultimatums. It stated, "I'm leaving you, Pat, because I can no longer tolerate your drinking." Armed with a list of demands he had to abide by before she would take him back. I was shocked to read she referenced me in her letter. "Stop taking up for JoAnn all the time." Her words held a sharp resentment concerning his feelings towards me. Dad and I were a lot alike in temperament, common sense, and loyalty. We both loved gardening and outdoors, however, that was the extent of our connection.

With Mom's incessant nagging and with no one in Dad's corner, I sided with him many times; however, I never condoned his drinking or running around.

In the fifties, men weren't expected to help with house work or kids. All the nurturing and discipline came from the mother. The man of the house stepped up to the plate only when extreme disciplinary action was warranted. For Dad to reprimand me for something I did made me ashamed, and I never wanted to disappoint him. When Dad spoke, I obeyed him and feared him but sadly, could never get close to him. Was it his stature or deep voice that made me apprehensive? I knew my place with Dad and he never crossed the invisible line of parent/child.

Dad believed in punishment but not the brutal kind. Dad never voiced a feeling of hatred towards us or backhanded us out of frustration or anger. He would lose his temper, but not with his kids, mostly with his job or Mom. If I misbehaved, the worst I can recall would be him stomping out and mumbling under his breath, "I'll handle you when I get back." Waiting for him to return seemed like eternity, and wondering what my punishment would be kept me in a fearful frame of mind which was punishment enough. But when he returned, he had calmed down and all was forgotten. If we needed to be spanked, he only spanked our fannies. Dad said, "That's what God made your back side for." But Mom sure made up for Dad's absence and leniency. We were Mom's whipping posts when she couldn't cope with life's disappointments, always letting her temper explode and blaming us for all her misery.

My friend brought to my attention that I never had anything unfavorable to say about Dad except for his drinking and womanizing. I was taken aback by her perception of my feelings toward him, but she was right. I had subconsciously put Dad on a pedestal, flaws and all. In my heart, I knew he was essentially a good man and father. The drama between him and Mom had no bearing on how he treated me. My only explanation was that even though there had been times he had disappointed me, Dad didn't hit me, curse me, and never said he hated me, or wished I'd never been born. Never. Was he truly thankful for his children or had he accepted the fact we were his responsibility. He kept his feelings to himself. *Much can be forgiven if you haven't been beaten down with hateful words and fists.*

Each time I look at the photographs of my youth, I smile for a moment only to realize unlike the negatives, certain memories haven't faded. I vividly recall the feel of each outfit; it's color, pattern, and texture leaving each memory dressed in its own unique feel. I am taken back to a time when my younger days should have been carefree instead of living in fear of my mother. The dismal portion of my youth sprouted from so many of my days growing up that triggered sadness and emptiness. *How can you feel secure at home or obtain confident in yourself?*

REALITY
WHISPERED IN MY EAR

I was young, but I remember overhearing phone conversations between Mom and other housewives sharing their forbidden curiosity on what steps needed to be taken if someone decided to end an unwanted pregnancy. Frightened, yet determined, they cautiously whispered woman to woman about different choices that existed such as pills, home remedies, and metal coat hangers. Not even society's taboos could stop the actions of a woman who felt she had reached the end of her rope. It wasn't until the sixties that women had freedom and options concerning their bodies.

Woven in a common bond of desperation, Mom nervously knew who to call each time a pregnancy scare surfaced. "Well, yes, I'm Catholic, but I married outside my faith. Yes, I believe it's a sin. No, I haven't told Pat yet. It's hard enough to feed the ones we've got. Yeah, I heard about that technique. She did? It did? I'll think about it and let you know; take care, thanks, bye."

Sundays were reserved for dinner at Grandma's house but it didn't feel special. We were people who just happened to be visiting our grandparents on the same day as the rest of the clan. All our relatives could not fit inside their small framed, shingled house. When it came time to eat, a seating arrangement was devised: the men were served first, the kids second, and the women ate last.

We didn't visit our kinfolk much outside the perimeter of Grandma's house so I never really connected with any of my cousins. Catching up became the platform of the women's conversations veiled under the pretense of family bonding. They exchanged polite small talk: "How y'all doing? Good to see you again. Yes, its been a while. My goodness, your kids have grown." As they wove through each other's chitchat, they became privy to all the latest gossip, repeating the superficial ending: "We need to get together more often." On the ride home, Mom would fill Dad's ears full of who said what about whom, which family showed up late again, whose cake was dry, who arrived empty handed, which one had put on pounds, whose kids behaved bratty, and who was pregnant again. Mom's most objectionable complaint was which aunt acted snooty and ignored her. Mom proclaimed, "You don't want to be the one who doesn't show up, or you'll be the one they gossip about." There was a lot of truth in that statement. It was like Mom needed to hear some dirt on a family member for leverage so she could justify the imperfections in Dad's family. Mom had little self-worth. She still felt ill at ease around them.

Mom's brash tongue never failed to piss someone off leaving her at odds within Dad's family. If Mom thought someone had slighted her in any way, her comeback would be, "They think their shit don't stink!" Just another one of her damning expressions that left me baffled. Mom reasoned, "None of them are angels. They need to clean up their own damn backyard and stop snoopin' around mine." They were no better than my mom, and if they thought they were, shame on them.

As my grandparents got older, Dad's family fanned out, seeding their own family customs. We saw less of them except for the yearly family bar-b-cue or an ill-fated funeral. I can't blame them for keeping their distance; no one wanted to be involved in my parents' destructive melodramas. Besides, they had their families to look after and their own share of troubles to deal with.

Dad would fix things around the house, only for Mom to demean his work. How humiliating to witness a grown man being belittled and shamed in front of his kids. Dad may have been physically strong, but Mom's constant verbal bashing left him beaten down. Nothing Dad did would ever be good enough to please her.

Dad did his share of flying off the handle with Mom as well. When Mom needed extra money to buy household necessities, Dad would decide that she didn't need it, and since he controlled the purse strings, she was forced to come up with creative ways to get what she needed. With each purchase came a conflict on what was deemed a necessity. Mom wasn't extravagant by any means, but she needed to hide a slew of things from Dad, like the time she bought a vacuum cleaner from the Jewel T man. Mom managed to keep it out of his sight for a year. Occasionally, she would buy herself an outfit and keep it hidden in the back of her closet. Mom had to defend her spending each time we had a growth spurt and needed a new pair of shoes. He selfishly begrudged her something new. Could this be his way of punishing her for not contributing monetarily to the family? On the other hand, he believed women should not work outside the home. Could that be a ruse to keep her under his control? No wonder Mom felt trapped.

I was keenly aware of the challenges my parents faced having to raise five kids. I'd hear them arguing over money, wondering how they were going to make it until the next paycheck. Somehow, they did.

When Dad was away at work, we ate simple meals like noodles mixed in butter, kidney beans, or tomato soup. It was inexpensive, filled our tummies, and easy for us kids to prepare. We never went hungry. If Mom served Dad a meatless meal, he'd balk, "Where's the goddamn meat, Charlotte?" Realistically, I understood they sacrificed amply to provide for us; making sure our basic needs were met, but it was the nurturing side of our lives that was consistently neglected. We had been cheated out of life's essential gifts; feeling loved and secure.

It wasn't always chaotic in our home. There were a lot of good times and Mom and Dad had various happy moments together. Mom's softer side was her enjoyment of music and she passed down an appreciation for music from the World War II era. As a teenager, Mom enjoyed going to clubs that highlighted the big bands and various up and coming singers like Frank Sinatra and Perry Como. Mom also loved show tunes. We sang and danced around the living room to the soundtrack of Camelot and Oklahoma. She adored Robert Goulet and owned most of his albums.

One example of Mom's kindness was that after dinner, she rationed equally between the five of us treats such as M&Ms; guaranteeing a treat each night until the bag was empty. This was how I measured Mom's love for me. Much like following crumbs of bread down a path, I convinced myself that if I kept searching for another morsel of kindness, I wouldn't lose my way.

Mom's misfortune of not knowing how to drive made me realize we had missed out on a ton of good times. We never went places and we weren't involved with any organizations. We watched a lot of TV. Mom loved old movies and escaped into the world of film, swooning over her favorite movie stars that she watched over and over, in what she considered "The Classics." Her favorite movie star was Rock Hudson. Her heart broke when his being gay hit the news. She immediately replaced Rock with Robert Redford.

Mom had a fascination with soap operas. She was hooked like millions of women. The attention she gave to the daily dramas seemed more real to her than the needs of her own whining, snot-nosed kids. They provided the ultimate escape from reality for a few hours in her day. I, on the other hand, loathe them. In my opinion, they are time-devouring, mind sucking, melodramatic assaults on human intelligence with more unrealistic affairs than humanly possible. I can't understand why this mindless smut mesmerizes half the world. *Am I missing something?* Why haven't they all caught a venereal disease? Even my favorite comedian, Carol Burnett, is a big fan of the soaps. *I don't get it!*

As children, no matter what turmoil Mom's life was in, she rallied, and made sure each holiday wasn't forgotten. We celebrated Valentine's Day with a pink cake and "Be My Valentine" cards that we exchanged with each other. Easter renewed our spirits with a new outfit and a large wicker basket full of jellybeans, candied eggs, and (my favorite) a large hollow chocolate egg from the famous five and dime, Woolworths. Each egg was decorated with pink and blue pastel sugar flowers, curly green pastel leaves, and written in cursive, our name with white icing.

Later, we gathered at Grandma's house for lunch and the main event, the annual Easter egg hunt. Along with my cousins, we scrambled for dozens of colored eggs and the coveted prized golden egg.

Our birthdays were celebrated with a homemade cake, ice cream, and a chorus of "Happy Birthday To You," ending the song with an over-zealous pinch on your fanny from Mom saying, "Here's a pinch to grow an inch." I dreaded the celebratory pinch because she made damn sure you felt it.

For Halloween, we'd dress up in our homemade costumes and canvassed the entire neighborhood like deprived banshees not stopping until our pillow cases were filled to the brim. Thanksgiving, Mom cooked the traditional turkey with all the trimmings as we watched the Macy's Thanksgiving Day Parade.

Each Christmas, Mom made sure we had a Christmas tree, a ham and plenty of baked goods. I was seven years old when reality whispered in my ear that Santa Claus wasn't real. Late at night when they thought I was asleep, I overheard my parents arguing over where the money would come from to pay for our Christmas. Mom worried that if Dad got laid off, she wouldn't have the means to finish paying for our lay-a-ways. It was Dad's duty to supply the money for the presents. She nagged at him to borrow money from the bank so she could finish shopping. A fight unfolded over how much money Mom needed, opposed to how much money Dad thought she was spending on foolishness. It was a struggle to pay bills, let alone come up with extra money for Christmas. Many times they had done without for us, but we were never forgotten; they both made sure of that.

Many times Dad worked late on Christmas Eve and barely made it home in time to finish all the assembling required before we popped up and dashed into the living room to rip open our presents. Other times I'd overhear Mom warning Dad not to get drunk or stay gone too long; the toys needed to be but together. Somehow it all fell into place.

I was deeply grateful for all my gifts. The wrapped presents were from Mom and Dad and the unwrapped presents were from Santa (wink-wink). We each had a stocking filled with candy and trinkets, a few surprises, and a big blue/purple box with the store name, J. B. Whites written in silver. Inside was a pair of pajamas, slippers, underwear, and a new outfit. We always got that one *special* present you had asked Santa for. Each child was treated equally as to the value and number of presents received. Age determined many of our gifts. If you weren't old enough for, let's say, a bicycle, there was no need to pout or beg for one.

You knew your turn would come around. Whatever differences were festering between my parents, they did their best and were always fair to us.

One Christmas when I was about five, Dad tied a small velvet box onto a branch of the Christmas tree. He teased, "Charlotte, if you want your present, you have to hunt for it. Turn around; it's right under your nose." With her every turn, we'd shout, "You're cold, you're getting warm, warmer, you're hot!" The closer she got, the louder we squealed. After a minute, her eyes locked on the box. A long awaited set of wedding rings. *I knew it, he does love her!*

LIVING LIFE OUT OF LOVE OR DUTY

As a family, we didn't take many day trips, and vacations were just as sparse. My first memory of a getaway was to the Great Smokey Mountains when I was six. I loved the mountains; the crisp air, exquisite fall colors, and smell of apples and hay at each turn. It felt surreal to be away from home and not hear my parents quarrel. It did us all good to get away.

We took a day trip to Magnolia Springs when I was about ten. It started off as a beautiful day for a picnic and swim. Dad did his duty by providing the transportation as Mom did her duty packing lunch and getting everyone ready. It was up to us, as usual, to concoct our own fun. But we hadn't been there no time when Dad began chomping at the bit to get back home. Acting fidgety, Dad decided it was time to leave. He wouldn't relax and enjoy the day with his family. He barely saw us as it was. Other families seemed to be enjoying themselves. What's wrong with him? I'll always remember the disappointment turned anger on Mom's face. They fought the entire way home. Mom bitched, "You never take us anywhere except to your goddamn mother's on Sundays. When's the last time you spent a day with me and the kids? I'm the one stuck in the goddamn house with your five brats all week and never get to go anywhere."

Dad's justification, "I stay on the road all the goddamn time, Charlotte. I just want to rest and be left alone." They stayed at odds with nothing in common to hold their marriage together except the duty of raising five kids.

Soon after that incident, Mom gained enough confidence and eventually learned to drive. Now she had a little freedom to do as she pleased, but she was still going places without Dad, which only intensified her discontent. It was the opposite for Dad. His job kept him away, but truthfully, he had to feel free to be away from the incessant bickering that took place between them.

Getting her driver's license was a big deal for all of us. On long summer nights, we'd load the car with drinks and snacks and head to the drive-in movies; always being the first car in line. It seemed like eternity before the ticket agent opened the gate. Children twelve and under got in free so me and Rose would crunch down to appear younger; it made for a cheap outing. We enjoyed pleasant weather most of the time and were allowed to play on the playground under the movie screen. We had to be back to the car at dusk for the start of the movie. It was pointless to argue over who would covet the front seat. Mom made sure we took turns. She passed out the snacks as we settled down allowing Mom to escape from reality. If we became tired or bored with the movie, we simply fell asleep. As long as we didn't make noise while the movie played, it was safe to say everyone enjoyed themselves.

We all went on a second vacation to Daytona Beach, Florida. I had matured early and looked older than my true age of fourteen. Naturally, I began to notice the opposite sex. As I walked the beach, a boy pulled up on a motorcycle and asked, "Hey, cutie, wanna' ride?" I spontaneously put my hands on his shoulders, threw my left leg over the back of the seat, glanced up, and saw Dad staring down at me from the hotel balcony. Nothing needed to be said; I jumped off as quickly as I jumped on and that was the end of my summer escapade. At night, I would fall asleep listening to beach music. Even now when I hear a particular song, I can almost feel the breeze touching my cheeks and the ocean's unique smell. It was one of the few times my parents acted like they enjoyed themselves.

As a family, we didn't attend church but with Mom's Catholic upbringing, I was very aware of God's wrath. As a youngster, my aunt and uncle invited me to their Baptist church. On our way I began to sing a song I had learned from another kid. You remember, "There's a Place in France Where the Women Wear No Pants..." I never got invited back. I occasionally went to church by catching the neighborhood bus; however, going to church by myself proved to be perplexing. I trembled each time the preacher pounded his fist and bellowed damnation for the wicked. I'd walked up the aisle to be saved just about every Sunday. How many more times do I have to pray for forgiveness? When will I receive salvation? I don't feel any different but I sure don't want to burn in hell!

Mom made the effort when I was a pre-teen to start attending a Methodist church. She was adamant we must all be baptized. Mom was elected treasurer of her Sunday school class, but the responsibility made her extremely nervous. She surrendered her duty then eventually, stopped going altogether. I think church gossip, real or imagined, made her feel ashamed and unworthy. The only time I recall Dad going to church was when Mom had her nervous breakdown. He found comfort through a Methodist minister, but when the minister transferred to Atlanta, Dad lost interest and stopped going. We never could get our act together concerning worshiping as a family.

Mom had three faithful friends throughout her life: Jesse, Ann, and Birtie. They talked for hours on the phone and acted as Mom's lifeline by helping her get through each rough patch. She didn't have a relationship with Dad's family; they remained the enemy. She would forever be that *damn Yankee*. Mom only trusted Aunt LeeEllen; she loved her like a sister.

Mom met her oldest and dearest friend Jesse when they both lived at the YWCA. Jesse had taken pity on Mom when she learned of Mom's dilemma: pregnant and alone. It was only after Mom's death that Jesse kindly shared with me the truth about how Mom's life unfolded. They remained friends for over forty years through letters and phone conversations. Mom had chances to visit Jesse, but at the last minute, backed out. Why didn't Mom reunite with the one person who didn't abandon her in her bleakest moment? Did Mom envy Jesse's life? It read like a fairy tale; stable home, very successful husband, and a beautiful, intelligent, and obedient daughter. Had Mom shared too much, or had she hidden her sorrowful life from Jesse? Did Mom feel inferior and humiliated by how her life had fallen apart? After Mom's death, I felt compelled to explain to Jesse Mom's illness and personal struggles. I owed her that much. Jesse admitted she had been baffled by Mom's erratic communication. Sometimes, when Jesse called, Mom would abruptly cut the conversation short, giving no clarification. When Jesse received a letter from Mom, there wasn't an explanation for the time lapse between correspondences. The contents in the letters didn't mesh with previous letters. Jesse was at a loss not knowing about Mom's breakdown. Now, everything made sense.

Ann was also married to a railroad man. She and Mom compared notes on the vices of railroad husbands. This helped bolster Mom's belief that all railroad men treated their wives shitty. Ann had a kind heart.

I never saw her angry. Ann had no children so she bestowed an ample amount of attention on me. I dearly loved her. I wished Ann had been my mom, but I feared her husband more than my own Dad; they both exhibited a persona of rough, standoffish, and grumpy.

When my parents separated and were going through their darkest days, Mom almost lost Ann's friendship. Dad tried to intimidate and discredit Ann by spreading untrue rumors. Ann feared Dad would drag her into their court fight. She had no choice but to pull away from our family or her life would be ruined. Ann remained a dear friend, just at a distance.

The third lady was Birtie, another kind friend to Mom. Birtie never said a cross word or lost her temper with her boys. She fit the image of what *I thought* a good mother should be. Being a military family, they were transferred and moved out of state.

Mom's friends, if nothing else, had a sympathetic ear for her even if they didn't understand where she was coming from. I sensed they each felt sorry for *poor Charlotte*, their friend who had been so put upon by life. In spite of Mom's messy circumstances, they all remained friends. *And face it, we all need our friends.*

My parents personal struggles and constant quarrels were endless. Like a long drawn-out soap opera, they spouted heartless cutting words to each other fueled by stubbornness and wounded pride. Each fight spawned another with all of their past issues barreling ahead until they collided into one big *(sorry, Dad)* train wreck. The tension in our home grew and the self-inflicted hell they put each other through went beyond sad. This is how their twisted lives operated. Added to the drama were the unexpected and unavoidable bumps in the road that every family is plagued with at the most inconvenient times: taxes, car trouble, house repairs, job layoffs, doctor bills, and unexpected pregnancy scares. My parents viewed everything as a duty and it appeared there wasn't much done out of love. *Are duty and love one and the same?*

As hard as they tried to make things work, Mom and Dad had separated numerous times. Mom felt betrayed, neglected, and pinned down with five brats. Dad was burdened financially, trapped, and felt unappreciated. How did our family get to be so large if they were always fighting? The time spent alone at home fueled Mom's imagination on what Dad could be up to behind her back. Mom kept trying to catch Dad in a lie. She would accuse him of running around with different women: a neighbor's wife, a divorced nurse, a waitress he met while on the road, or some (rode hard, put away wet) whore in a bar. Mom stayed connected with other railroad wives. They all had to stay on their toes when it came to their husbands. They were quick to gossip about what *their* husband told them the *other* husbands were up to. It kept the heat off their imperfect spouse. Men gossip just as much as women; *really, they do.*

Mom told many people the saga of her stormy life with Dad, and it was no secret her kids were accidents. When Mom got mad enough, she made sure I knew it by aiming her sharpest (*you were never wanted*) arrow to inflict ultimate pain. If you were never told you were loved and never shown any outward affection, the burden falls on you to figure out why. *It's painful to know you weren't wanted. I've disappointed her. What can I do to change her mind about me?*

Being part of a big family wasn't entirely bad; I blended in and didn't get blamed for everything that went wrong. I had my sisters to play with, provided one of us wasn't on restriction. *Be fair, JoAnn, maybe Mom did love you. What is love exactly? If you are taken care of, then you are loved. If you weren't given up for adoption, then you are loved. Don't dwell, things could always be worse.*

YOU'RE A YOUNG LADY NOW: MY TURBULENT YEARS

I had entered the awkward age of pre-teen and I longed for the name brand clothes my schoolmates were wearing. But outfitting five children proved challenging. The dress I detested the most was purchased from the Jewel T man. He canvassed the neighborhood once a month in a tan truck that resembled a milk truck. You could order anything in the catalog from cleaning supplies, food, or clothes, however, the catalog carried a limited selection. He was a godsend to all house-bound women across America. The off-brand dress that Mom had chosen for me had large printed flowers in shades of brown, orange, and gold, with thick pleats around the waist that emphasized my wide hips and butt. The oversized belt with a huge gold buckle didn't help. I resembled a drab, middle-aged housewife in this type dress. Mom had no clue what trendy entailed, but I understood she did the best she could considering the budget she was given.

I began to mature early and by the age of eleven I was one of the girls in class who needed to wear a bra. Mom made a feeble attempt to prepare me for womanhood, but her unhealthy attitude toward sex did more harm than good. Plain and simple: Mom's portrayal of sex was distorted, and she wasn't shy in telling anyone how much she deemed sex as a woman's duty, void of pleasure, and bordering on sinful, yet it never stopped her from enjoying sex jokes with her friends. Mom lacked the fundamental wonder of nature and even viewed animal behavior as nasty. If Mom saw two dogs mating, she made us turn our heads. Dad used the word *frigid* quite often to describe Mom anytime the subject of sex came up.

I was clueless about the changes my body was going through so Mom took me to the health clinic. We picked up a pamphlet explaining a girl's monthly cycle entitled *You're a Young Lady Now*. "Read it," Mom said. I guess that's all she thought I needed to know, but her aloof approach to my body's changes left me bewildered, adding another layer of humiliation I had to suck up. Crossing over into womanhood should be a special time in every girl's life that is celebrated with their mother, but once again Mom fell short to bond with her girls.

Despite all the immature whispers and snickers about 'sex' being passed around school, it didn't sound that terrific to me. I couldn't understand what the big hoopla was all about. School didn't offer a sex education class, so I tried to decode the big "sex mystery" myself by relying on the encyclopedia. Not only could I not pronounce the words, the definitions were boring and the illustrations were confusing. So that, in a nutshell, was my sex education. I felt freakishly detached from myself. If I couldn't grasp the mechanics of human connection, at least I understood the logical assumption that Mom hammered into each of her girls, "Never trust any man. All men will lie to you, use you, and run around." It was left up to me by trial and error to figure out the rest for myself.

Dad on the other hand was a little too expressive toward sex and he embarrassed me one night in his attempt to enlighten me about the birds and the bees. I knew he had been drinking; that was nothing new. As I walked through the kitchen to see what was cooking, Dad abrasively blurted, "You better not let any boy get into your pants, do you hear me?" He caught me off guard, so I timidly replied, "Yes, sir." That was all I could think to say. *What does he mean? It sounded so vulgar. Why would he say that to me?* I was mortified. I hurried out of the room. That was Dad's only sex talk and I prayed their would never be another one. Dad had an unyielding rule that we girls could not date soldiers from the nearby fort. I didn't have a clue why, but I obeyed.

Dad bought a Stag magazine each month, and under the guise of cleaning the living room, I would sneak a peek. Splashed across the cover was a riveting, sensational title that pictured a young, beautiful, full-figured, sensual woman that was obviously in danger. These pictures could arouse any man's fantasies, especially Dad's. Each issue portrayed a damsel in distress being thrust into various amplified perils while dressed in skimpy, skin tight clothes that were conveniently torn in all the quintessential places. She was often being chased by a pack of animals (the two and four legged kind) through a jungle, desert, or forest, always with her long hair flowing in the breeze. Her wide eyes expressed a terrified foreboding fear. The dashing hero, who must try to save her from doom was placed as far in the background as the page allowed. Each story proved cheesier than the next; I promptly lost interest. I identified this smut the same as I did soap operas and cartoons: stupid mindless fiction. Seen one, seen 'em' all. Being analytical, I just didn't get it.

By the time I became a teenager, the realization of Dad running around on Mom had come to fruition. I would hear Mom telling her friends, and anyone who was in earshot, all the humiliating details of how she had once again caught him cheating. I wondered if the other woman was just a fling, or if he truly loved her. Maybe Dad had another family in another town and, if so, would he leave us for a happier existence with them? He was out of town as much as he was home, which made it easy to get away with plenty. Whatever he did when he was away from us was his secret. I naively rationalized his indiscretions. If Mom would stop being such a vindictive, nasty, cold bitch, Dad might stop looking elsewhere for affection. Was it her damn cold-heartedness that made him run around, or his damn running around the essence of her losing control? I prayed they would come to the realization that their life wasn't as bleak as they made it. Just look around, so many have it much worse.

My perception that Dad could do no wrong would inevitably be shattered. I was around eleven; we were heading home from an outing and we stopped for lunch at the Blue Bird Café in Waycross, Georgia. It was then I witnessed a distasteful experience: When it came time to pay the bill, out of the corner of my eye, I caught Dad flirting with our bubbly waitress. She wore her bleached blond curly hair pinned up with a dazzling rhinestone barrette that also held her pencil in place. Her bright red lips and nail polish matched. The name tag pined to her collar read Loretta. But It was her shapely figure in that short tight pink uniform that stirred the shit show. Dad threw a wink with his sparkling blue eyes, as he simultaneously thanked her for her service, folded her tip, and slipped the money into the crease of her cleavage. She clearly played her part in their eye tango. Mortified, had I been the only one at the table who witnessed his boorish behavior? What possessed Dad (other than her enormous exposed breasts) to act reckless with his family present? Does he know her from his railroad stops? She must be one of those whores Mom is forever obsessing about. If Mom had caught Dad flirting; no one could have stopped her before a few punches and claw marks would find their way to Loretta's painted face. Simultaneously a hand full of Loretta's bleached curls would get snatched out by their dark roots-only for Mom's wrath to be turned on Dad-all the while spewing a plethora of vulgarities at the hussy until the police arrived. Mom's fate would be jail, and I couldn't envision what ours would be. Dad's crude impulsive actions hurt deeply. I lost respect for him that day. Mom was right; he was a womanizer and a drunkard, and having her heart broken would be a never-ending reality.

Most life's experiences were thrust on me at home or school. There wasn't anyone in my life to encourage or influence me, and I'll admit, I wasn't blessed with a vivid imagination. With no best friend to lean on, I mastered this rationality by embracing the art of keeping to myself. *I don't need anyone.* They pretend they're my friend, and then repeat to others the secrets I begged them not to tell. So much for trust. All they do is talk about their looks and boys and brag about what clubs they belong to and which brand of clothes they wear; either Villager or Bobbie Brooks. Besides. How did they know which brand of clothes to buy? Who showed them how to put on makeup or fix their hair? I haven't the time for their silly nonsense; I have a mountain of chores waiting for me.

Growing up, if you weren't a cheerleader, you were a nobody. Girl's sports weren't as prominent as they are today. I wanted to play high school basketball, however with no transportation to the games, no family support, or confidence in myself, sports were excluded from my life. Instead, I enrolled in cosmetology thinking it would be a good trade to fall back on. I could open a beauty parlor within my home and support my children in case my marriage failed. It seemed like a practical idea, not that silly happy-ever-after Pollyanna crap, but a mature, prag-matic (in a positive sense) way of preparing for the future.

There was just one glitch; I hated every aspect of cosmetology. I had mastered the technique of making pin curls and finger waves but I found them repetitive and boring. They had gone out of style in the early sixties and the school hadn't kept up with the modern hairdos. I lacked *the knack* for creating bouffant swirls that were all the rage in the sixties. It took skill to keep the height of their hair in proportion to the size of their heads, and knowing the exact amount of lacquer to apply so their beehive wouldn't deflate midway through the evening. I dreaded the haughty white haired old biddies giving you a tongue lashing if their tint wasn't the right shade of blue. Fixing hair didn't come natural and besides, my heart just wasn't in it. Just like an ill-fated bouffant hairdo, my only dream for the future quickly deflated. Cosmetology would not be my vocation.

Conflicts at home had grown too intense for me to concentrate on my studies; somehow I passed school, but I felt like a failure. At least school took up most of my day. *Where do I go from here? What would I do after graduation? I didn't prepare for a career. I'm frightened.* I hadn't allow myself the luxury of dreaming about my future. Any goal seemed impossible to reach and as distant as the stars. *If your life is predestined, then what is there to prepare for anyway?*

In the mid-sixties, besides ball games or movies, many high school kids hung out at the local community center, Teen Town. It was open on Friday and Saturday night with a DJ spinning the top forty tunes. Occasionally, a local band, *Johnny Hensley and the Red Hots* would play. A cop at the door checked IDs and made sure the night remained fight and alcohol-free. It was *the place* to be and meet new people from neigh-boring schools. I learned different dances by watching Dick Clark's

American Bandstand, like the Twist, Stroll, or whatever was popular at the time. My only dilemma was finding a ride to Teen Town and bumming a way home. Somehow, each week I lucked out. I held back enough lunch money to pay for my admission. For most of my teen years, it served as a social lifeline that kept me out of trouble, a decent trade-off since I rarely had a date. I would hang out with friends and share the latest gossip on which couples were going steady or breaking up. It became a place I could enjoy instead of spending the weekend at home.

When I did snag a date, Dad would bark orders, "Jo is not allowed at the downtown movie house. You can take her to the drive-in movies, where it's safe." In the sixties, integration had just begun in the South, and Dad would go ballistic thinking I might have to sit next to a black man in a dark movie theater. Damn, the looks on my dates' faces. They couldn't believe their ears. What luck, to be given permission to go to the drive-in cinema that had earned the dubious distinction of being the make-out destination for lovers, and the local pick-up spot for sluttish girls. Dad didn't realize that his overzealous rule to protect his daughter trumped his good intentions. I'd roll my eyes and when we left my house, we went where we pleased.

I am amazed how people can effortlessly recall their childhood classmates. On the other hand, the people that drifted into my life seemed trivial and temporary since I placed no importance on my existence. Going through adolescence, I needed stability and encouragement from my parents; inversely they were my main problem. I had mastered the art of suppressing my feelings; not realizing how much I ached inside. I strived to erase hurtful memories that didn't need mentioning ever again, for they serve no good purpose. I dealt with reality by comparing my woes to others. This logic kept me grounded. I adapted this method to endure by reminding myself; some have it better and some have it worse. Everyone's life will experience twists and turns, but unless you recognize each encounter for what it is, you will be wandering aimlessly, and face it, life's your journey; it is what you make of it.

AN OLD
FAMILIAR PAIN

Mom tried to visit her family in New York every five years. One of the perks Dad had working for the railroad was that the entire family could travel by train anywhere in the United States for free. But traveling with five kids and having to come up with enough money for all the other expenses proved to be an ordeal. Dad stayed home each time we traveled to New York. In fact, he never returned to the North after being discharged from the Navy. He used the excuse, "I ain't lost a goddamn thing up there, Charlotte. I ride the rails most days and I'm sick of travelin." So, it was always *poor Charlotte* making the long trip with her brood. Mom made three trips in fifteen years, putting the emphasis on *needing* to see her father. But infrequent visits coupled with the passing of time couldn't repair their already damaged relationship.

We stayed with Uncle Sal and his family. Most of the trip was spent going to Coney Island, Chinatown, and visiting relatives. Mom's only sibling I never met was her half-brother, Willie. While making our rounds Mom would ask if anyone heard from Willie, but each conversation ended in a smirk and "no." Willie broke from the family early on so keeping in contact or his whereabouts wasn't noteworthy. It stirred up more curiosity than concern whenever his name was mentioned.

Mom spent a day with her cousin, Margie. They were as close as sisters. Mom barely spent any time with her dad and going to his apartment was considered a duty that she neglected up until the final day of our trip. We traveled all that way to spend just one afternoon visiting with our grandpa. No wonder he treated us like strangers; we were.

Grandpa still lived on the top floor of the apartment building in Brooklyn. Mom reaffirmed, "He prefers the top floor because the higher the floor, the cheaper the rent, and Pop's a goddamn cheapskate about everything." The neglect to himself and his apartment was overwhelmingly apparent the moment he opened the door. The foul aroma inundated my nose. I instinctively shut my mouth fearing if I swallowed any smidgen of the emerging smells I would die from a bizarre and incurable plague. His apartment reeked of mold, lingering remnants of stale cigar smoke, old wallpaper glue, urine, dust, and bird droppings. Thick, shabby drapes remained drawn, making the room darker and creepier than it needed to be. My eyes quickly fixated on huge stacks of old yellowed newspapers and brown paper bags that devoured every chair and corner. There was no place to sit except on top of the papers. I feared a rat would run out from under the seat and bite me. Later Mom confessed, "I bet that's where he hides his goddamn money."

Grandpa had a gorgeous golden-orange canary. I felt sorry for the bird and its dreary surroundings. It appeared the cage had never been cleaned. Did Grandpa ever let the bird out of its cage or play with it? Did it have a name? Was its existence just as lonely as Grandpas'? Could the bird be the only companion left in his life? He had run everyone off with his nasty disposition. How could Grandpa be so heartless to his own flesh and blood, yet have compassion for a small bird?

Mom ordered, "Go kiss your grandpa." I didn't want to get too close, but what else could an eight year old do but obey. I glanced over at Mom who kept a guarded distance. Grandpa was a dismal decrepit sight. His hands trembled as he gestured for me to come to him. His undershirt was dingy with layers of embedded particles of food and a variety of stains that blended down the front. His bedding reeked of urine and it appeared as if he hadn't bathed for awhile. His foul breath smelled of cigar, salami, garlic, and onions all rolled into one. His salt and pepper stubble pricked my face so I pulled away from him quicker than I should have. This frail unkempt stranger frightened me.

Many times I overheard Mom call him a monster as she damned him to hell in the same breath. But he appeared too puny to be any kind of a threat to anyone. His bed consumed the majority of his days. My first impression upon meeting him clashed with Mom's portrayal of him. Mom repeatedly affirmed she could see the hate in his eyes. But I couldn't. They appeared to be clouded amid years of loneliness and remorse. Had *Mom gotten her dark brown eyes from him?*

I savored a lemon anise cookie from the corner bakery and played with his canary while he and Mom rehashed their family's past. He maintained his Sicilian accent infused with broken English even though he had been in America fifty plus years. I couldn't understand a word he spoke due to his low raspy voice. He utilized his rickety arms to orchestrate each sentence while tears flowed down his cheeks. Mom cried too. *Were they crying about the deplorable way he treated his wife or the way he treated Mom? Did he regret his behavior? Had he missed her? Did he ever admit being wrong? Did he ask for her forgiveness? Did he love Mom? Did Mom love him? She said she didn't. Had she finally forgiven him? She said she never would.*

Could all those things Mom said about him be true? Perhaps long ago they were, but Grandpa withered through the years into a feeble, harmless, and pitiful old man. I now wonder if he knew that Mom had to get married. *Is that why he kept his distance from us, because shame had been brought to his name once again? And if so, would he ever forgive Mom?* I observed a different side of Mom that I had never seen before. It hurt that I knew so little about either of them.

It was no secret that Mom held contempt for her father and I later learned that her siblings despised him as well. They, too, had endured his wrath and witnessed him lashing out against their mother. As the years crept on, declining health and his hard-hearted personality transformed him into a recluse. Any connection with Mom remained piss-poor. He never traveled to Georgia to visit. He overlooked our birthdays and holidays. He made no effort to bond with his grandchildren. *What's the use? When would he see us again? He doesn't even remember our names.*

Over the years, Mom lost touch with most of her family except for Margie, but as much as Mom loved Margie, she kept her at a distance. I'd ask, "Why don't you go and visit Margie?" She's say, "She could just as easily visit me."

I had been to New York twice; once when I was eight and the other when I was twelve. I couldn't wait to go back, but in 1965, Grandpa died. He was in his nineties and I was fifteen. Mom took Rose with her to his funeral. They were gone a week, leaving me in charge of the house and siblings. Dad stayed MIA most of the time Mom was away, and I truthfully, didn't know his whereabouts.

Mom had hopes of inheriting something from her father but that fantasy was quickly shattered. He was a tailor by trade but retired from the phone company. He made a good living throughout his life so there should have been a decent nest egg, or so Mom thought. Her brother, Sal, lived around the corner from their dad. He took care of all his finances and personal needs. Mom divulged, "Your grandpa was a tightwad his whole goddamn life. I never expected anything from him, alive or dead." Mom suspected that he had hidden his money all through his apartment, but by the time she had arrived, there was nothing but mounds of trash intertwined with her dismal memories waiting to be discarded. The truth about his nest egg accompanied him to his grave.

BEYOND SAD

Mom returned from her father's funeral furious over the outcome. Once again I absorbed the brunt of her frustration. She bitched at me for leaving the ironing board out, giving no recognition for all I had done. She fixated on the damn ironing board. Her friend Ann spoke up for me and told Mom I had done a great job taking care of the kids and house while she was gone. Ann defused our standoff by suggesting I attend her church camp for a week. I wanted to go, even if it meant I would probably have to get saved again. Mom agreed to let me go and that is when I met Johnny, my first, true boyfriend.

I couldn't officially start dating until I was sixteen (six months away), so Johnny would come to the house to visit. I never understood how waking up one morning and being one year (actually one day) older, would magically make me ready to be left alone with a boy and simultaneously mature enough to embark upon the real world. Naturally, I kept this theory to myself.

I have a fond memory of my sixteenth birthday, and looking back, I felt (in her own way) Mom made an attempt to be a part of my life. It was one of the few times I felt like she cared about me. I had some friends over and one person was Frank. His mother was a family friend. As we slow danced, he gave me a birthday kiss. Mom caught us kissing and worried that we might be getting too serious. She didn't have to worry. Frank was a wonderful person but he was leaving for the Army and, besides, I loved Johnny.

Soon after my birthday, Mom and I started clashing-big time. Mom had a few intervals of normalcy, but her illness had begun to take hold. I could tell that each day was a struggle to keep her emotions in check. Instinctively, I felt close to Johnny and I began leaning on him more. He became my world, as small as it was. This was my first taste of what happiness felt like. We dated for six months, then he suddenly broke up with me. He justified his decision by telling me I reminded him of a song about a lemon tree. I played the song over and over hoping to decipher a hidden message so that I could link the lyrics to our relationship and hopefully turn my blunder around before it was too late. The only logic I could come up with was spelled out in the chorus: no matter how pretty the lemon tree is or how sweet its aroma, the fruit is impossible to eat. Did he mean it was the drama in my family or my erratic behavior that made our future hopelessly sour? Had I demanded too much of his time and leaned on him too much? Did I not pay him enough attention or did I act too immature? Whatever I'd done, I didn't know how to fix any of it.

Johnny was my first-love and I had gotten too serious, too soon. I simply didn't know the boundaries, so for whatever his reason, it was over. He began dating another girl. Trying to survive a broken heart for the first time brought endless tears. I moped around the house all summer. To have Mom on my side would have been a godsend. On the contrary, Mom was becoming more unpredictable. At times she acted obtuse, or so I thought, to what was going on in my life-then other times, she wouldn't stop breathing down my neck.

As Mom's resentment toward me had accelerated, I instinctively placed more distance between us. I stayed with a friend for a week. That's when Johnny's wedding announcement appeared in the Sunday paper. A picture of the bride-to-be in a beautiful wedding dress proclaiming their matrimony to the world. Mom's eyes locked on to the article and made damn sure I would see it as well. She mailed the newspaper clipping to me and wrote all over the picture in bold black ink, "HA, HA, HA, TOO BAD IT WASN'T YOU!" That was the defining moment in my life when I decided to isolate myself from Mom. *She was either crazy or just pure evil. What mother couldn't feel her own daughter's pain and intentionally not be there for her?*

I once read of a term the German people have for this called Shadenfrueude: getting pleasure or satisfaction from the pain and misfortune of others. It was upsetting that she hadn't shown any interest in my heartache except to belittle me or mock at my distress. I did my damnedest to not reveal anything concerning my true feelings, and to NEVER let her see me cry, EVER. I felt like I had lost my mother at sixteen, just as she had lost hers, except her mother died, while mine vindictively turned her back on me. *It felt like a death just the same.*

Rose was the oldest but she wasn't interested in dating, so my conduct with boys became the catalyst that fueled Mom's abnormal judgment. I had been grounded enough to know that actions held consequences. Her noxious remarks held no merit any longer. My new strategy of defense turned to indifference. I continued to keep my distance; however, I still had to deal with her cutting words and swift backhand.

I tried out my new-found independence by staying away from home as much as possible. Most of my time was absorbed between school and hanging out with friends. I dated anyone who asked me-whatever it took to be gone from Mom's presence. Mom started accusing me of things that simply were not true. Like the time I wrote in my diary that I had spent the day at a quaint hotel downtown. My friend worked as a lifeguard and he invited my girlfriend and me to swim in the hotel's pool. When Mom read this in my diary, her inherent reaction was to slap my face, call me a whore, and forbid me to see my friends again. Her accusation made me loathe her more. *Why wouldn't she believe me? How in the hell could she take the leap from a day of swimming to being a whore?* Ricky, who was nine at the time, witnessed Mom's assault on me, only to mimic her words, "You're a whore." To be a whore in Mom's perverse mind was the ultimate sin. She must have believed that her daughters would travel down the wrong path.

Each time Mom called me a whore, I wondered if she could faintly hear her father's voice shamefully repeating the same; allowing his condemnation of her still dwell in her mind? Did she believe he placed an *old world* curse that rendered her and her descendants forever tarnished? She didn't believe me; so how could I convince her otherwise? She had already made up her mind. She couldn't understand that accusing someone of being a whore doesn't make them one, nor would it stop them from becoming one. Her father's damning judgment of her character left Mom oblivious to how insensitive she treated her own daughters. Mom never recognized the correlation of her actions she placed upon her girls with the interactions of herself and her father.

I can't grasp what pleasure anyone willfully takes in spewing vindictive words except for the sole purpose of trying to wound them. Only to have to take back the words that lacked value or truth to begin with. "I'm sorry, I didn't mean it," or, "I only said it because I was so upset." What utterly cruel and immature behavior we reduce ourselves to. I remained perplexed because Mom never apologized or took back any words, especially the hurtful ones. I was demoralized each time Mom screamed in my face the affirmations of hate she had for me. I silently took all her words to heart because I take everything literally; in my mind if you say it, you mean it. *What else was I to think? Why else would she say them if she didn't mean them?*

I won't say things I don't mean, especially to my family. It's not in me to get back at someone through hurtful words just for spite. When I have a disagreement, I try to stick to my initial gripe, say what's on my mind, and not reduce myself to insulting name-calling. That would further damage the relationship and erode my credibility; it's nonproductive and causes added chaos. I'll never know if Mom genuinely meant: *she wished the hell that I'd never been born.* It was the repetitiveness of her remarks that gave the reassurance her words held truth. *Did she listen to the stinging words spewing from her mouth? Were they for shock value only? Did she ever wish she could take them back?*

As I transformed from a dirty ragamuffin to a young lady I continued to kept my distance from Mom. I had no clue how a normal person was supposed to act, but I knew I didn't want to be like her. If someone perceived even the slightest resemblance to Mom and me in looks or personality, I cringed. I saw only evil in her.

Kathy became the next in line to inherit Mom's perverted suspicions making her life equally harrowing as she, too, got pulled into the cross hairs of Mom's accusations and wrath. Kathy's feisty disposition clashed with Mom, leaving me apprehensive about her safety while I visibly kept my distance. We were both going through our confusing adolescent years, peppered with doses of rebellion.

Mom knew my freedom meant everything to me and to be placed on restriction felt like a prison sentence. I quit keeping a diary and I stayed clear of her as best I could. Each time our paths crossed, she tried to stare me down. I learned to freeze, not take my eyes off her, and never rebut what she was accusing me of. I had grown as tall as Mom; no more mother dominating child, but rather person to person confrontations. Her threats took on a whole new meaning. If Mom's dark, brown eyes could kill, I would have been pushing up daisies before I reached womanhood. I remember thinking, "Just slap me and get it over with!" What am I expected to say? WHAT? Do I stand here and take it, run, cry, yell, tell Dad, or say I'm sorry? How can I fix this? What does she expect from me? I wished she knew how I really felt about her. If she could read my mind she would know, "I'm sick of your malicious accusations and your brutality. I can't stand to be near you. *Just leave me the hell alone, you crazy, heartless excuse for a mother!*"

I compared her illness to a kudzu vine, her problems to water, and her hatred to fertilizer. If you are familiar with this particular Southern plant, then you know how prolific the plant is. It grabs hold of anything, covers it completely, deprives it of sunlight, and chokes the life right out of it. Given the right conditions (pain and rejection), her illness took root like the kudzu on a tree (her life) encompassing everything in its path. Her illness, like the kudzu vine, was unrelenting.

Like most teenagers, I acquired a sassy mouth. When provoked by Mom, I mustered enough courage to sling a zinger or two while making sure I was near an exit. "Well, you made me," was my comeback. Why didn't she have a response? That wasn't like her. My intended analogy went over her head. *Wow, JoAnn, you really told her!* Expressing her disgust in me implied pure evil but I didn't have it in me to come back with hurtful words. But there were times I did lose control and I felt myself slipping into her depraved way of thinking. It sickened me as I struggled against a never ending lure not to mimic her actions. How easy it would be to succumb to her conduct; her beliefs were all I had known.

I also kept a healthy distance from Dad, especially when he drank, which by now had turned into a routine with him. I despised how his views of women were distorted when he was under the influence of alcohol. After witnessing the Blue Bird Café incident, I realized Mom was right about his womanizing. I felt uncomfortable observing him flirting with my girlfriends, so when Dad was home, I stayed gone.

Late one night, Dad staggered into my bedroom drunk, leaned over my bed, and tried to kiss me good night. I wanted to scream for him to get out but I was frozen with uncertainty. Mom appeared at the door with her cold, cutting Sicilian eyes; stared straight at Dad and yelled, "Get the hell out of this room Pat, and leave her alone." This time, her feisty perception was on target. I was determined I would never forget his drunken display. I scratched my inner arm with my fingernails so that when I woke up the next morning, I couldn't delude my memory as a dream; however, I cowardly never mentioned the incident to either of them. When he drank, he was too strong for me to handle and too drunk to reason with. I kept my guard up from then on.

I BRUISE YOU,
YOU BRUISE ME

S oon after Mom's father's death, she found an inner strength to look for a job. All us kids were growing like weeds, eating more, and needing more things. A persistent factor of their woes was the lack of money. Mom was determined to start making her own way and not remain dependent on Dad any longer. Mom was hired by the state hospital to take care of mentally disabled patients. When she received her first paycheck, she kept it for herself, launching a fresh conflict between her and Dad.

Dad had shouldered the financial responsibility of his family from the beginning, and he felt it wasn't right for her not to contribute to the bills. However, he also believed a woman's place was to take care of family and home. Any talk of women's lib and bra burning made his blood boil. The more independence Mom acquired, the less control Dad had over her and the more rejected he felt. Mom had also done without for our sakes so everything she earned would now be hers to do with as she pleased. So what if she didn't share; by her way of thinking, everything balanced out. She wouldn't have to beg him for any spending money, therefore, leaving Dad with more money in his pocket. Dad grumbled over Mom's stinginess while Mom gloated over her slice of independence. Her comeback to Dad rang true, "You bitched when I wasn't making any money and you bitch when I do." I understood each one's point of view, but it left me trapped in the middle to witness their bruising each other.

Mom's cocky stance not to contribute drove a deeper wedge between them allowing resentment on both sides to fester. Oh how she loved to throw in his face that she was now capable of making it on her own. This could've been a turning point in their lives if they would only come together. But neither one could put their own feelings aside or concede that all the sacrifices they each made for the family were just as deserving as the other. They betrayed two essential rules of marriage: respect and support for each other.

Mom worked the midnight shift in charge of a cottage of patients. Although they were referred to as children, they ranged in age from pre-teen to elderly and would call that place home until their deaths. In their world, a normal day consisted of cursing, fighting, and eating. Her duty was to monitor their habits, distribute medications, and help them settle in for the night. Mom described the patients' behavior as unpredictable. You needed to stay alert at all times. Mom expressed concern when she learned a patient had turned his brute strength on a worker. It's a widely accepted belief that patients became more agitated and their aggression escalated during a full moon. One night, on a full moon, a patient twice Mom's size picked her up and threw her 105 pound body against the wall. If a co-worker hadn't come to her aid, he could have killed her.

That one year of working took its toll on Mom's physical and mental well-being. The stress affected her sleep. She worried about what Dad was doing, or *whom* he was doing, while she worked. His outings to *who knows where* increased leaving Mom to endure another betrayal. Mom was hanging on by a thread to her already strained marriage; so she resigned. Her hold on her kids was slipping. I sensed something was about to emerge, but I was too naive to be of any help. Mom's full-blown breakdown lurked right around the corner.

Mom and Dad's big break-up came in 1965 when I was almost seventeen. I had lost count of the endless fights, separations, and threats of divorce that set an avalanche of distrust in motion. The discovery of another tryst was the last straw. Dad moved out and stayed with his older sister, LeeEllen, for fifteen dollars a week. A faded blue pickup truck and five kids all under the age of eighteen were all he had to show for eighteen years of marriage.

We hadn't seen Dad in over three weeks when he called and told Kathy for all of us to get ready; he wanted to take us all to lunch. Kathy begged, "Mom too...please?" She swore she heard him say yes; we eagerly got dressed to go. The moment Dad drove up, we ran to the car excited to be with Dad. Mom locked the front door and had made her way to the car when Dad asked Kathy in a boisterous voice to make sure Mom would hear, "Who in the hell told her she could come?" Mom burst into tears and ran back into the house. Kathy began sobbing, knowing she was to blame for relaying the message to Mom. Did Kathy hear Dad correctly, or by wanting us all to be together, had she just thought she heard "yes." Had Dad maliciously lied about inviting Mom to lunch, using Kathy as a pawn?

At the court hearing I was terrified just by being in the presence of such prominent intelligent people. I trembled when I spoke to the judge. How humiliating for a stranger to know our family's personal problems.

The judge informed Dad of his duty to take care of the family he had created. Once again, a person of authority (a goddamn, know-it-all outsider) stepped into Dad's life and altered his fate.

I overheard Mom divulge to a friend, "Pat can't afford to leave me, thanks to the judge. He awarded me the house, car, and alimony. Plus, Pat must pay child support for his damn kids until they reach the age of eighteen." Then, in an imperious tone, she boasted, "The judge really stuck it to that son-of-a-bitch. It serves him right for all the heartache he put me through all those goddamn years. I hope he's suffering."

They put the house up for sale, however, each time the real estate agent placed the FOR SALE sign in the front yard, feisty little Kathy would wait for them to leave, then run and take it down. My parents would spite each other at any opportunity. Dad stopped paying the car note so the bank repossessed our only means of transportation. They both played a part in some nasty mind games and mudslinging while they shamefully overlooked the trepidation they placed on their kids. Each one, in random moments of malice and despair, threatened to kill each other. Not knowing their outcome; our future hung in the balance. No one had mentioned what would become of us.

I prayed the madness would end. It didn't matter who they dragged through their miserable hell. They kept score on how many people sided with or blamed the other for the latest screw-up, and the winner would be whomever accumulated the most sympathy. Are they finally going to call it quits? I hope she goes back to New York. Would Dad turn his back on us? Will Mom ever let him go? Damn her for all the shit she stirred up and damn him for leaving. Damn them both for burdening their kids with all their exhausting self-inflicted drama.

Mom once again, choking back the humiliation, agreed to try and make another go of it. Poor Charlotte took him back. His baggage of previous indiscretions, fostered lies, drinking issues, and emotional abandonment followed close behind. She had to love him if you compare the vile ultimatums she spewed at Dad when they fought, to the contradictory way she exhibited her hysterical behavior each time he left. Dad stayed away about eight weeks, although it didn't feel unusually long considering he'd been absent from our lives a great deal of the time.

I remained cautiously optimistic the day Dad came home, but when he did, he wasn't the same man I knew. He appeared to have aged ten years; his face portrayed a defeated look. He headed straight to his chair and never uttered a word. Dad walked back into our lives a broken man. I glared into his eyes, and saw a reflective plea for forgiveness, but before I could say anything, he dropped his head in shame. The wringing of his hands was the only outward clue that revealed his despair. He resigned himself to the fact that his life would remain in a hellish limbo until the kids were grown. *Here I go again feeling sorry for him.*

Dad's decision to come back seemed noble, but was it in our best interest or his own? We were five notches on his belt that confirmed his manhood, his posterity, and his burden. Had his commitment to his family been bound by guilt or duty? Had our existence carved out a purpose for him? Were we ever his pride and joy? Did he resent us as much as Mom had? Perhaps if he had known what was just over the horizon and how it would impact the family, he may have given more thought before he reconciled with Mom.

Their marriage morphed into a dance of its own. Mom was trying to not lose the love of her life and Dad struggling to reclaim his lost freedom; while trying to do the right thing by his family. Dad made attempts to appease Mom but wouldn't give up the root of his problem, drinking. I doubted if it was worth the price they paid by staying together. Both were lonely, beaten down, miserable, and undeniably trapped. The problem with a sour relationship is that no one on either side is willing to compromise or consider the other person's perspective. The longer the problem lingers unresolved, the deeper the root of the matter blurs until you can't recall what created the fracture in the first place. No matted how hard you try, you're not able to make things work. You can't keep beating yourself up if the other person, for whatever reason, isn't willing to relinquish their disdain, forgive, and meet you halfway. A broken relationship typically remains two-sided. As Mom worried about the fragile state of her marriage, she had to concede she had no means to support herself and five kids. Her main skills were giving birth and causing chaos.

Allowing Dad to return from their last separation proved to be a quandary. In addition to her looming problems and her escalating temper, life threw her another snare. At thirty-eight-years-old, Mom needed a hysterectomy. She still had her ovaries but her hormones were never regulated after the operation. This betrayal of her body turned her emotionally upside down and her mood swings bounced from one end of the spectrum to the other. How long would it take for her body to complete the cycle of change and return to normal? Mom battled with her inability to adjust to the "change of life" while Dad damned menopause for her irrational behavior. Dad's repeated drinking and rumored infidelity, and her rebellious kids kept her emotions stirred up. Her perception of reality and her inner demons clashed, distorting the balancing act in her mind. Any rational thinking began to slip away.

Mom and Rose were at each other's throats, so Rose abruptly moved out. This caused more unsettling drama for my parents. They remained trapped in a volatile marriage now with four kids but their quarrels were never-ending. Doesn't everyone's father curse, drink, and run around? Doesn't everyone's mother scream obscenities, beat their kids, and voice she wished the hell she never had them? Were their "I wish you were dead" out burst to each other real, or are they just spouting words in anger?

With graduation being just around the corner; I realized if I wanted to be a part of the ceremonies, I better get busy and find a way to pay for all the incidentals. I got a part-time job as a waitress at Shoney's. I placed my tips in my dresser drawer but when I checked, some of the money was missing. I'd complain to Mom, "One of the brats stole my money." Mom's only solution, "You should have hid it better." I realized I was in this alone; my existence carried no weight with her. I managed to save enough to buy my cap and gown, graduation dress, invitations, and thank you notes. This was my senior year of school and so far, the biggest event in my life. I should have been enjoying every moment. My senior year was treated as just another untimely burden without any thought for celebrating. They weren't supportive, however, they did buy my class ring, only because it was ordered a year in advance and they had bought one for Rose. The safety net of school would soon be behind me and I wished that I had recognized the importance of an education sooner.

Even as a teenager, I took no interest in my appearance. Makeup and fashion was never my strong point. *What's wrong with me? Who would want me? No one so far.* I never seemed to blend into any public setting. It appeared others were effortlessly in tune with life, while I marched out of step. My parents' screw-ups had seeped into my thoughts and undermined my perception of what kind of person I should be. I lived with a constant worry, questioning my own worth. I perceived myself as too good to be bad, but too bad to be good. I believed in God, yet I felt inadequate around the company of Christians, specifically how they gave the guise of their lives being perfect in every way. They appeared smug and self-righteous. That in turn, made me feel like I was on the outside, not worthy enough to belong.

I was at my wits' end dodging Mom's erratic flare-ups, knowing what little connection we shared was crumbling at an accelerated rate. Mom is always crying and she glares at me so hatefully, as if I'm the one that ruined her life. I was also fed-up with Dad's drunken habits. Would he get wasted again and start another brawl at Snuffy's Bar? Will he drive drunk, get into another wreck, and be locked up for a DUI? Will he get fired? Will he leave again? That's when the conflict flared up: loving them, resenting them, and putting up with their shameful conduct while trying to mold a life for myself. If I had learned anything, it was that I didn't want my life to mimic theirs. I did my best to shut both of them out of my life.

As other people were going about their own adventures, I felt somehow paralyzed by an invisible force of uncertainty. My life will never change until I stop tripping over my own fears and move far enough away where my past can't follow. People do it every day. But how do they find the courage to leave? Where would I go? How would I get there or support myself? Where would I live? I wouldn't know anyone. What if things go wrong and I have to beg to come home? Would they let me come back? The irony of it all was that even a sad existence is safer than the fear of the unknown. Rose never called home, so I had no way of knowing if she was happy, safe, or in danger. Damn Rose for bolting. *Had she regretted leaving?* Rose had put our parents through a magnitude of anguish; I couldn't have them go through that again. I kept reminding myself, it could always be worse.

Graduation was finally upon me. That's when my life should have had a clear vision for my future. I carried a halfhearted notion that I wanted to become a teacher, but I didn't have a clue on how to prepare for college, nor did I have the means to pay for college. I knew nothing of grants or scholarships and I believed in a half-baked idea only the richest and smartest people were accepted. College wasn't discussed or encouraged in our home, and I hadn't known anyone that had been.

Dad preached, "If you're not gonna' be a nurse, there's no need for any more schoolin'." One solution to my dilemma was to get married and have children. But I had no love in my life to start making wedding plans. The cosmetology course I barely passed didn't interest me or provide any notable skills to pursue a different career. My duty to take care of my parents prevailed. My graduation took a back seat to their drama.

Dad didn't attend my graduation. I think he had to work that day. I'm pretty sure they were separated at the time. I'm still haunted by a picture of Mom taken at my graduation. She looked ghastly, like a walking skeleton. She weighed ninety five pounds and lived off cigarettes and coffee. Mom's nerves were shot and her mental pain was evident. I could see the anguish in her eyes.

There are numerous occurrences that I simply can't recall, especially the episodes that involved my siblings. Even now, when my sisters and I ask each other when did such and such happen or if we remembered a certain incident, our reply is matching, "No, I don't remember." *How do you put chaos in order?* Memories tumble through my mind like nonsensical dreams drifting through. I can't evoke the specific order of when they transpired, especially my senior year. That's the time everything came crashing down. My love life was in turmoil. Rose had left home. Mom and Dad separated only to get back together. Dad's drinking worsened. It was also the time leading up to and going through Mom's nervous breakdown making 1966, 1967, and 1968 the most traumatic years of my life.

THE ILLNESS AND
THE AFTERMATH

Mom invited my friend Sue to have dinner with us, but she had to work late so I decided to take dinner to her. I started to leave when Mom stopped me and demanded to know, "Where in the hell do you think you're going with my spaghetti?" Stunned by her irritated inquiry I answered, "I'm taking Sue dinner and then we're going to the movies. Mom, you're the one that invited her." My response provoked Mom that instantly sent her into a hysterical tantrum. Wrong answer, JoAnn. She was all over me in an instant, cursing and beating me, and with her wild arms she robustly yanked my hair, then took her nails and clawed my face. I instinctively fought back and broke free. I stayed at Sue's house and skipped school until my face healed. I was too terrified to go back home. *Where had this fierce rage come from?*

I tried to explain to Dad how bizarre Mom had acted, but he responded in a clueless manner. My bitching was so insignificant in comparison to his misery; he couldn't connect with what I had gone through. Dad never knew about the prior incidents when Mom pulled a knife on Rose, and attacked Kathy in one of her impulsive outburst. I had witnessed plenty and wished I had told him sooner about Mom's brutality to us while he was working, but I remained under his spell of obedience. Open your eyes, Dad. Mom's violence had already run Rose off. Just because he never observed her attacks on us didn't mean I was lying. I lived through more than enough sorrow than to want to purposely fabricate any more drama. All he had to do was look at my clawed face and realize that Mom had become dangerous to be around. *Was he in denial?*

Of course Mom got to Dad first with her version of our fight. Dad promptly sided with Mom. I had to endure his lecture, "Jo, you let me down; you don't ever fight your mother. You should know better. Just because you two butt heads don't give you the right to disrespect her." *I guess it was my fault; I must have provoked her in some way.* His lack of support alarmed me as well. I had no choice but to go back home and endure Mom's evil gaze. You couldn't appease her and her distrust toward everyone intensified. I felt helpless and frightened for my siblings and myself. I kept my guard up the nights Dad worked.

Shortly after the food sharing incident, Mom flipped out on Dad. Dad called her doctor and told him she was acting deranged and needed help before she killed someone. *Now he gets it.* Mom went by cab to her doctor's office, but the doctor sent her home, telling Dad she seemed fine to him. Within the hour, she again called a cab and left for three hours only to come back wild-eyed and full of rage. During her outing, she phoned her doctor and cursed him out, cursed the taxi cab driver, and anyone else that crossed her path. The doctor was now willing to sign the papers to have Mom committed to the mental hospital. As the ambulance drove off, I could hear Mom scream, "I'm gonna' kill you, you goddamn son of a bitch! I hate you! I hope you rot in hell!" I muttered under my breath, "My God, has she gone crazy? Has she lost her mind?" Little did I know; *she really had lost her mind in the most unimaginable way.*

The only thing I knew about crazy people was what I had seen in the movies: they were sent to an insane asylum and locked away, never to be heard from again. They dressed each patient in white gowns and pumped with endless amounts of drugs that altered them into submissive, mindless zombies, or raging screaming lunatics. A wave of panic like nothing I had ever experienced before came over me. She had tipped the scale with her anger. We were informed that Mom had suffered a nervous breakdown, and was diagnosed with paranoid schizophrenia and manic-depressive disorder. The prognosis horrified and saddened me. I believed she was lost forever.

The doctors chose a series of shock treatments to be administered as Mom's therapy. She stayed hospitalized eight weeks. Her illness and treatment were foreign to me and my ignorance on the subject made it nearly impossible to absorb. Being told her condition was a mental illness instead of thinking she was pure evil didn't diminish my being terrified of her. Just because a label was put on Mom's condition didn't mean her violence had ended. It had taken me a lifetime to build a wall of defense. I was determined not to let my guard down. No one could predict how she'd cope after being released, especially when she was returning to her same environment. I could only surmise that all our lives would be radically altered.

Back in the sixties, mental illness was a taboo that carried a stigma far worse than going to jail for mass murder. If it was discussed at all, it would be in a disturbing whisper. I carried around so much shame I could barely hold my head up as I walked down the school halls. My weighted problems were embarrassing. Why are my peers staring at me? Am I the one they're whispering about? Has everyone heard about my mother's meltdown? *Do they think I'm crazy too? I can't trust anyone.* I couldn't describe my misery to anyone mainly because I didn't understand it myself. No one ever talked about their problems, so I assumed they didn't have any. They all seemed to be into themselves enjoying their teenage rite of passage, talking about what they would wear to the game, what pop singer they had a crush on, which boy asked them to the prom, and who was going steady with whom.

While Mom was being treated in the Cleckley psychiatric ward, she wasn't allowed visitors; still Dad never failed to stay on top of her progress. I overheard him telling Aunt LeeEllen that he peered through the window on the door and saw Mom and another patient giggling, holding hands, and skipping down the corridor. They acted like little children without a care in the world.

Mom came out of the hospital less than human and her life as she once knew it came to a screeching halt. The shock treatments seized Mom's old personality only for her mind to emerge like a box of melted crayons that had been left out in the sun. The original colors were still there, only fused together in a clotted swirl, transformed into a hue that was difficult to recognize. Her freakish transformation was perplexing to witness. This became Mom's new shade of life. There was no way their original composite could be restored. I doubted she would ever have clarity again.

All of this made Dad grapple with whether or not he had made the right decision by having Mom committed. What other alternatives did he have? If he had waited much longer, her threats of killing him, committing suicide, or harming her kids would have come to fruition. He either agreed to the treatments with hopes she would be cured within a short period of time, or have her committed to a mental hospital indefinitely. Each choice carried its own weighty consequence. Will Mom get better or be sent away? If she gets to come home, will she remember us? Are we to blame? Does Dad feel responsible for her flipping out? Will he bolt and leave me running the show? I wouldn't wish this illness on my worst enemy.

In my convoluted vision of realism, I pictured everyone's life in constant motion and floating perfectly (or so it seemed) into place, except mine. By this time, many of my girlfriends were paired up with the love of their lives, had received engagement rings, and were making wedding plans. After graduation, friends were packing for beach trips, preparing for college, or beginning careers. I envied their carefree persona as I peered through rose-colored glasses. My mind was at a standstill, while the days swirled around me like a tornado. *Weren't these supposed to be the best years of my life? Where do I go from here? What path do I take? What career do I choose?* My inaccurate perceptions of other peoples' lives caused frequent and unnecessary anguish. I believed my family was the only family in the world with a drunken father and a mother fresh out of the crazy house. It was terrifying to think what else would crumple. If I couldn't unravel this fear, I might lose my mind just like Mom did.

After Mom's stay in the psychiatric ward, she continued treatment under her doctor's care. We never met her psychiatrist. What value was going to a shrink if he only heard one side of the story-and the crazy one's point of view at that. I could have shared plenty. After several appointments, Mom abruptly stopped going. When I think about the physical and mental pain that Mom endured as a child, my heart deeply aches for her. She didn't have a positive environment growing up, so how could she create one for us? She kept her distance and she never connected emotionally past a mother's duty. She rejected love from the very ones that could have loved her unconditionally.

Mom gave the impression of confusion with an unwavering reservoir of paranoia. Any question you asked her had a guarded answer, as if answering incorrectly would land her back in the *loony ward*. Only once did she divulge what the psychiatrists told her. He instructed Mom to release her inner feelings instead of keeping them locked inside, to always speak her mind, and never hold anything back. *Wow...that should cure her.* So Mom blurted out to anyone, anywhere, exactly what she was thinking and it didn't matter if she embarrassed you or hurt your feelings. Not even a look of disapproval could shut her up. This entitled behavior fed her gratification for all the stares and whispers she had endured.

Months passed while Mom continued to be out of touch with the world. What good were the shock treatments? I assumed Mom's hospital stay would be as basic as getting a car fixed. The car goes in the shop, gets worked on, and it runs as good as new; only it didn't work that way. The general observation concerning her behavior was, "Oh, you know Charlotte; that's just the way she is", or "Poor Charlotte, she just needs to rest more; she's been through so much." But the diehard gossips unveiled the obvious, Herbert had finally driven Charlotte over the edge.

All I knew was this woman had been very cruel to me and my siblings and I believed she was pure evil. Her glaring eyes hadn't left; I think she still hates me. She told me enough times, she beat me enough times. I was her good-for-nothing shit-ass daughter. The one that made her sick to look at. It never occurred to me that I should seek professional help to sort through my state of mind. *Why should I?* Mom was the crazy one, not me, and to suggest I needed help would label me 'crazy' equal to the person that I hated and feared.

Needless to say, after Mom's nervous breakdown the whole family fell apart. Dad was visibly shaken by Mom's mental collapse with no clue on how to handle her new rituals. The outcome of their future must have weighed heavy on his mind. Had he accepted that his drinking and infidelity contributed significantly to her crisis? Dad continued to work out of town. I'm sure he had many sleepless nights wondering about the safety of his kids being alone with her, not knowing what she would do to us, or not do for us. Dad couldn't afford a housekeeper so the burden fell on me.

I was seventeen, still in school, and saddled non-stop with the responsibility of taking care of the house, three siblings (ages fourteen, ten, and seven), and a mother, fresh out of the nut house. I felt overwhelmed and trapped–being as much in the dark as Dad was. My every thought was consumed by panic. My fear and reality had collided. Would she snap again and try to hurt any of us? Does she remember her kids? Would she fall asleep and have a neglected cigarette catch the house on fire? Would she overdose? Would a stranger break in our house while Dad was away? You read in the newspaper about these types of horrors happening every day, so don't label me paranoid.

Before my mother's breakdown, I was very fearful by her level of violence and what I might walk into each time I came home. After her breakdown, I was still frightened, just with different concerns. The fusion of shock treatments and powerful medications had diminished her violent flare-ups, but instead of her thoughts sustaining logic, a paradoxical side effect created a negligent repercussion that wove through her mind and distorted her ability to function. The doctor had her drugged with Thorazine, Lithium, and Valium. When she needed to get up and walk somewhere she stumbled around like a drunk. Her communication diminished. She would only stare at you like a mindless zombie. That was the extent of her response. I was petrified of her. It never occurred to me that my siblings might be frightened of her as well. If they were, they never let on, at least not around me. Surely Mom's appearance and unwillingness to respond was enough to conjure up scary thoughts in their naive minds. The younger two weren't as caught up in Mom's wrath like Rose, Kathy and me, but after her nervous breakdown, Ricky and Gail got drawn into an altered wave of neglect and misery. They were much too young for emotional abandonment.

Mom's appearance would make you cry. It was one of the most heart-wrenching sights I've ever witnessed. She appeared to have aged twenty years. The shock treatments seemed to suck her soul right out of her frail body, leaving only a shell of my mother. Her cheeks were hollowed, giving her eyes an exaggerated protrusion under their fidgety lids. She had lost so much weight, it looked as if she had emerged from a concentration camp. How was she capable of reclaiming her life when her mind seemed to be suspended in space, and her body too weak to protect her? *I don't know this person, she's beyond pitiful, and I'm sick with worry.*

Mom had never neglected her appearance, but after the shock treatments, taking care of herself no longer held any worth. The treatments caused peculiar side-effects, one being Mom's eyebrows fell out and never grew back. Mom stopped wearing makeup. The only regimen she didn't neglect was making sure no one saw her before she penciled in her eyebrows. Why she was self-conscious about her eyebrows but not by the rest of her appearance baffled me. It made no difference that her hair was dirty so when Mom sat up after her long bouts of sleep, her wiry, gray hair would be smashed flat against the side of her head that she had lain on, poking straight out on the other side, and sticking up and out on the top. Mom stopped bathing on a regular basis, and I couldn't talk her into changing her nightgown or panties. "You'll feel much better, Mom, if you would bathe." But for whatever reason, she disregarded any comfort for herself.

Mom remained in a constant daze; her eyes had a wild, fixed stare, yet deep inside, they looked empty and oblivious to the world around her. She preferred not to make eye contact. Instead she kept her eyes fixated on any object that could not harm her. Her mouth remained dry and open as she made involuntary movements with the back of her lower jaw like a guppy gasping for its last taste of air. She couldn't control her fidgety hands, unsure of where to place them. She sat with her hairy legs wrapped around each other with the top foot supporting one bedroom slipper that flapped nervously in the air.

If someone came to visit, Mom popped up like a cork on the end of a fishing line and sealed an insincere smile on her lips, but again, wouldn't make eye contact. She tried to focus on the moment even though her mind was incapable of holding any thought or interest. Her skeletal frame revealed a nervous tremble as she instinctively reached for a pack of cigarettes from the carton that never left her side. Her cigarettes were the only familiar thing she clung to. She simultaneously fumbled with the buttons on her bathrobe to cover up parts of her scrawny body that would poke through exposing her physical deterioration. Her anxiety escalated with each passing minute as she strived to light a cigarette.

The shock treatments prohibited Mom from expressing her feelings; all emotion in her voice ceased. She gave a one-word reply to any simple question that was asked her but never asked anything in return. If Mom felt pressed to answer, she simply agreed with what was being said just to shut you up and leave her be. As she became more panicky, the conversation quickly turned one-sided, placing any guest in an uncomfortable position and drawing the visit to an abrupt halt. Mom's quick "Well bye," gave the cue it was time for them to leave. We made feeble excuses for Mom's behavior as we saw each person to the door, always thanking them for coming and suggesting they come back when Mom felt better.

Some dropped by out of curiosity, others afraid that her condition might rub off on them, and I was one of them. Could her disease be virus-related, contagious, or worse, hereditary? But no one ever questioned us directly about her sickness. Any judgments or quarrels anyone previously had concerning Mom evaporated in the aftermath of her mental breakdown, allowing new speculations to swarm after witnessing her broken spirit for themselves.

The visits began to taper off and soon people stopped coming altogether, except for aunt LeeEllen. She visited Mom the most, and even though Mom loved her, not even LeeEllen could get through to Mom. My aunt would kiss her goodbye, and before the door closed behind her, Mom would be lying down in a fetal position with her face turned toward the back of our big green sofa. Mom's damaged mind sought refuge, convinced everyone had deserted her. I wondered if her delusions of betrayal would be her protection or destruction. She wrapped herself in an afghan, a.k.a. her security blanket that lured her to retreat to a safe silent place as far back as her mother's womb.

All of Mom's living was executed on the sofa. Her daily activities consisted of sleeping, smoking, eating, and watching TV. I don't think she even comprehend what she was watching. Each time Mom turned to face the back of the sofa, she tuned the world out. When she chose to turn back around, it was on her terms, still with very limited interaction. Administering to her basic needs was all that was required of us. No one could penetrate her world, and she wasn't in any frame of mind to reconnect with ours. Safe in her mental cocoon, she wanted nothing more than to be left alone.

When she did emerge she struggled with having only her muddled and bewildered bits of memory to sort through. To what extent had her mental awareness slipped away? Was she grieving for the stolen memories? How much of the wonderful had she lost with the excruciating? Were they the memories of her childhood or only the later years when she was at her sickest? Had she surrendered the traumatic chapters of her life that had put her in peril in the first place? Does she remember any fragments of how horrible she treated us, or how vile her words were to us? And if so, did any of it matter? She was in no condition to sort things out. She had lost her desire to live.

Whatever abnormalities the doctors claimed the shock treatments should cure proved futile, in fact, they made things worse. I watched helplessly as Mom blindly declined deeper into her illness, yet simultaneously had not relinquished the bitterness she possessed for Dad's past indiscretions. The emotional hell he put her through, and her deep belief that Dad would leave her for someone else didn't diminish in spite of the numerous rounds of shock treatments. The hospital stay added a fresh contention: Dad's role in committing her to the *loony house* would never be forgiven or forgotten. Her paranoia conjured up a tangled new phobia: Dad held the power to have her institutionalized at any time. That's how tenacious her psyche ran.

I wondered why Mom never reached out to at least one of her children; instead her distrust in people shut everyone out. Not even her friends could bring her out of her darkness, so they, feeling just as helpless as we did, drifted away with nothing left to contribute except an occasional phone call to say hello and to please relay that they were thinking of her. She never discussed her menacing illness so I assumed she felt demoralized for mentally breaking down. Looking back now, I believe she must have been terrified.

Mom's mind linked through a contrived alarm clock programmed to instinctively ring when it was time for her to pop up for each meal. In a child-like mannerism, she'd timidly ask, "What are you cooking? Is it ready yet?" We were expected to fix her plate and bring it to her. When Dad cooked, he would announce dinner was ready and demand that she come to the table; submissively she complied. Mom ate everything on her plate and when finished, she retreated back to the sofa like a mouse running to its cubbyhole for safety. At times, she smiled sheepishly like a child relishing in the small victory of getting her way. Other times, she glared at you and you felt the rebirth of her hate penetrate right through your body.

At first, I worried about Mom not eating when we were away, but the empty cheese wrappers in the trash let me know she had sense enough to eat when she was hungry. Whatever filtered through her mind was cryptic, and you never knew where her distorted thoughts took her, but they were all she desired to keep herself company. I never knew if she was relieved or terrified with each retreat. We, like Mom, were surviving by ingesting whichever state of mind she chose to be in.

One peculiar behavior of hers was each time the phone rang, she asked, "Who were you talking to?" That's all she wanted to know; who had called–curious I guess. She intently listened to each word being said. Occasionally she'd ask, "What did they want?" I would reply, "Just seeing how you're doing." She wouldn't respond. Mom never talked to the caller, nor would she call them back. I could tell they didn't make any impact. She positioned herself once again retreating back into her safe world on the big, green sofa.

Mom's demeanor could be summarized into three stages of her life. The first outwardly sign was the hostility she showed to her family and others. Her perception towards people teetered on paranoia and distrust. I was about fifteen when I witnessed a noticeable transformation in Mom's personality. Her emotions began escalating into hysterical odious rages, especially when they involved Dad. There would be no deviation; if anyone disagreed with her, she took it as a personal assault. She was desperately trying to defend herself against the outside world.

This psychotic behavior caused the second stage, an unmistakable descent into a full-blown nervous breakdown that turned her life upside down, withdrawing from everyone around her. This was the darkest time of our lives.

As she slowly emerged from this deep depression, the third stage of illness manifested, bipolar symptoms. This caused her personality to have erratic periods of up swings followed by down sways. In the final stage of her life, she mellowed somewhat from the facets of her diseases; unfortunately, they never completely went away. The paranoia remained by her side like a trusty silhouette.

After Mom's nervous breakdown in 1967, we tip-toed around her illness; none of us spoke about her shock treatments or medications. That in itself is idiotic. If we couldn't grasp a plausible understanding, how could we be expected to cope or be of any help? How much longer will her illness last? I think she's being over-medicated. Will her memory ever return? Will she become aggressive again? Are we safe being around her?

As her bizarre conduct blossomed I still couldn't see any positive results from the shock treatments, in fact, new complications emerged. How naïve I was to think the new Mom had been cured of her mental illness. I couldn't keep her illnesses separated or understand which personality represented which behavior. We were dealing with schizo-phrenia, paranoia, hormone imbalance, depression, and bipolar disorder. The illnesses enveloped her body and collided like a perfect storm. I hadn't observed the bipolar symptoms before her nervous breakdown; they manifested after she underwent shock treatments. For the rest of my life, I would be branded with the stigma of having a crazy person, a loon, a nut, a maniac, a psychopath as my mother. Was she born with mental illness or had it evolved from her traumatic teenage years? How many more mutations are there going to be before it releases its grip on her? Will her mind ever be free of the burden of distrust? Why can't her mind heal itself? *Will she find peace before she dies?*

When the bipolar disorder put Mom in an up mood, she managed to summon her feisty (but diluted) roar, cursing and still threatening to slap the shit out of you, knowing full well she no longer had the strength to follow through. She also had an uncanny ability to keep her guard up around everyone, especially Dad. She lost all trust in him.

It was only when the bipolar disorder threw Mom in a down mood that she retreated into her emotional void with no will to fight back. She took refuge in her bedroom only to zip out for something to eat, wearing the same clothes she had on a week prior along with no visible signs of grooming. Her down wave was the only time there was peace in the house, a pathetic trade off with no victory for either side.

Throughout her illness, she was still taking all the powerful drugs that had been previously prescribed to a mentally ill person plus a cocktail of other pills to help her sleep and replace the hormones her body had stopped producing. I never knew which medications Mom was ingesting, but no matter the dosage or combination, she was left with large gaps in her memory and an inability to function normally.

Oh, mental illness, such a taboo and frightening subject to confront. Tread softly around Mom; she could teeter either way. I wish I had found the courage to educate myself regarding her illness instead of sticking my head in the sand while waiting for a miracle. Her nervous breakdown played like a cheap "B" horror movie except this nightmare had no end in sight. When I cleaned out their home after their deaths, I didn't find a single piece of documentation referencing Mom's illness. No bills, receipts, or hospital reports, nothing. All evidence of her sickness had been purged, just like her memory.

On one occasion, I was forced to call Dad home from work for an emergency involving Mom. I checked on her around 2 P.M., and when I tried to wake her, she wouldn't respond. When properly taken, the combination of the drugs left her groggy and lethargic, but this time was different; she appeared to be unconscious. I panicked. Had she taken too many pills? Was this an accident or intentional?

Dad called LeeEllen to intervene, knowing it would take him three hours to drive home. She and my uncle arrived immediately, but I dismissed their help. I became very protective of Mom and insisted that I would take care of her until the ambulance arrived. But I did need them. How stupid of me to push help away. My frantic guilt wouldn't allow anyone to get involved. I carried the added burden that I had neglected Mom and let Dad down. *Why did this happen on my watch?* The sooner I could make things right, the sooner this nightmare would be behind me.

I sat in the hospital's emergency room waiting for word on Mom's condition and expecting Dad to arrive at any moment, when unexpectedly the emergency doors thrust open and the paramedics wheeled a man right past me that had apparently been in an accident. The horror of seeing Dad injured took my breath away. I fixated on the man's boots. They're exactly like Dad's black leather, lace-up work boots. Then I saw the same dark shaded blue Dickey jeans that Dad wore. Even his build was the same as Dad's. My heart raced but my mind reacted in slow motion. I tried to stand but I couldn't untangle my legs quick enough from underneath the chair. They were froze. Then, in a split second, an obscure strength instinctively pushed my head down and forced me to focus on the man's face. What a twist of fate. While Mom tried to take her life, Dad could be fighting for his.

I felt extremely responsible and helpless for each event that was set in motion. *What is happening to my family?* I don't even know if Mom is okay, and now I could be thrown into another calamity. I should've monitored Mom's medicine more closely. If I had taken better care of her, Dad wouldn't have raced home and wrecked. What if he is badly injured or dies? What if he gets fired because I called him off his job?

Thank God it wasn't Dad, though I blamed myself for the entire incident. The guilt had never left me. I had already adopted a healthy dose of shame for my family's conduct, and as the occurrences became more frequent, I became more depressed. I didn't have a clue how to help either one of them. I remained emotionally drained. What triggered Mom to take such a drastic measure? Will she try and overdose again? Was it something I said or did? Why can't I fix what's wrong? I functioned in a never-ending fog of despair and every direction I turned, held nothing but uncertainty for my future. I dreaded the start of each morning, wondering, "What will I walk into today?" I didn't want the responsibility of taking care of the family. What about my life? I'm stuck in this nightmare but worst of all, I'm trapped by guilt and duty.

We did the best any child could do considering how young we were when mental illness and alcoholism were woven into our lives. My parents' behavior thrust each child into an automatic survival mode where we protected ourselves and became self-centered; kind of like, every man for himself. We were ill-equipped and couldn't understand the magnitude of what was happening around us. The growing gloom in our home was enough to bring anyone down. I was trying to make it from one day to the next, except a barrage of abnormal incidents kept occurring and I didn't have the answers or control over the outcomes. Regardless, each crisis had to be dealt with. My personal response instinctively fell on the side of logic. I turned inside myself, willing my emotions to shut down. If you don't feel anything, you can't be hurt. *Simple logic, don't you think?*

Even when life seemed calm, the fear of what might happen next lurked around each corner, zapping my energy and leaving me feeling drained with no desire to enjoy life. We were blind-sided by Mom's disease and not prepared for the energy her illness would deplete from us. Sense Rose had already left home, Dad had no choice but to once again depend on me and Kathy. We had been doing all the chores and cooking for a very long time; the only noticeable difference in the house was a new drug-induced fixture, Mom. Truthfully, I was still very afraid to be alone with Mom.

Dad's life was unraveling as he helplessly watched events take a turn for the worse. There didn't seem to be an end in sight. Realizing he was powerless to alter his past, and not being able to make things right with his family, he fell into a deceptive need to drink his troubles away. Dad's drinking found a path of its own and escalated to the point of his being sloppy, passed-out drunk every night. His intoxication started the moment his workday ended, fueled by tension from his job, Mom's erratic behavior, and Rose breaking ties with the family; it all took a toll.

Dad called the house one night to see if everything was okay. I told him things were fine, then I left to go to a party. He called a second time and Ricky told him I wasn't in the house; maybe someone had kidnapped me. Once again, Dad had to leave his job, borrow a car, and drive three hours, worried the unthinkable had happened. Only then did I realize what torment he must have gone through not knowing what to expect each time he walked through the door. This time it was my fault, but surprisingly I wasn't punished. Maybe he identified with the heavy burden that he placed on me. I remained in fear of 'what if', and all I wanted to do was get out of the house, to escape the gloom and enjoy my youth.

Kathy was a teenager and with house rules and discipline nonexistent, she began running wild. *Wouldn't you?* We both stayed away from home as much as we could, stumbling around and tripping over our shortcomings. We each spread our wings and jumped off the edge as quickly as our turn rolled around, only to realize no one had taught us how to fly. Our lives were left to chance.

We still hadn't heard from Rose so she had no clue what had happened to Mom. I don't remember much about the youngest two. They were old enough to care for themselves but too young to be on their own. My teen years were turbulent, but it wasn't from my behavior as much as it was from my parents. I carried the dubious burden that part of their madness had to be my fault.

Who am I? What does life have in store for me? I'm lonely and restless. Where am I headed? I tried to make my own way and my own fun, and I made my share of mistakes; hell, we all did. I had my first drink of liquor a week before graduation and from that moment on, had no problem with drinking. I never connected my new habit with Dad's. Freedom and youth were slipping away. It was my time to party, hang out, let loose, have some fun, and break away from the freak show I lived in.

Six months before graduation, I began dating a boy named Harry. Not only did I fall in love with him, I fell in love with his family. His parents were awesome. His mom was a very caring person and his dad was a comic. Sure, they had their share of problems, but I felt safe in their home. We were eighteen and straight out of high school, I should have known our relationship wouldn't last. By the middle of summer, I was alone again nursing a heart broken for the second time. I hung around with his older sister. This made my life exceedingly miserable by knowing every move Harry made. All I did was pine away the rest of the year for someone who didn't care about me. Is there something wrong with me? Is my family situation too intimidating for my boyfriends? Am I too needy? How is it so easy for the other girls to find a boyfriend? Am I cursed? *Will anyone ever love me or will I end up an old maid?*

After graduation, I looked for a full-time job. Unfortunately, with no guidance, I turned job hunting into a summer of play. I spent hours at the lake soaking up the sun and watching the clouds breeze by, taking my youth with them. I was out of step with the rest of the world and had no inkling where I would land. I found myself wishing for prince charming to come and rescue me, but he never came. What a stupid hypocrite I am; serves me right. I must be pretty damn desperate believing in a prince to begin with. I've just reached a new low.

I wandered through my days and nights with no direction. I found myself back at my old familiar hang out, Teen Town, however, I didn't recognize anyone except for the cop at the door. Everyone had moved on with their lives. A new wave of teens had taken over and I had nothing to reclaim except abstract nostalgia. It quickly sunk in, I had outgrown Teen Town. So, reluctantly, I relinquished my past, which left a large void that I didn't know how to fill.

There wasn't even a life lesson to salvage from the flood of memories that rolled in like the tide with no restraint, triggering an anxiety of being emotionally alone. Still dating any guy who would ask me out just to have someplace to go, I'd find myself in some precarious situations, all with unrelated outcomes. Yet by the grace of God, I managed to make it safely home. If I didn't have a date for the night, I would find a girlfriend and we would hit the bars. It didn't matter where we perched, I couldn't stay in that dreary house another minute and allow it to suck any more life out of me. Physically, I kept in motion with uncertainty and fear as the only driving force for my survival. It had been a dispirited and lonely road and any number of paths could have led me to self-destruct. But I didn't want to repeat the same mistakes my parents made. I didn't want to live a sorrowful life, but with no guidance I stumbled many times, even though I longed for a normal existence.

MY BIG SISTER, ROSE

Rose, being the first born, was destined to take the brunt of every form of punishment my parents handed down. By establishing a strict regiment they hoped to keep us all in line. Mom had never been flexible with her rules or punishment. Wrath was swift-when it wasn't directed at Rose, it came to rest on me. Although Rose and I were close in age, you might think we were inseparable, but we clashed a majority of our youth. Our personalities were like night and day, so we reacted to Mom and Dad's demands differently. Truth be told, Rose was born with a stubborn streak. She brought excessive anguish upon herself by not keeping her sassy mouth shut or doing what she was told. Dad would say, "Rose would argue with a fence post if it could talk." And she, like Mom, persisted on always being right and having the last word. It baffled me why Rose was so defiant; she only hurt herself. I had my share of busted lips but quickly learned the art of restraint; why hadn't she? It didn't seem to bother her that she stayed on restriction for most of her teenage years. I kept telling her to keep her sassy mouth shut, make passing grades, and do her chores; this would be her ticket to freedom, but she wouldn't listen to me or change her behavior for reasons only she knows. Rose and I looked at life differently; me with my realistic thinking, and her with her pie-in-the-sky dreams kept us at cross-purposes. We coped with our unhappiness in our own way, but her irrational decisions and my lack of imagination served neither one of us well in life.

Rose was never content in her adolescent years. Always fantasizing about leaving home as fast as she could, move to Hollywood, and become a famous actress. She spent endless hours thinking of ways to meet Michael Landon, the actor who played Little Joe Cartwright on the TV show Bonanza. She wrote herself into a script and boldly sent it to him. He would (naturally) fall in love with the script and her. I asked, "Rose, have you considered the age difference between you two, and doesn't he already have a trophy wife?" It baffled me where her grandiose ideas came from. She stayed so out of touch with reality and it didn't seem healthy. I left Rose to dream the impossible while I went about trying to stay under Mom's radar.

People say you should follow your dream, but how? How can you distinguish when dream-chasing and reality mesh? What happens when they collide? How will you know which road to take? *Don't you get it, JoAnn? That's the adventure, the search in not knowing, but witnessing, discovering, making waves, loving, learning, and moving on with life.* My problems weren't unique, or my existence doomed. My dilemma was just being scared and not knowing how to move forward.

Rose and Mom's personalities were so similar that, as Rose got older, the power struggle between the two amplified. They butted heads causing them to come to blows quite often. Mom's mental instability distorted any logic of how to interact with her girls. Rose was thirteen and struggling with adolescence when her testy disposition caused Mom's already frayed nerves to erupt. One day, fresh after a beating, Rose decided she had endured enough of Mom's brutality, and she bolted and hid at a neighbor's house. Mom franticly went from house to house searching for Rose. When Mom found Rose, she beat her again and told her if she ever ran away a second time, that she would get much worse. I was terrified for Rose. I decided I would never run away, no matter how bad things got. The beating caused Rose to leave, then when Mom found Rose, she beat her again. Damn, Mom made no sense.

Rose was eighteen and had graduated from high school when she decided she wanted to enroll in an airline school in Kansas City. The classified ad read like a seductive travel brochure exuding allusions that all your dreams would come true. While traveling the world, you would meet famous people, visit interesting places, savor exotic foods, earn a terrific salary, and have independence. All that was required was two thousand dollars, eight short weeks of your time, and if you passed the course, you *could* (not would) become a flight attendant. This was just the ticket (not counting the round trip airline ticket my parents paid for) Rose dreamed of: to be free from the insanity of our parents. She begged them to let her go and even skeptic Dad realized it would be a great opportunity, and much cheaper than four years of college. Rose had concerns about the school's height requirement, but she qualified by an inch.

This was the first real thing Rose had shown any interest in, so reluctantly, Mom and Dad scrounged up the money and sent her on her dream. Just like Dad, this was Rose's first time away from home and she relished her new-found freedom along with a taste for the Kansas City nightlife. The inevitable happened: She partied endlessly, met a man, fell in love, had her heart broken, and failed the course. My parents were furious. They felt she didn't try hard enough or appreciated the sacrifice they had made for her. Rose had no choice but to return home, and when she did, Mom had a laundry list of rules awaiting her.

Mom was adamant that Rose be punished for her blunder. Now that she had graduated, she must get a job to pay for her room and board.

119

My parents had to support themselves at an early age, and Mom made it clear Rose wouldn't sponge off them. The phone company hired Rose as a switchboard operator but her biggest obstacle was not having transportation. Mom wouldn't let her use the family car. She had sacrificed enough for her damn kids and allowing Rose to take the car meant she would once again be stranded at home, and that wasn't going to happen. The phone company had inconsistent work schedules for peak hours of business. Rose worked a split shift, making it two round trips to work each day. Since Rose needed Mom as a chauffeur, it turned into four round trips, ruining any plans Mom might have for the day, not to mention the gas and the wear and tear on the car.

Mom's nonsensical demands and rigid, excessive rules were the reasons Rose bolted. Rose couldn't use the phone after nine P.M., had to be home by eleven P.M. on weekdays, and twelve midnight on weekends. She still had chores, pay rent, buy her own clothes, and fill the car's gas tank. It was time for Rose to make her way in the world; it just wasn't the world my parents wanted for her. Like most family rifts, Rose didn't leave with their blessing.

One night at dinner, Mom pushed Rose to the limit when she ordered Rose to eat her green beans. Rose told Mom she didn't want any beans, and the argument escalated. They went back and forth as Mom insisted, "As long as you live under my goddamn roof, you'll do as I say." Rose, determined to secure her freedom forged ahead with unrelenting stubbornness. What an utterly asinine thing to fight about, but obviously it went far beyond green beans. With each ongoing battle, they allowed their pride to further damage their relationship. That was the last straw. Rose was fed up with Mom's demands. The heated confrontation ended with Rose packing her bags and leaving. Dad begged Rose to stay, but once she made up her mind, she never looked back. Mom was losing control over her kids; we were growing up.

Rose immediately got an apartment downtown within walking distance to her job and the bars. Logically, Mom should've been glad to have one less brat to worry about, but it was quite the contrary; Mom constantly cried over her parting. In spite of the malicious way Mom treated Rose, she was, after all, her first born. Rose's leaving broke her heart. Mom, for reasons known only to her, never bonded with her children, but deep down on some misconstrued level, she must have loved us.

I listened to my parents blame each other for Rose's departure I wondered if it ever entered their minds that their strict upbringing, lack of empathy, and constant belittling caused her to bolt. Why couldn't they see that they were part of the problem and admit they were partly to blame? Mom tried to control Rose's life, as if she was still a child. They each took Rose's leaving hard.

When Rose first experienced the night life in Kansas City, she developed an unquenchable passion to enjoy the unfamiliar. Being a late bloomer, she felt that she had missed out on so much in her teen years and had a compelling desire to make up for lost time. She craved the excitement of partying. However, her approach to freedom came at a price. She tried to find happiness in her own way, but her free and easy choices soon infringed upon my life.

The senior boys at school bragged about how over the weekend, they slipped into a "Go Go" bar downtown by using fake IDs. They described how blown away they were by a girl named Rose, in a skimpy outfit, dancing in a cage to Purple Haze by Jimi Hendrix. Humiliated and speechless; I quickly turned and walked away. I felt the need to throw up. Why in the hell are they telling me this? Did they suspect that she's my sister? I don't care what she does with her life as long as I'm not dragged into her misdeeds-and besides, she has never taken dancing lessons in her life. Furthermore, they're just as bad; they broke the law by using fake IDs. Did the entire school know about Rose's new recreational diversion? It would devastate my parents if they caught wind that she was running wild.

Night life had greatly influenced Rose and she became trapped by her own naive illusions of what self worth and happiness really meant. She began spending more time in bars and less time at work. She eventually got fired. Had Dad's lewd behavior with women subconsciously influenced Rose? Had Mom's non-stop fixation with her girls becoming whores distorted Rose's perception of her true self?

Still living in a fantasy world, she believed all the bullshit the men dished out. Added to her remnants of disappointments, gullible Rose had her heart broken several times. I reminded Rose, "How do you know when a man is lying? When his lips are moving!" I'd never believed what guys had to say. Rose made many faux pas that led her to one day leave Georgia and vanish from our lives. *I wish I knew where she went. I miss her. I need her. I love her.* I was envious that she got to leave and I didn't. It had been two years since anyone had spoken to Rose so she didn't know about Mom's illness. For a brief time, I blamed Mom's breakdown on Rose, but my heart knew the truth. Rose's actions may have been the straw that broke the camel's back, but my parents' problems ran too deep for their children to shoulder the burden of blame. Complicated doesn't begin to describe the ongoing tribulations in their lives.

Mom had no voice in preventing Rose from making her own mistakes, but it didn't stop her from incessantly worrying about Rose. It appeared she had fallen off the face of the earth. Fearing the worst, Dad hired a private detective to try and find her. I guess Rose had her reasons for not wanting to be found.

Out of the blue, Rose returned home and in our usual way of (not) dealing with family situations, no one asked where she had been for so long. It was enough to have her back, safe and alive. Rose soon moved to Baltimore, Maryland, where she met and married a man named Ray and shortly after, gave birth to a baby girl she named Jacqueline. Rose hoped, like I did, that a grandchild would be just the spark to get Mom to snap out of her depression and end Dad's drinking. She'd visit Mom and Dad each summer. Although they were glad to have Rose back in their lives, nothing for them changed.

FALLING APART AND FALLING IN PLACE: MY LIFE

At nineteen, I got my first real job at the phone company, and just like Rose, I too had a complicated schedule. I needed my own transportation so I asked Dad if he would co-sign for me to buy a car. Dad made it clear he helped Rose and had gotten burned, so he wouldn't make that mistake again. *But I wasn't Rose.* Being let down by Dad, I had no alternative but to quit. I didn't like their schedule anyway.

I snagged a job at a bank working in the proof department and immediately began looking for a place to live. I had to get on with my life before I fell any further into their fractured way of living. I felt guilty leaving since Mom was still confined to the sofa, but it was time for my siblings to pitch in and help. With my clothes packed and a friend waiting in the drive, I sprang it on Mom that I was moving out. She just stared at me. She didn't ask where I was going and I can't recall if I told her. Dad was at work so I didn't have to face him with my news. I moved into the YWCA, free from all of my burdens. I lived five blocks down and two streets over from work. Since I didn't own a car, walking to work would have to do. I rationalized, just another trade off for freedom.

I had concerns the "Y" would not let me live there since I was a local, so I devised an elaborate (I thought) story about needing a place to stay while my parents were away for the summer in Europe. Damn, I think the manager actually fell for that line. If she checks my story, she'll know I lied. It was never brought to my attention.

The dread my life would mimic Mom's had already taken hold. She didn't get along with her dad, or I with her. Mom lived at the "Y" and now I'm doing the same. I had nowhere else to live. The "Y" was all I could afford. The "Y" was her shelter in her time of need, and it became mine as well. *God help me to not have my life go down the same path as Moms'.*

I lived at the "Y" for one year, however, being off the beaten path, most of my friends wouldn't go out of their way to pick me up, leaving my social life limited. Feeling out of place and alone resurfaced. With no pot of gold to dip into, I diligently began saving money. So began the birth of my thrifty ways. I paid cash for a 1964 Chevrolet Corvair. I continued saving for any unexpected emergency that lurked around each corner. I couldn't afford rent and utilities on a banker's salary so I began looking for girls to share an apartment and expenses. As fate would have it, two co-workers, a friend, and myself rented a townhouse, splitting the bills four ways. It was the sixties (hippie explosion) and between the four of us, we had some wild characters coming through, but it was far from living carefree. I couldn't foresee thirty days into the future what life had in store. I worried constantly. Is my car going to break again and cause me to be late for work? How much will the repairs cost? The car insurance is due. What if someone moves out? How will I afford next month's rent? Will I get fired? The only difference between home life and being on my own was the absence of violence. I had just as many responsibilities and worries with no stability, especially from renters.

They moved in and out depending on who needed a place to stay, who could afford the rent, who broke up with their boyfriend, or who had met the man of their dreams and committed to marriage. I constantly had to take on new renters, and each time they gave no assurance on how long they could commit. This went on for about eighteen months before everything began to fall apart and fall into place all at the same time.

When the last roommate left, I had to act quickly and find somewhere to live. I stayed with a friend who needed money with the understanding that I could only crash at her place for one month. With nowhere to turn my living conditions turned desperate. Then, out of the blue Dad called, "Jo, I need you home to help with your mother and the kids." Wow, Dad and I were both in a pickle and required something from each other. He needed a housekeeper and I needed a roof over my head.

Dad was losing ground. Not being able to fix Mom's condition left him reeling. I felt simultaneously needed by Dad and, sadly, pity for him. Could I have swallowed my pride and asked to come back home? I'll never know, but I was able to save face; for all that's worth. When I moved back, I wasn't as afraid of Mom; I wasn't her target any longer. By then she had given up on her family. Mom still clung to all of her past troubles; the ones that had pushed her over the edge in the first place. If she could only put them to rest, maybe she could heal.

Aside from the fact I had nowhere else to go, why in the hell did I agree to move back? I had become my own worst enemy, staying trapped in my self-induced shortcomings. I should have joined the armed forces, and then I could have traveled the world, furthered my education, and gotten away from their maddening existence. *There must be something wrong with me to intentionally slide back into hell.*

I worked during the day and at night did as I pleased; that usually consisted of hanging out with my girlfriends at a local bar. I felt older than my years and worrying about my parents' fate consumed my thoughts. I constantly prayed for their well being and for my fate. Oh God, will I end up like her? Will I have lots of babies, turn bitter, and end up with a nervous breakdown? Will my husband cheat on me? Will I grow to detest him? That's how I envisioned my future. If my faith in God had been stronger, I could have let go of my fears and realized that life held many gifts, but I didn't believe my life held worth.

Between Dad working and Mom's illness, there was zero control over the younger brats. They wouldn't obey me, so other than fixing meals and washing clothes, I wasn't much help to Dad. Mom replaced abuse with neglect. She abandoned all of her motherly responsibilities leaving the kids to defy all the established rules that had once been staunchly imbedded in our brains. The kids wouldn't help with any housework, ignored curfew, slept late, skipped school, and neglected their homework. They had the run of the house without any supervision or discipline. I couldn't keep tabs on them. Everyone functioned on a different level of chaos. As we each left home, it became inevitable that the obligation to take care of Mom would fall back on Dad. The months rolled on as Dad struggled through the mechanics of living with no enjoyment in his life. It was all he could do to get off work, make it home, then escape into his solitary world of drink. Much of his torment had been brought on by his own actions, but it was depressing to watch such a stoic man stumble, because in my eyes, Dad, the rugged railroad man, was larger than life and had always taken care of us. *Isn't that how every daughter views her dad, at least in her adolescent years?* Dad's duty was to take care of his family, and with three siblings still to raise, he was looking at ten more years before any peace was in sight.

LET NATURE TAKE ITS COURSE

E ach day overlapped onto another, void of any momentum and leaving me to feel adrift in a motionless sea, but how can that be when the tide's pull is in constant motion, and the wind can blow in from any direction a storm on any given day? There is nothing constant but change, and all life's changes created new chapters, whether orchestrated by fate or purposely formed through our actions. The truth, my life was moving in a constant progression; it began to take a turn. I met my future husband, LeRoy (Lee), at a local bar. He had just returned from Vietnam. I sensed he was just as lonely as I was. His high school sweetheart had dumped him in the middle of his military tour via a classic "Dear John" letter. Lee confided in me that his mother had never written to him while he was away, just his dad. When I asked why, he shrugged his shoulders and changed the subject. I didn't pursue the issue; I had my own dilemmas to deal with.

When we first started dating, I'd be ready and waiting for Lee to arrive. The moment he pulled into the driveway, I'd dash out the door and off we went. I'd be damned if I was going to let him see the condition my parents were in. It was always a toss-up; one or the other would be indisposed. Lee's war duty had ended, but meeting Herbert and Charlotte invoked a different kind of war.

The first time I met his parents, they acted as bizarre as mine. As soon as his dad walked in the back door, his mother jumped over my feet, bolted down the hall, slammed the bedroom door, and didn't come out the rest of the night. Lee said his mother's actions were customary, and staying isolated from her family for weeks at a time was reluctantly tolerated. His father waited until Lee made it safely home from Nam before affirming he was divorcing Anita. Lee wasn't shocked that his dad wanted to leave his mother; he was surprised it took him so long. Lee had just as many family problems as I did.

We dated for eleven months when Lee asked me to marry him. I said yes. Events were falling into place at just the right time. With his parents' divorce came the sale of their home, so Lee purchased a house instead of renting. He lived in the house and finished the remodeling by the time we married.

My year-end bonus helped pay for our honeymoon. I was approaching twenty-one, and in the seventies if you were twenty-one and single you were labeled an old maid; creating one more fallacy that fed my insecurities. Those were the only logical *(not)* reasons for choosing to marry in mid winter. Everyone we knew was married and some had started a family, including Lee's younger brother, Marshall. We both felt life was passing us by and I believe we needed each other more than we loved each other. *I'm scared and I'm lonely and I think he is too.* And what is love, exactly? My only understanding about love was my parent's blue print of their marriage. I assumed Dad loved us. He upheld his duty and met all his family's needs. Even though he would leave, he always came back. I guess Mom loved us because she defended us from anyone that tried to hurt us, and until her illness, kept holidays alive. *Yes, I think we were loved.*

I experienced a sobering slice into normalcy one night when Lee and I visited his brother and his family. Their three-year old daughter, Tammie, was getting ready for bed and her mom, Sandra, suggested she kiss me goodnight. She put her arms around me, gave me a kiss, and told me she loved me. I tried to say I loved her too but I choked on my words. I couldn't say *I love you* back; it wouldn't come out. I was so moved by her warmth that I began tearing up. As a child, those words were never said to me. My parents were unapproachable and kept their true feelings hidden. I hadn't been hugged or kissed either, *honestly, never.* Except for Lee saying he loved me, and we all know that's a given (especially in the heat of the moment), I realized I hadn't experienced physical bonding with anyone in my family. A child opened my eyes.

Lee and I carried around a lot of sorrow from our childhoods and we only had each other to lean on, and that was enough for the moment. No one really knows what he or she is getting into and we were no exception. We moved forward with hopes of a happier life that had eluded us both for so long. But I must confess, I struggled with my decision. How did I know this was what I wanted? Was I looking for a way out of my house? Did I love Lee enough to be married to him for the rest of my life? It didn't feel wrong; I just didn't know how "right" should feel. Did he honestly love me or was he also trying to fill a void?

I told my parents we were getting married and once again, they were too involved in their own woes to show any interest in my happiness. Dad wouldn't pay for my wedding and my pride would never allow me to ask him why. I never dreamed of or asked for a lavish wedding; that would be selfish to impose such a frivolous debt on my parents. I did what I learned at a very early age; I swallowed my disappointment. This made the third time they both let me down: my graduation, not helping me buy a car, and now my wedding.

Mom and I were not communicating. She stayed locked in her mental frailty and took no interest in my life, and I, in turn, took no interest in hers. With Rose gone, I made all the arrangements. I dipped into my savings and paid for my flowers, cake, and napkins, that I had engraved; *LeRoy & JoAnn, January 16, 1971*. I rented a white lace dress and veil. My entire wedding cost one hundred and fifty dollars.

Lee didn't belong to any church. I did, however, I hadn't attended since Mom's breakdown. I had been too ashamed to face the (perfect) congregation. But I was determined to be married in church by a clergy. I believed that traditions equaled normality and I would not say my vows to a justice of the peace like my parents had done. I would not allow my future to be jinxed. That would make the third endeavor in my life that paralleled with Mom's. First, the "whore" comparison, then living at the "Y" parallel; our similarities had to end.

My wedding day played out just like previous celebrations, a fiasco. Dad didn't walk me down the aisle. I assume he stood up behind me and responded to the preacher's question of who was to give the bride away. My pride wouldn't allow me to look back. I felt let down by not having my parents' full support, especially on the most important day of my life. I wanted them to play a bigger part in my wedding. Did they care about my happiness? Maybe they disliked Lee? They barely knew him. Are they going to miss their built-in maid? I lived twenty years of disappointments and I prayed my marriage would be a new start to a normal existence.

I don't know who in the family persuaded them, but my parents did have a small reception at their home for us after the wedding. Lee's parents were in the middle of a divorce so his mother didn't attend the wedding. His father brought a lady-friend who we later learned had been involved in his life longer than anyone realized. I forgot to ask someone to take pictures so I only have one faded Polaroid photo of my wedding.

We drove to the big city of Atlanta, Georgia, for our weekend honeymoon. We arrived late that Saturday at the Hyatt Regency. I observed the guests in their expensive cars and fancy clothes, and once again, I felt out of place. When I made our reservation; I neglected to request the honeymoon suite. I felt too intimidated by my surroundings to think I could request a change so we settled for a drab generic room. That night, we dined on the top floor of the hotel's restaurant, the Polaris, that turned 360 degrees, giving us a breathtaking view of the city.

The next day, we went to the Atlanta Zoo, and God only knows why, but every animal at the zoo appeared agitated. The monkeys screeched, bit, and pulled each other's tails, ears, and hair. Willie B, the gorilla threw a temper tantrum. The zebras kicked other zebras, and the lions growled and charged at their mates. The birds flapped their wings wildly and even their songs squawked loudly out of tune. I had lived through enough fighting to last a lifetime. I prayed this display of discord wasn't an omen of how my marriage would play out.

Mom and I had a lot in common. We loved cooking, music, and old movies. I hoped we could somehow reconnect, so when we got back in town, I invited Mom to join me at the Woolworth's lunch counter. During lunch, she blind-sided me with her only question, "Do you like sex?" Stunned, I timidly replied, "Well, yes." She audaciously responded, "Well, I don't." That was the only time we exchanged views on intimacy. Perplexed, I'd hear Mom tell a dirty joke and also took pleasure in hearing one, yet she would shout to anyone in hearing distance how much she disliked sex.

Rose, Mom and I took a girl's trip to Atlanta to shop for my new house. I enjoyed the trip and Mom's company but getting together for future trips would be nil. Any meaningful bonding would prove to be an elusive.

Mom took every advantage to shame her girls; it didn't matter that we had grown into womanhood. Her criticism ran nonstop with never a word of praise. I read that some mothers envy their daughter's happiness. They resent any joy that comes to their daughters: beauty, popularity, job opportunities, happy marriage, etc., while swallowing old regrets and begrudging lost dreams they once had for themselves.

I asked Mom to run an errand with me when we bumped into Lee's Aunt Pearl. As I introduced them, Aunt Pearl said to Mom, "We're delighted to have such a lovely person in our family." Mom mocked, "Well, you don't know her like I do." That's why I hated going anywhere with her. She took an unhealthy pleasure criticizing me in public. Would it kill her to be nice once in a while? Why must she put me down in front of Lee's family? She embarrassed me; bringing back feelings of childhood shame.

In another instance, Mom dropped by the bank where I worked as the branch manager. I introduced her to my co-workers all the while agonizing over what disparaging reply might roll off her tongue. They expressed how much they enjoyed working with me. Again, Mom didn't disappoint. She disputed their compliment with a malicious retort, "Well, she's got you fooled." I wanted to scream, "Damn, why do you have to humiliate me in front of my peers? Have I not done anything meaningful in your eyes? You belittle me every time you get the chance. I hate being around you!" Why do I even try to include her in my life?

I sensed Mom's loathing each time any attention was given to me. I swear she's jealous of the life I have made for myself. She wishes my life would be as embittered as hers. I became so focused on her abrasive approach that I shut out any chance for further bonding. *She's the one that threw her happiness away.* I tried to hold on to any glimpse of approval that (I thought) resembled love from Mom. At the same time, I had to let go of the fallacy that a relationship didn't exist between us. Of course one existed, just not in the conventional aspect of a normal mother/daughter relationship. I needed affirmation that she did love me.

I quickly settled into my new home and role as a wife, and like Vesta, the mythical Roman goddess of the hearth, home, and family, I strived to be a perfect wife. Lee and I were married six months when I learned I was pregnant. Planning for the future, whether it concerned education, marriage, career, or children, had never been discussed. I lived in the moment and never gave myself the luxury of dreaming about which direction my life would take or what the future held. I assumed that once you married, nature took its course, and it did. I was thrilled to be pregnant. My baby might be the spark needed to turn their lives around.

I was so grateful to be having a baby but, in my fifth month of pregnancy, something went terribly wrong. I was too naive to think anything bad could happen. After all, Mom had five healthy children and she didn't want any of them. She said it enough times; it must be true. The doctor insisted that I go home and rest. Lee had just left for work so I just missed him. I fell asleep only to wake up in unbearable pain. I called my parents and within minutes, Dad placed me into the back seat of his car, running red lights while Mom was begged him to slow down before he killed us.

I don't remember much of when we got to the hospital except looking up from the stretcher in time to see Lee bursting through the doors with a bewildered and panicked look on his face. When I woke, I was told I had lost a little girl. *How could that be?* I was five months along. I truly wanted this baby. I took care of myself. I was never sick, didn't smoke, ate well, exercised, and I never cursed my pregnancy. That was Mom, not me. It had never entered my mind that I could lose a baby. What had gone wrong? Am I being punished?

I went home and grieved alone. Even though Mom came and sat with me; she wasn't any comfort emotionally. I stayed in my bedroom crying and sleeping the days away; she sat in the living room smoking and watching soaps. I must take the blame for this sorrow because I deliberately shut Mom out.

In Mom's usual brazen style she blurted out, "Poor Lee. He signed the hospital's consent papers to dispose of the baby's body." Neither the doctor, nor Lee, revealed to me what followed and for whatever reason, I hadn't thought past the miscarriage. I was to heartbroken to ask. I could have gone my entire life without knowing the outcome; especially from her mouth. Her thoughtless utterance pierced straight through my heart. It served no purpose except to cause me more heartache. Damn her for telling me. Was she deliberately trying to torment me or was that just the way her crazy obtuse mind worked? Maybe she meant no harm, but her continual lack of respect for my feelings drove the wedge deeper between us. I would not include Mom in my realm of grief; nothing she might say could heal my wound. My heartbreak shifted to resentment. I wrestled with one question: *How was Mom able to bear children but I couldn't?*

I hadn't forgotten that Mom was emotionally absent, leaving me alone to muddle through my first heartbreak. I was disheartened that my own mother expressed no interest in helping me with my wedding. But my lowest moment was the emptiness I felt when I lost my first child. Knowing that life could be so unfair tormented me.

A classmate had given birth to a stillborn; I compared our misfortunes and knew her heartache proved far more devastating than mine. In an abstract and perverted way, Mom had been there for me. I could hear her voice in my mind shaming me into facing all the "what ifs." I realized that as sad as my situation was, it could always be worse. That conviction saved me from slipping into Mom's dark world.

My OB-GYN doctor suggested I get back in the saddle, so I did. When my first son, Matthew, was born, Dad came to the hospital proud and drunk. Mom seemed happy but still too disconnected to be of any help. Deep inside, I always needed her. I never lost my yearning for Mom's love in spite of all she had put me through. That's when my feelings of emotional abandonment re-surfaced. *How do you obtain motherly skills? Would I lack the motherly/child bond like Mom did? Aren't they as natural as breathing?* I was on my own. I walked around the house holding Matthew in my arms repeating over and over, "I love you, I love you, I love you," until the words flowed naturally from my lips and harmonized with my heart. I could finally, without wavering say out loud, "I love you," and truly mean it. By God's grace, my motherly instincts had awakened.

Seventeen months later, my second son, Daniel, was born. I had an opportunity to work part time, so with both boys in cloth diapers and bottles, being home with them was a Godsend. This lasted a year, before I returned to work full time. I dreaded having to leave my boys allowing my bitterness for Mom to grow stronger. I couldn't identify with Mom's misery. She had been blessed with healthy babies but remained uncaring. She was able to be home with her family and not have to shuffle time, energy, or put up with the demanding public in the working world. If she wasn't so self-absorbed, she could help me out with her grandsons, but she wouldn't. She quipped, "I've raised five brats and I'm not about to be tied down again." I heard you, Mama, loud and clear. By now, I didn't expect anything from her. I'm afraid she might hurt them or at the very least, neglect them. So that's just the way it will have to be. I'll get by. I have so far. Just one more rejection to suck up. *Don't wallow in self-pity JoAnn; move on.*

Once again, an alarm sounded with the possibility that my life might mimic hers. Six months after Daniel was born I thought I might be pregnant again. This would be my fourth pregnancy in less than five years and I was panic-stricken. Would I have five kids, resent my life, and grow to hate my kids as Mom had done? I loved children, but my body was tired. It was a false alarm, so with sad reluctance, I had my tubes tied. I got busy molding my life into what I assumed a "family" was supposed to be; still determined not to duplicate Mom's way of living.

My heart still aches for my precious baby girl that didn't make it into this world:

To My Unborn Bebe.

You were on my mind today, my little Bebe,
No particular reason why.
I just miss you and yearn for you to be here.
The years quickly pass and
With each day behind me,
I wonder what your life would have been like.
Your laughs, hugs, joys, thoughts, and dreams are all tucked away
As the world continues without your smile.
I cry each time you drift in and out of my thoughts.
My eyes struggle to absorb each tear
before they have the chance to roll down my cheeks,

But I must let them flow.
No amount of tears are able to turn back time
For the little one I never got to hold,
I never got to know.
I end each thought with a sigh of what could have been.
You were on my mind today, my little Bebe.

Each day was like building a house from scratch with no blueprints. Every decision was mine alone. The only guidance I had was my past, but I longed to tear that structure down. I formed new insights and grew hungry for fresh ideas and values.

I understand living backwards is never productive and void of any stopping point. Reliving fragments of my childhood kept me in turmoil but I didn't have the know-how to resolve my sorrow. All I attained was my inherited stubbornness, and that never got me anywhere. Each time a memory plays in my head, the frustrating reality is that there isn't any degree of difference, it will never get worse, never get better, but it will never diminish either. It is what it is. Most everyone I know has admitted having at some point a personal conflict of varying degree. I gained perspective, believing my family's woes weren't as aberrant as I imagined. I realized a life is shaped by what our memory recalls but even that gets distorted, as no two people view a memory the same. *Is each memory what we will them to be?* All things matter and mold our lives, but what counts the most are the people in our lives.

Please don't think I was a saint in my roles as daughter, wife, and mother. I made my share of mistakes. I read a quote that hit home: Good judgment comes from experience, and experience comes from bad judgment. It wasn't until I had my own children that the negative dialogue from childhood re-emerged, taunting my motherly instincts.

It sickened me to relive each episode. I trembled at the thought that I could easily repeat Mom's coldhearted outlook. It took constant prayer and restraint not to emulate the violence I had suffered as a child onto my boys. I made a solemn promise to God that even though the seed had already been planted in me, the cycle of abuse would end with my parents' generation.

My boys got their share of spankings but I never hit them out of anger. If they needed to be disciplined, I made them go to their room, allowing me time to calm down before I carried out their punishment. If my frustration boiled over, it had to be released somehow, so flexing my vocals seemed the lesser of all evils. When reprimanding my sons, I carried over the art of *hollering...hollering...hollering*. I deeply regret yelling at my boys because they truly weren't bad children.

When I did fly off the handle or realized I was in the wrong, I quickly apologized to them. I meant it with all my heart. But words do emotional damage and leave invisible scars too. I never told my boys that I wished the hell they were never born, nor did I call them names like stupid little good-for-nothings, little shit asses, or dirty little ragamuffins. I wouldn't degrade them in public or in front of their friends. I never said to them, "You make me sick; I wish the hell I never had you," as Mom had spouted to me throughout my childhood.

As the boys got older, they let me know how much they hated my rants. It was best defined in a Mother's Day card when they were about ten and twelve. Matthew drew a blue face with bugged eyes and a large tongue hanging out. His rhyme was original, "You always yell and yell till your face turns blue...but I still love you. You get me so mad I think you're an old buzzard watching every move...but I still love you, but the best thing was, you had me!" Talk about feeling like a tyrant and a failure; that broke my heart. They were right; all the *I love yous'* in the world couldn't take back my brash screams in my frazzled moments. Trying to raise the boys while being under a mountain of stress from my job, parents, in-laws, demanding husband, house duties, and fluctuating hormones, while trying to sort out my own state of mind left me beaten down. I found myself, more often than not, functioning in an irritable wave of helplessness. I reminded the boys that they shared some of the blame; if they had minded me more, I wouldn't need to holler. The boys couldn't understand what burdens I carried, but it wasn't fair to inflect unhappiness onto them by letting my frustrations spill over into their childhood.

At the age of three, Matthew needed an operation. He stayed in the hospital seven days. I bonded with the night nurse. Like a jolt of electricity, I realized a caring person was what had been lacking in my life. It was refreshing to be able to talk to another adult without being shamed or having to defend myself. I felt confident around her. I wished in some way that she could be a part of my life; my neighbor, friend, sister, or even my mother. I knew professionals couldn't get close to their patients, but she was everything Mom wasn't. *There you go again looking through those rose-colored glasses.* I seem to gravitate to older ladies for the wisdom and comfort they exude. Their natural uniqueness inspires me there is a softer and more beautiful side to life.

Until my sons were old enough for school, Ms. Mancillas was their sitter. She took excellent care of them. I'll never forget her kindness to the boys and me. I felt secure and loved in her presence. Each time I think of her, a sensation of warmth comes to mind. I hold her friendship close to my heart; I love her dearly. *Shame on me for wishing she had been my mother, but I often did.*

In spite of the drama going on in my parent's life, I took pride in my home, and caring for my family gave me enormous satisfaction. I couldn't bear ever being separated from my boys. But I felt every child should experience camp at least once in their life. So when they turned nine and ten, my friend Lorraine and I sent our boys to an Episcopal Church camp for a week. This would be the first time they had been away from (me) home. They had no sooner left when I mailed them a "miss you/love you" card. The front of the card had a cartoon firefly that read, *When you are gone I'm all dressed up*...and the inside read, *with nowhere to GLOW.* I hovered over my boys like a mother hen, barely letting them out of my sight. To think about them being away left me weepy and I cried most of the week they were gone. I realized they would soon be grown, leave (me) home, and make their own path. Knowing that day would come, I held onto the notion: one door must close for another door to open. So when the time came, reluctantly I let go. *Their life is their adventure, let them enjoy it...I pray they enjoy it.*

Face it; daily living is a struggle. When I wake each morning, I must put into perspective any senseless dream or flashback before being drenched in fear. I have as much control over which way the wind will blow as I do over my frame of mind. I have an instant to shake this sentiment or else it will be a toss-up between which emotion will consume my actions. Will I be covered in a blanket of melancholy, or achieve satisfaction today? I try to make plans the night before so I can be in better control. If I don't, that's when my day gets squandered. It takes every ounce of courage I can muster to shed my insecurities and tackle each qualm. There's also the nagging panic for what's lurking around the corner; any surprises or disappointments must be faced head-on. There's a plaque hanging on my wall that reads: *To be afraid is to believe in evil more than you believe in God.* I find myself reading this quote often. You're no different from anyone else JoAnn; it's called life, get a handle on it. There is no crystal ball to peer into for the day's outcome; pick yourself up; move on. No one is promised tomorrow; enjoy today.

Looking back on my life, I tried to erase all the painful actions involving my family, especially anything pertaining to my mother. One clue is the noted activities throughout my "Week at a Glance" appointment book. It's dotted with doctor appointments, meetings, ball games, birthday parties, play rehearsals, and the monthly star (*) to validate the timely arrival of my monthly period. You can read between the lines in the subtle notations of events, or lack thereof concerning family connections. They reveal so much of what I deliberately masked from myself. One entry in particular stands out, September 15, 1987, and it reads: shopping trip with Mom. Two thoughts came to mind: there were very few outings with Mom, and, I had shared something with her that I considered important enough to remember.

I often encounter a mother and daughter out shopping. Inadvertently, I will overhear bits of their conversation. They appear to be in tune with each other's lives. The mom compliments her daughter on how beautiful her new outfit looks, and with sincere interest notes it would match her red shoes perfectly. The mutual respect shared by both shocks me and makes me ache for the emotional bonding I had missed.

Some moms live miles away or have died, but it's a disturbing kind of void when your mother lives three miles away and your lives don't connect. My envy fuses with emptiness and that's then when I realize all the bonding that should have been customary with us would never be. I tell myself, *"Stop staring, JoAnn. Stop feeling sorry for yourself. You should be ashamed. A whole lot of people have it a hell of a lot worse than you."* Don't envy others and wish you had their life. Take off those rose-colored glasses and stop fantasizing over every relationship you observe. You don't know what goes on behind closed doors. No life is perfect, no ones'. My insight into other lives clash like a battle: one side craves harmony, the other side stabs like a knife. I just want the emptiness to stop gnawing at my gut. I return home determined to put this mini-drama behind me. JoAnn, *this damn pity party must end.*

When it came to us girls, the common thread that intertwined throughout our lives: we all shared similar abuse and rejection by Mom. However, they didn't let Mom get under their skin like I did. I was the only one at the time married with children while the others were free and living in party heaven. Kathy would tell me Mom could be so much fun, still, I stayed guarded. I wouldn't open up around her. When they were smoking, drinking, and joking around with Mom, they adopted a *who gives a shit* attitude, but I couldn't. I wasn't included in their excursions. In fact, many times I felt left out and the butt of their jokes. But, you see, someone always had to be, making me an easy target. I wore my feelings on my sleeve, held my tongue, and didn't stand up for myself. I couldn't shake Mom's voice inside my head murmuring, *"You're worthless."* How could my sisters act so cozy around Mom? She beat and cursed them too. Am I overly sensitive or had I blown things out of proportion? We each embrace sentiment in a unique way. I spent all my life trying to distance myself from Mom. In my youth, I tried to hide from her wrath, during my teens, I felt abandoned by her, and in my adult years, I was ashamed of her. Yet Mom was a major force in my life that affected every decision I made in raising my boys. Her conduct was the only burdensome tool I had to compare my actions to and I resisted any interpretation that I may be emulating her behavior.

It has never been my intention to bash Mom every step of the way. I was just trying to make sense of her lifelong rejection toward me so I could get on with my life. I struggled to find balance and shake the lingering unrest that was floating in my mind, questioning my sanity and doing its damnedest to bring me down. I needed to place value on my existence if the feeling of worthlessness was ever going to dissipate. My apathetic mood led me to a lot of soul searching. I confessed to my priest how depressed my parents made me feel every time I visited them. He responded, "If you knew of a wreck up the road, would you deliberately drive into its path or find a way around the chaos?"

People say you can't keep living in the past; it will only bring you down, it's nonproductive, can't be changed, and a waste of time; so why dwell on it? If that's the case, then why do people lean on their past accomplishments as stepping stones to achieve a better life? You certainly wouldn't ignore all the good experiences, so why bury the painful ones? There is no denying or hiding your past, and if you try to, you're only fooling yourself. All experiences convey a lesson to be learned. I believe your past is the map that determines what degree of wisdom you absorb throughout life; ultimately molding who you become. *I can't move forward if I haven't taken the time to understand my past.*

It was a challenge to pick out a present for Mom. She was hard to buy for, and truthfully, I hadn't allowed myself to get close enough to hear her wishes. Since I felt neglected, choosing any gift for her felt like a thorn in my side. Besides, in her later years, there was nothing she needed or wanted, and that held true for me too.

I dreaded buying greeting cards for Mom, no matter what the occasion. Finding a truthful message that connected with her personality was damn near impossible. Mother's Day was the worst. I'd get nauseated thinking about having to pick out a card. Each card had a sappy rhyme like, "You are the best mother in the world; you mean everything to me," or "I could never repay you for all your love," or "What would I do without you in my life?" etc. How could I give her a card filled with adulation for something I felt she didn't deserve? I wanted a card that reflected my true feelings, but finding one that relayed my sincerity was hopeless; they didn't sell that kind. I'd settle for a card leaning towards a generic sentiment like, "I hope this is a happy day for you-enjoy," or "I hope your day is filled with sunshine and surprises." On their fiftieth anniversary, I found a card of the famous *American Gothic* painting. On the front, the couple were standing side by side, showing no expression. It read, "*All I can say is...*," and the inside read, "*What's done is done.*" It was one of those ha-ha funny phrases that revealed a true sentiment that pretty much summed up their marriage.

Occasionally, I'd find a humorous card with a silly rhyme thinking we could all enjoy a big laugh, but even that backfired. On Mom's seventieth birthday, I picked out a card. The front had a flying fairy waving her wand and when opened, the inside read "*The Bitch is back. Happy Birthday.*" Mom assumed I was referring to her as '*the bitch.*' I tried to make her understand, "Get it, Mom? No one likes the birthday fairy to come around each year. That's why it reads the bitch is back." My efforts never made the connection. She couldn't comprehend its true meaning; again her paranoia ruled. I'd have a temporary reprieve until the next holiday rolled around. I did however, sign all her cards: Love Always, JoAnn, LeRoy, and the boys. *That I meant.*

I WANT
THE WHOLE PIE

I was married with my own family before I opened my mind to this
big, beautiful world. I tried to take in as much as I could on our
trips and to preserve every bit of beauty, though they were few and far
between. I snapped endless photos to be able to relive each outing. If I
missed the perfect shot, I was devastated. I'd be up at the crack of dawn,
go nonstop, and milk the day for all its worth. I crammed as many activities as I could into the weekend before we had to head home. I'd squeeze
every drop of fragrance out of each day and lingered till the very end. I
soaked in every sunset and wouldn't leave till the band stopped playing.
It saddened me to leave any place I visited only to promise myself I'd
someday return. I wonder, in another life, have I passed this way before,
or ever will again? I hope so.

I want the whole of everything. Not a thin slice, but the whole pie,
crumbs and all. I felt I missed out on so much growing up, I developed
a quirkiness to run a perpetual race trying to catch up. I'd get upset if
even the smallest clouds floated by; afraid the weather might ruin my
trip. I finally realized there will always be clouds in the sky, especially
near the coast. Now that I am older, I am grateful to be going anywhere,
no matter what the weather. I try to never miss event: a picnic, play, ball

game, day at the lake, a wedding, or a concert. To be healthy enough to get around is a blessing in itself. It saddens me to think of all the places I'll never see on this magnificent planet.

I wanted to share with my children all the earth's beauty, so Lee and I included the boys on every excursion. Living in Augusta, Georgia, is an ideal geographic location for beaches, mountains, lakes, and big cities. Kathy thought we were crazy, "You two need to get away and have some time to yourselves." But I needed my boys near me. In our early years of marriage, we were poor (wasn't everyone), so vacations consisted of weekend camping trips to not so very exotic places, but no less enjoyable. My happiest memories are the outings shared with my family.

We began camping as an inexpensive adventure, hoping to expose the boys to nature and normalcy. As long as I had my family around, I was in heaven. I knew if we stayed in town, we would be expected to share the weekend at my parents. They thought we were nuts for always being on the go. Dad said we should rest after working all week. I thought they were the foolish ones for staying home.

I wished my parents had gone somewhere, anywhere, and enjoyed themselves, but they didn't. They both had their freedom, and so much living still ahead of them. I invited them to the lake countless times, but to no avail. Mom didn't like the outdoors, especially the humidity and the bugs. Dad, well, I never knew why he stayed home except that his job was demanding and he remained exhausted or hung over.

They acted much older than their actual ages, choosing to stay in their dismal cocoon, allowing day to day living whittle away and wearing themselves down. They had become disillusioned with life, generating little effort to savor pleasure for themselves, yet it was theirs for the taking.

My parents put themselves in a perpetual rut and their only traveling was the same routine each day; pick up groceries, go to the doctor, drop by the bank, run to Sears, or step out for a haircut. We shouldn't allow routine to dictate our lives, yet we put such importance on routine. It turned into an excuse to hide behind, consequently, they remained chained down.

It occurred to me they almost never took any trips together. It was mostly Dad calling the shots with his same tune, "Charlotte, I've been gone all damn week. I'm tired. I just want to stay home and rest." I think when he was younger, he enjoyed riding the rails, if only to get back the feeling of freedom he believed he had been cheated out of. They had forgone a honeymoon and except for one trip to the mountains and two trips to the beach, they had no desire to travel anywhere. They both deserved enjoyment, however, plays, concerts, or movies didn't hold Dad's interest, and sporting events and bars didn't hold Mom's. They shared no hobbies except for a brief time fishing. They had nothing in common except being locked in their own routine of regrets.

THE MOON PULLS ON MOM'S MIND

Fifteen years had passed since Mom's nervous breakdown, yet her psyche still controlled when to withdraw from life and when to emerge from her zombie state. It was baffling how she could blend back into rhythm as quickly as flipping a light switch and intuitively pick up where she had left off. The oddity being, so did we. Being grateful she was back among the living, I didn't dare question her conduct. I feared any mention of her aberrant behavior might send her spiraling back down, and the burden of another pitfall being my fault would be devastating. I was still dealing with my guilt of not being able to help her, or at the least, understand her illness.

If you needed Mom while she was down, you were S.O.L. Until she was ready to re-enter the universe, she was reduced to just another piece of furniture. Each time Mom withdrew into her solitary place, I perceived her as weak. I was perplexed why she would give up on life. But each time she made a comeback, she would harvest a thunder of strength that could only come from a strong-willed person. Her determination gave me hope until her next downward spin. We had no choice but to move forward with our own lives. So the cycle continued like seasons of the year, except hers were giddy spring and silent winter. I too, was riding a parallel wave of emotion, depending on which frame of mind she displayed at the time. I either felt deep sorrow for Mom or intense animosity, but either way, my conflicting emotions were taking a toll on me. It wasn't that I had given up on her, I just believed she had given up on herself.

Her daily routine never deviated until her bipolar clock signaled it was once again time to forfeit sides. I never uncovered a pattern or knew what triggered her mood changes, but sleeping, eating, and smoking were still the only constant things she cared about when she was down. Then, out of the blue, her up mood would emerge and she would call me on the phone, jabbering, laughing, and asking a million questions about Lee and the boys. Mom struggled to reclaim lost time and catch up on all she had missed. She babbled her way back into our lives, pretending nothing had changed; hence there was never a need to explain or apologize for her absence from reality. Her first act of normalcy would be to invite all of us over for her signature dish, spaghetti and meatballs. I never could turn down her invitation. Did she realize how long she had checked out of this world? Was she haunted by how much living she had lost and that life was passing her by? Had she missed us? Was she glad to be back? By not questioning her behavior, had we become her enablers?

I don't think she could ever control when to leave or come back because there was never a rhyme or reason in her departure or arrival. As for the length of time for being captive in either domain, would be anyone's guess. Mom's psyche was the dominant mechanism that controlled her internal clock that ultimately betrayed her. The conflict she must have gone through to leave her silent world and re-enter her family's lives had to be gut wrenching. Like a caterpillar going through metamorphosis as it struggles to puncture through its cocoon. Will it break through and be free or suffocate inside its own protective layers? You can't call this living. Watching her struggle broke my heart.

I wondered what she thought of when she took those long mind journeys or how much she remembered. Was she happy being there? Was it peaceful? Was it colorful and could she hear tranquil music playing? It had to give her some sort of comfort; why else would she stay gone so long? She never mentioned her two different worlds, and they never overlapped each other. As one shut down, the other one took over like the ebb and flow of the ocean's tide. Maybe this would be the last time she would be down. After all, she's up now. Sadly, she functioned in this bilateral way of living for so long, it became the norm for her and us. *She can't stay this way forever, can she? It has to end eventually.*

There were times, in different situations, I observed Mom acting normal, so why couldn't she find the strength to hold herself together for the sake of her family? I am left once again with the same bewildering belief: those damn shock treatments didn't do Mom a bit of good. I didn't see any positive changes emerge from her treatments. Was she leaning on her sickness as a crutch? For all that was erased from her mind, it didn't diminish her distrust in people. The side effects were just as damaging as the sickness. The only shred of confidence she retained was her instinct to think she was always right trusting paranoia as her defender from the cynics. Mom's inability to connect with reality fluctuated according to the degree of chaos in her life at that moment, or what conflicts were taking place in her children's lives. Either way, watching her struggle just to stay afloat was tormenting.

Mom happened to be in her down mood when her brother, Tony, from California came for his first and only visit. Mom seldom mentioned him and if she did, it was never flattering. Mom's deep-seated issues with Tony never wavered. She never forgave him for missing their mother's funeral and she detested the way he treated his first wife. You would think his visit would make an impact on her, but she barely spoke to him. In fairness, during this stage of her illness, no one mattered.

A great deal of Mom's misery seemed self-inflicted. Had she ever looked inside her soul to own up to any mistakes she made? I only know she never took blame for any portion of her actions. Mom kept score of all the hurtful events but didn't counterbalance all the good that came her way. I strongly believed if she were truly *grateful enough,* it could've been a stepping stone for happiness. Mom's obsessed and dispirited belief that her feelings were being trampled upon were only hurting herself and her family. She never made the connection that she was the one stirring each conflict.

Mom remained tormented over the loss of her mother and rejected by her father. Her marriage proved to be equally as painful; betrayed by her husband and unappreciated by her children. All this emotional baggage had taken its toll. Again, I tried to rationalize her feelings, yet couldn't grasp why her life stayed on a collision course with everyone she came in contact with. Did she feel unworthy of love or that we weren't deserving of her love? I believe the mental illness clouded her happiness and short-circuited all of her natural instincts that damaged her perception of people.

When Mom got mad at one of Dad's relatives, she took tremendous satisfaction in cutting their faces out of photographs. She went one step further and cut their pictures into tiny pieces mailing them to the person as if to say, I'm rid of you; you don't exist in my life anymore! Insecurity and paranoia had turned her bitter while her willpower remained one-sided; not even the shock treatments could cure her.

Mom gradually emerged from the mental trauma that held her captive. The worst of the ordeal seemed to be behind her as her down time became less frequent, though remnants of her illness still lingered. A combination of coming off of so many mind-controlling drugs and finding the right combination of medication to regulate her hormones are what helped her regain a somewhat manageable life where she could function on a level that allowed her to drive again. She became a little more outgoing but there was no way to know if the illness had ended. Her children's lives were settling down, so there weren't as many crises for Mom to deal with, just the drawn-out quarrels with Dad that knocked her from solid ground and caused her to rehash, "I wish the hell I had left him years ago." *Will she ever be the person she dreams to be?* Whatever kept luring Mom back remained a mystery. How uncanny and exhausting to not have any control over where your mind would take you while both domains had equal pull.

In Mom's struggle to reclaim some measure of control, a new habit morphed: impulse buying, giving us one more unforeseen repercussion to deal with. Mom favored Walmart as her one-stop utopia. She spent money on items that were overpriced, not needed, never used, not practical, and just pure junky. Dad grumbled excessively about her wasteful spending, but it didn't matter. Mom now had her own cut of his railroad pension, which was hers to do with as she damn well pleased, and she damn well did.

FOUR GIRLS
AND A SISTER

I admit to being overly protective of my boys, and in one of the doleful episodes in my life, I needed to explain to them that my brother, Rick, was gay. Having seven years between us and with him living in another town, I hadn't given any credence to his lifestyle. That is until an incident happened with my boys and Rick that left me livid. I didn't recognize this person or his behavior, so reluctantly while riding in the car, I chose to enlighten my boys with the truth; *once again; "The truth according to JoAnn.* "The car was the place I had so many times passed down my motherly words of wisdom—besides, they were trapped and had no choice but to hear me out. I explained as best I could and hoped their naive minds could comprehend my concern over their safety. Saddened by the news, Daniel sighed then meekly remarked, "Oh, Mom, I wish you hadn't told us." But I had to. The anxiety of all the *"what ifs"* crept into my thoughts and my motherly instinct to protect my boys took over.

Rick was eighteen when he joined the Navy. He lived in San Francisco, then Atlanta before settling in Savannah. One summer in the late seventies while on leave, he returned home and broke the news to Mom that he had come out of the closet. It broke Mom's heart. I don't know how Dad learned of Rick's lifestyle but he was equally devastated.

Well, back to the incident. Mom, Rick, my boys, and I were going shopping when Rick leaned his head out the car's window and let out a piercing wolf-whistle to a handsome male jogger wearing nothing but a pair of skimpy, red nylon shorts, socks, and running shoes. I was incensed at Rick's brazen display and for the lack of respect he had shown our Mom. It was one thing to choose that lifestyle, but it was humiliating to have him flaunt his loutish actions around us. Why can't he keep his private life private? Maybe by being defiant he was trying to get Mom's approval; God knows, we all had issues.

After that incident I worried, "Could I trust Rick around my boys?" I wasn't about to take any chances. I didn't want my boys exposed to Rick's rebellious nature that included drinking, drugs, smoking pot, or be blindsided by any inappropriate behavior. We kept our distance. You know what they say when a child is molested: it's usually a family member, a friend, or a neighbor. *Right?* This created a larger wedge between Mom and me. She didn't approve of Rick's lifestyle, but he was still her only son and she defended him no matter what.

Rick's coming out couldn't have been at a worse time. My parents' relationship was hanging by a thread and this news added another devastating blow to their marriage; their only son *turned gay*. Then came the blame game; if Mom hadn't babied him and defended his every action. If Dad had taken more interest in his life and taught him how to be a man. To add insult to injury, they couldn't recall a single gay relative on either side of their families to place blame on. You know the myth: there's one in every family.

In the seventies and from a Southerners' perspective, gays were very much misunderstood and despised. The stigma of having a *gay* in the family brought another layer of shame to bear, sending Mom deeper into depression and Dad deeper into the bottle. Dad viewed all gays as perverted. How could a big strapping ex-sailor/mighty railroad man, who loved the ladies, one and only son be gay?

I shamelessly teased Rick when we were growing up. I would be angry with him for tattling or hitting me, and I was jealous of Mom forever taking his side, so I retaliated by calling him a sissy. I sensed there was something peculiar about Rick, but again, these things were never talked about. Why doesn't he play sports? Why did he drop out of swimming lessons? He acts like a sissy and giggles like a girl, and he's even too afraid to climb a tree. He's nothing but a mama's boy and a cry-baby. Had his four sisters harassed him to the point of homosexuality? Were we to blame?

I tried to be open-minded but Rick's lifestyle hit too close to home. I didn't hate him; I simply had no tolerance for any of his vices or conduct. But deep down I grappled with my illogical attitude toward homosexuality. I was just as ignorant about "gay life" as most until I transformed my inherent stance from prejudice to open-mindedness and acceptance.

In spite of all the years we were estranged, I loved my brother. Our relationship healed after our parents died. The disrespect Rick showed for our parents is what upset me more than his sexual preference. Rick's life is his own and I may not understand his world but I am not intimidated by or ashamed of him either. However, things were never the same between him and my parents. Dad and Rick barely communicated. Mom stayed in contact with Rick but their relationship remained strained. In reality, it's shocking when a member of your family exposes you to something atypical. Deferent behaviors are easier to accept when they morph in other families. Mom and Dad never came to terms with his choices in life because of their beliefs and the era in which they were raised.

I can't walk in my brother's shoes, but I know in his early years he endured a private torment from my parents' actions. Then he battled his own unmatched demons throughout his adult life. Different from what we girls went through, but still an anguished, lonely, and neglected existence.

OMISSION IS A SIN

I made three mistakes in the beginning of my marriage. The first: I wouldn't take any shortcuts in home-making or insist Lee share any of the house duties. I had to prove to myself that I could be a strong wife and mother. This was a gratifying time in my life to be caring for my family. I enjoyed cooking and felt I had moved beyond my upbringing; determined to show Mom I could create a normal, happy home.

My second mistake: I played the "it's not fair" card. I resented Mom for not appreciating her family, but what fulfills one person's desire causes another's burden. Mom didn't have to work, had her freedom, owned a decent home, and birthed five healthy children. Sadly, she felt trapped and miserable by her own inability to find any blessing from her surroundings. I was naive in thinking that most of Mom's problems stemmed from her being indolent. I believed that if she would only take the initiative to embrace life, her sadness would magically evaporate. Then perhaps she would feel better about herself.

I didn't have a choice between a career or housewife. Lee had a seasonal job as a carpenter that didn't provide medical benefits. He had been laid off twice, triggering an unhealthy dose of the 'what ifs' life might throw at us. We witnessed our parents' struggle throughout their lives so job security held priority. I gave heed to Dad's advice, "Don't

confuse your needs with your wants; if you don't need it; don't buy it."
We had our share of doing without and we were quite creative in making
things work. I became a thrifty shopper, paid every bill on time, and was
perfectly content being home with my family. Lee's handyman skills
saved us lots of money. It wasn't that we were to proud to ask for help,
we knew it was our obligation to work things out.

My third mistake: I tried to hide my own family's flaws. I hadn't
intentionally set out to create a false impression however, inadvertently,
it made my home life appear perfect. My goal was to construct a stable
peaceful home. Mom would make snide remarks, "You think you're so
damn perfect," or "You think you know it all," in a condescending tone
that wavered between resentment and disdain. Just like my childhood;
that worthless feeling came flooding back. I never thought of myself as
better; she concocted this notion on her own. She didn't acknowledge
how hard I worked or what sacrifices I made for my family. *To be fair, I
hadn't acknowledged her sacrifices either.*

But omission is a sin. I never let on that Lee and I had disagreements.
It's natural that all young couples quarrel at times *right?* I hadn't forgotten the promise I made to myself, never expose my personal feelings
to her again. The more I concealed my failings from Mom, the more
they (somehow) surfaced and exposed my blemishes. Any tidbits of discontent in my life gave Mom something to sneer about. By keeping my
distance was I simply trying to avoid any more clashes with her? *There's
no contest between the two of you. When are you and your mother going
to end this emotional tug of war?*

One night, Lee and I had a rare but explosive fight that even upset
the boys. I kept busy in my bedroom to avoid his tantrum when who
do you think made a surprise drop by visit? You guessed it, my parents.
Ironically, they never visited, especially unannounced.

Lee had been talking to Dad in the kitchen when Mom hastily entered my bedroom with a smirk on her face. She took immense satisfaction to witness the discord that was unfolding in my house. Mom knew all too well what I was going through. She imagined me treading through the same dysfunctional mire she had lived her entire life. My troubles equaled her misery as only she could relate. Damn, her fallacy of thinking my home was perfect just backfired on me.

They left in a hurry, but as soon as they arrived home, Dad called and said, "I'll come get you and the boys, and ya'll come stay here *if things get too rough*." What did Dad mean if things get too rough? What in the hell is going on? I was mortified! What had Lee said to my dad for him to get the impression we were in danger? I'd unwittingly gotten blindsided in my own home; left exposed and betrayed by my husband.

The next morning, Mom called deviously asking, "How are the boys? Is Lee feeling okay?" I didn't want to appear vulnerable in her eyes, so I tried to act indifferent. I wouldn't give her the satisfaction of rubbing salt in my wound. The small tolerance I had for Mom hinged on duty and it took all my volition to keep my wounded pride hidden. She wouldn't know how deeply her words affected me, nor would she see me cry. I had perfected the art of hiding my feelings while growing shamefully cynical. Through our impossible moments, I would catch myself (mentally) confessing, "Why can't you shut the hell up and stay out of my life. You are no help to me; you make me sick." but the moment I thought it, regret flooded in, leaving me washed in shame. I must deflect these thoughts that I don't mean. I didn't elaborate about what went on after they left; their was nothing to concede. I did however reluctantly confess Lee had been drinking; that was no secret. All Mom knew was what little she heard Lee say and whatever Dad told her, and they both saw and heard more than I knew.

This wouldn't be the first time Mom exploited my failings. She knew how to push my buttons. The only time Mom felt connected to me was through my pain, but a caring mother shouldn't delight in witnessing her child's strife. Lee was talking out of his head so I deliberately avoided him the rest of the evening. I assumed he had passed out in his chair. I went to bed. I never asked Lee what was said to Dad that night; he wouldn't have remembered anyway. *Shame on me for trying to portray a perfect family and shame on Lee for humiliating me in front of my parents!*

Mom didn't spend time with her grandsons, even though in her own way she loved them. Due to her bouts with depression, I wasn't comfortable leaving them alone with her. I always imagined the worst might happen. What if she fell asleep with a cigarette in her hand and the house caught fire? What if the boys upset her and she beat them like she beat us? What if the boys got into her medicine? What if she was lying down and they ran into the street, *what if.*

Lee and I endured a multitude of stormy days putting up with each others' parents. We felt put upon and worn out by their ongoing feuds that were no fault of ours, and had no clue on how to keep their troubles from bleeding into our life. Our parents should have been our rock; instead, we felt abandoned. My strength came from my faith in God and the love for my family.

In spite of my journal being deliberately blank, most of my memories eventually resurfaced and had to be dealt with one by one; the drinking, fighting, separations, and Mom's illness. I battled how to forgive Mom and move on, yet I intuitively (still) pulled away from her every time she tried to hug me. The trepidation that I had for Mom remained embedded deep in my bones. Wanting to hug Mom and run from her in the same instant felt insane. Think about it, a mother and daughter who had never physically connected or shared something as sincere as an embrace; *it's unnatural.*

I wouldn't go to Mom with any personal problems. If she couldn't handle her own life, then how could she help me with my woes? *Don't go back on the promise you made to yourself, JoAnn, keep your feelings hidden, one less sorrow to endure.* I couldn't let go of the mistrust that had built up over my lifetime. No matter how hard I tried to keep peace, her illness twisted everything I said. My intent was always taken the wrong way, making it appear I was her enemy; not a good daughter. As much as I needed Mom in my childhood, woman to woman, I now needed her just as much. I needed her as my rock, but I knew that would never be. We both lost out. It took the best part of both of our lives for me to salvage a tolerance for Mom without the animosity I harbored to resurface.

People at times would tell me that Mom was proud of me, but I couldn't identify with the compliment. My presumption was based on her never saying it directly to me. I passed it off thinking Mom may have been talking about one of my other sisters and simply mixed our names up, We assume as a culture that self-pity is an entitlement, but that's the one emotion that isn't genetic. We alone indulge ourselves in its destruction. To be fair, perhaps she was proud of me. *I hope so.*

The haunting of our family screw-ups, I hoped, would be left by the wayside. But memories trickled in at the most mundane times and reminded me of the shame and anguish associated with my family. We all carry a secret we would like to keep hush-hush, a wound only we can cradle, while knowing it needs to be resolved. I've been privy to many of my friend's damaging situations and that's what kept me grounded, always comparing notes if you will. *A belief is shared: we have all felt unloved and trampled upon at one time or another.* My flawed perception influenced what degree of neglect constituted my inner sorrow. I assumed, "If they only knew how lucky they were with their uncomplicated lives." Shame on you, JoAnn; looking through those rose-colored glasses again; stop comparing lives. We're all just trying to get by, and who's to say their way is all that virtuous. I read a letter written by a confederate soldier that stated, "If our cause was so noble, how could we (the Confederates) have lost the war?" Conceivably, I too, have inflicted hurt on others.

I struggled through each day as feelings of failure hung over me like a cloud allowing sadness to fill the void where confidence and strength should have shielded me; while I struggled to keep my emotions under control. I never invited feelings of despair into my head to distort my views, but childhood memories unexpectedly crept in, taking hold, and reducing my mood to a level of dejection that made me second guess any joy that came my way.

My trepidation just to get out of bed, face myself, and accept the challenges the day might bring left me panicked. The craziness was I had to shame myself into tackling my responsibilities. The very thing I feared about Mom's illness was what kept me motivated. The incessant turmoil and fear fueled my determination to hold on. I bombarded myself with house projects and outings with the boys. If I stumbled, I might just as easily have a nervous breakdown.

By never hearing any praise or encouragement growing up, I didn't feel confident in my surroundings. I also didn't feel deserving of happiness. I felt like a phony anytime someone gave me a compliment. I'd assume, "They have it all wrong, surely they don't mean it, I'm not as great as they think." I'd force a friendly smile to mask my insecurities as I warily made it through each day. *I don't think anyone noticed.* A stranger once told me I was pretty. I was totally taken aback by the compliment. Past affirmations came from relatives that compared my looks to Dads' or my skin tone to Mom's. I didn't know how to see myself and hadn't placed any significance on how I looked to others. *It's called pride, JoAnn; not to be confused with vanity.*

As a young adult, I began the ritual of subconsciously criticizing myself; taking over where Mom's undermining left off. Stop being so damn lazy, clean your dirty house. You're getting fat. You look like a ragamuffin. Put on some makeup. Your hair is a mess. Endless guilt kept me in a constant state of melancholy. I felt I had failed everyone, including myself. An ordinary trip to the farmers market would trigger guilt for buying from one vender and not supporting the others. I loathed wasting time, but I would get caught in the trap of feeling morose, and that sent me into a voided state of actually wasting time, only to (naturally) beat myself up about it. As hard as I tried, I never reached a level of contentment.

I worked for a financial institution and I held the top sales position for over ten years. Each time I won an award, I would be proud, only to have my success short lived. Mom showed no enthusiasm and I wondered if it was jealousy or apathy on her part. I lacked confidence and doubted my own success by undermining my ability. It's a fluke I won. Surely it can't happen two months in a row. Maybe there was a mistake in calculating my points. I hope they don't think I cheated. What makes me so special? How can I possibly be better than the other sales reps? I'll be ashamed if I fail next month. My secret to success was I tried in every way to please everyone; managers and customers. No matter what I did for them, I felt it was never enough. My dread of failing fed my obsession to try harder. I feared being reprimanded or embarrassed in public. It placed needless pressure on myself making it my fault for not believing in myself. I sincerely cared about my customers and I appreciated everyone's loyalty. I acquired numerous and lasting friendships that I deeply cherish.

My biggest drawback was my trepidation and it didn't serve me well in the work place. I cowered to authority. I loathed not being assertive. I didn't think I had the right to speak up for myself, so by my failure to not act, I got passed over many times. I also detested confrontations. The get-ahead wannabes, insecure bullies, and ambitious managers with over-inflated egos caused me many sleepless nights. If caught off-guard, anxiety took hold, and I instinctively froze like a scared cornered mouse. After I calmed down could I think for myself, but by then, it was too late. I never could defend myself. I'm my own worst enemy.

Each of us have our unique personalities developed through daily living experiences. I adapted a different understanding from the life that I was born into. Memories have long been watered down and who is to say they are correct or unbiased; over the years, accuracy fades. But the balancing act is maddening. Sometimes, I think I will lose my mind: too much to take in, not enough time, not enough emotional support, endless demands, so many disappointments, too much sickness, too many painful memories, and on and on. Lighten up. Stop dwelling on the past, stop feeling sorry for yourself, stay focused, make better use of your time, and be thankful for everything in your life. Nothing lasts forever, just keep moving forward and learn how to enjoy each day.

I have to be fair; not all of my life was sorrowful. It was the waves of unforeseen turmoil that kept my emotions stirred up. As I said before, so many people had it a lot worse. I recognized my parent's struggled to take care of our basic needs and worried for our well-being. I can't say they mastered the art of harmony or stability in our home, because there were ongoing conflicts coming from different directions that needed to be dealt with. They did, however, try the best they could with what they extracted from their past, and that in itself is genuine. I know my life had more opportunities than theirs and their lives were better than their parents' were, but many of their struggles were self-inflicted. That's what made their relationship so miserable. Human frailties inflict havoc on the human spirit, creating a ripple effect that harms everyone in their path.

Without stepping on anyone's beliefs, I question, "How did I become the person I am today?" Luck, destiny, resolve, or God's plan? Some don't give it a second thought, but life is a precious gift, and we all have the ability within ourselves to make our existence worthy. *I'm not wanting pity; only closure and peace.* I must face reality, keep striving for better, lose the negativity, and tackle each obstacle that comes my way. It takes courage to change; we have to want it bad enough...*and I do.*

LIFE DOESN'T HAVE TO BE SO DAMN CHEERLESS

My parents looked forward to a one-on-one visit from us siblings, but when the entire family got together, the mood turned tense. We allowed our nervous energy to explode into giddy nonsensical chatter, teasing and cracking jokes at each other's expense until my parents couldn't tolerate our mindless foolishness any longer. At other times, my parents played the role of instigator using insults wrapped in the guise of teasing, but even in jest, their words turned hurtful and someone would inescapably be chastised for their shortcomings. Each cynical remark ushered me back to my forlorn childhood where their strict rules and harsh, misguided punishment tried to shape us into what they considered obedient kids.

Each parent felt the need to divulge to one of us the fall out between themselves and another sibling. Mom bitched to me about Dad's drinking or about Rosemary and Ricky driving her crazy, so logically she must have channeled her woes about me to one of them. Dad criticized my siblings' imperfections and Mom's unpredictable moods but would do an about face and defend her unconditionally. Our visits together were never enjoyable or beneficial. I selectively shared portions of what was happening in my life. Mustn't let my guard down or divulge too much of what's going on; it will come back to bite me. We didn't support each other like siblings should have. In fact, we acted like a pack of wolves pulling down the weakest, with Mom more times than not acting as the pack leader. I felt a wave of relief each time I was skipped over but I knew my turn would come around.

It was a sick feeling driving to my parents' house with all the resentment for Mom flooding back. The closer we got, I'd break out in a cold sweat and my stomach would begin to churn. Robbed once more of time that I could be sharing with my own family. Lee grumbled how my entire persona changed each time we visited. I admit, I allowed much of their burden to fall on my shoulders. It's insane to keep punishing my family and myself. The next time they call, I'll tell them we can't make it. But I can't lie. Instinctively I knew what I would walk into but I always went back. After all, grandparents need to see their grandkids. *Don't they?* Maybe things will change soon. *They could, couldn't they?*

As we unloaded the car, I had already fabricated an excuse as to why we needed to leave early. Then, I'd plaster a bogus smile that served more as a shield to hide my true feelings, than elation for being there. As I entered the house, I'd give Mom a quick cheek hug, then promptly pull away using the food or gifts in my hands as an alibi. It felt intimidating getting close to Mom. I never shook the natural instinct to pull back when she got too close to me, even after all the years. *When had "hugging" become part of this family's ritual?*

Nothing in our family exhibited normality; even mealtime tilted off balance. Dinners planned for 1:00 P.M. typically meant we ate at 3:00 P.M. I never knew why we couldn't eat at 12 P.M. or 6 P.M. like normal folk. Forget about making any other plans because the day was shot in more ways than one. There was simply no way to salvage any part of the day. From the time you were invited until the time you arrived, the atmosphere in their home did a U-turn leaving me to wonder, "What the hell am I walking into today? Why did I say yes to her request?" My parents sincerely believed we were abandoning them if we didn't show up at their command.

You never knew from day to day what frame of mind Mom would be in. She could turn as fast as the wind and I would be trapped for the duration with whichever mood she saw fit to expose. Each time she emerged from her down mood, you could hear the anticipation in her voice wanting to get together with her family. As if her excitement was contagious, I responded with the same enthusiasm of needing to see her as well. To tolerate Mom, you had to endure her illness. When Mom invited us for dinner, we discussed what we each would bring, but it didn't matter how carefully we planned, by the time we came together, she had worked herself into a tizzy and the mood soured. The preparation proved overwhelming and the anxiety grated on her nerves. Damn, what happened this time? I just spoke to her three hours ago and she was fine. If it's too much for her to handle, why did she invite us over?

Just like Mom's unpredictable conduct, the same held true about Dad. When she was up, it would be his turn to disrupt the evening. He grumbled, "Why do you wanna' go to all this damn fuss for?" But, when she was down, he would be the one wanting you to come, practically begging, and wouldn't take 'NO' for an answer. At times, his request was more like a command, but most of the time it was reduced to a pitiful plea. By the time we arrived, he would be drunk, insulting, combative, or passed out. He hasn't even started cooking. We'll be stuck here all damn night. *Nothing changes, they're not going to change; STUPID, you have to be the one to change...SHIT!*

Why would any parent want their kids and grandkids to see them in such a loathsome state by exposing their innermost flaws? It never clicked with them that most of our family's miseries were spawned from their abrasive tug-of-war behavior that ignited most of the discord in the first place. Their actions were an absolute waste of human spirit.

Drop-in visits were equally hard to endure. I felt an oppressive sadness surrounding their house. Many times I'd walk into the middle of a meltdown that couldn't be dealt with rationally. Either Mom was hysterical or Dad was raging drunk. I became the sounding board for whatever had gone wrong in their lives. They both had an uncanny way of not owning up to their mistakes. Do you know how frustrating it is to watch your parents trying to destroy each other? By pecking order, they have lived longer and have experienced more than me. I was expected to stay and witness their degrading each other, grumblings, and despair, but forbidden to intervene. Children didn't stick their nose in their parents' business.

No matter when I dropped by, I blamed myself for not having the answer to any of their problems. Each time I left, I felt remorse that I wasn't grateful for the time we spent together. My sympathetic side reminded me it was the right thing to do. After all, they were my parents. They spent the prime of their lives raising me. How selfish to not spend time with them. If I stayed an hour, I felt guilty for not staying two. When I shared half a pound cake, I scolded myself for not bringing the entire cake. I'd leave with a nagging, sick sensation that I hadn't done enough for either of them. But you can't atone for what was never your liability to begin with.

My logical side signaled for me to flee the madness and not look back, but I didn't know how to stop the chaos. So I inevitability carried their troubles home with me. I kept telling myself that one day they will wake up and realize how blessed they are.

The more my parents exposed each others short comings, the more their grudges mounted. My obsessive pity for them outweighed my pledge to stay away. How could I fix their problems when I could barely understand where their pain was coming from? *Ahh, the endless cycle of blame and abandonment.*

It was a long-standing belief that we could never do anything right in their eyes and each flaw was verbally noted. *Did they expect too much? Did we give too little?* I was spineless when it came to confronting my parents so I'd devise an excuse to leave. They'd look at me with a puzzled frown and say, "Why do you have to go? You just got here." Their disturbing way of communicating was normal to them; they never understood my feelings were hurt. Or, to add insult to injury, they would laugh at me for being so sensitive.

They had nothing in common except for spitefulness. I don't know what kept them together for so long except the obvious, five kids. Mom bought single beds and moved into the empty bedroom. They may have lived under one roof, but they couldn't have been further apart. We'd comment about their relationship and concluded; they couldn't possibly have had sex more than five times in thirty years. The joke was ha-ha funny, yet a sad insight into their marriage.

Everyone in my family smoked except me. Years of their chain smoking saturated every inch of space in their house and no amount of air freshener could disguise the stale aroma. Their clothes, bedding, and curtains reeked of saturated smoke. Even porous containers, fresh foods, and cooked dished absorbed the odor. My eyes would begin to burn from the lingering smoke the moment I entered the house. In Mom's obtuse manner, she'd ask, "What's the matter with you?" I blamed it on allergies. What else could I say? She knew. I had complained enough times, but all she'd give up was a scoff. Then her smoke craving instinctively kicked in. She never delayed lighting up on my behalf so why give her the satisfaction by asking her to please refrain? After enduring all I could, I knew I had to bolt. Staying any length of time evoked a coughing fit.

Once outside, I'd gasp for fresh air, and from my coughing fit you would think I was a chain smoker. Then in a welcoming relief, a gust of wind would fill my lungs and blow much of the smell out of my hair and clothes. I'd drive straight home with my windows rolled all the way down to keep the air circulating. This worked well except in winter. I'd leave my belongings inside the car so they wouldn't absorb the smell. I detested transferring the stench odor into my house. Without delay I'd head straight to the bathroom, strip down, and lather from head to toe. As I washed away the residue from my parents' house, I'd tell myself it was the smoke smell in my hair and clothes that made me nauseated. Subconsciously, I knew it was a cleansing ritual I must go through. I either cried all the way home or wept in the shower. Only then did I feel relieved from sorrow until the next visit. *Shit, who needs this? Is it out of pity, guilt, or duty that I remain trapped?*

Each one of us, at one time or another, had caused our parents a lot of anguish, leaving no stones of rebellion unturned. They had let us down so many times, yet they viewed things differently. Bewildered, they didn't have a clue what part they played in our personal sagas and heartache. They took the stance that their kids were ungrateful in spite of all they had sacrificed. There had never been a time that something wasn't erupting in the family that kept all of us off-balance. I've watched movies on dysfunctional families reuniting during a holiday, and no matter how quirky the characters were portrayed, the woven thread in their closeness was the love they had for each other. Every family has issues, so what exactly does normal encompass? In a bizarre way, I knew we held that common thread, it simply got tangled in a mire of personal anguish.

How depressing, to sit in their dismal house witnessing them tear into each other, spewing spiteful accusations and dragging up old wounds; driving a wedge deeper into their marriage. I felt tremendous sorrow for both of them, but the fact that they could never put any quarrel to rest kept all their conflicts energized. Their years together grew complicated with so many missed opportunities; sadly, they weren't there for one another. I had an understanding of their pain, but not their actions. In the end, their declining health proved heartbreaking enough, but it took a back seat to their real problems: alcoholism and mental illness. They lived in a ominous vacuum long before the encroaching assurance of death moved in. In their eyes, I am still their child so what good could I be to them? What could I say that would make a difference or possibly teach them any of life's lessons that they hadn't already been exposed to?

Routinely, I'd burst out crying while driving home. But tears possess no worth, no insight, or power. So what good were my tears except to make me realize how helpless I was. One night while leaving their house I turned the radio on. A song about a young couple who promised to meet at a certain time and place to elope began to play. The message: if you get there before I do, wait for me. The sentiment of their love for each other carried over to their death. Talk about a tearjerker, I sobbed (again) as I branded my parents' stormy marriage against the song's lyrics that tore me apart. I didn't have the skills to help them turn their lives around, especially towards the end. They didn't have a clue the sorrow I carried for them. I then realized I can't save them and there was nothing

I could do to make life easier for them. It was their journey, however it played out.

What I am trying to say is I despise waste, waste of any kind, and their years together had *runneth* over with waste. When you total all the time fighting, money squandered, kids ignored, memories trampled, dreams abandoned, emotions neglected it was all an overwhelming fucking waste.

HOMEGROWN
HOLIDAY HELL

Holidays...what can I say except that in their later years, each celebration became increasingly stressful. We tried to hold on to our family traditions, but the only tradition that had been perfected was carrying out the emotional impasse of duty that dominated with barely a whisper of normalcy. My parents also expected us to celebrate their anniversary and each others' birthdays together.

Mom had shed many of her quirks, but she continued to struggle to stay on an even keel that proved wearisome. She continued her retreats to her bedroom, locking herself in if anyone upset her. Dad would be passed out in his recliner in an undershirt, work pants, no belt, shoes, no socks, and a half smoked cigarette that somehow managed to stay between his two fingers and put itself out. I put my boys through so much hell dragging them to their grandparents' house with the naive intention that things would get better. I hoped being around their grandsons would bring them joy, but I was only fooling myself. They expected us to come and it didn't matter that the atmosphere in their home had deteriorated to beyond sad. If guilt was the driving force that kept me returning, then hope was my prayer that maybe they would soon snap out of their despair. After all, you can't live in muck forever, can you? *Why would you want to?*

As the boys became more inquisitive, I prevented them from seeing Mom in her unkempt condition, and from seeing Dad staggering drunk. Their clashes and bitter words grew tiresome leaving very little quality time. *Damn it*, why couldn't they be grateful, focus on how truly blessed they were? Why couldn't they figure out their lives didn't have to be so damn cheerless?

Easter was the first holiday of the year that brought the family together. It made no sense; no matter what conflict either one of them demonstrated, there was still that compelling need that each holiday must be shared with family.

Each sibling handled holidays differently, making their appearances at separate times, arriving late, leaving early, or not showing up at all. Often-times, a sibling would take issue with another sibling and ultimately, someone's feelings would be trampled. I walked on eggshells hoping not to say the wrong thing that might get the ball rolling. But as sure as an approaching storm, an argument would erupt, and we each would be trapped in the torrent. The offended one decided it was time to leave by abruptly snatching their belongings while swearing out loud, "Why in the hell do I keep coming back to this hornet's nest?" They believed that *family was* the most important thing in life. What other reason could there be to keep inviting us? Why couldn't they hold it together for he sake of the holidays?

I wanted our family to continue to share Christmas but it was the hardest holiday to endure. I prayed they would come to the realization that their life wasn't as bleak as they made it. Just look around, so many have it much worse. Rick and Kathy lived in Savannah, but Ricky rarely attended any family events. He had distanced himself from the family years ago. If he came, it would be Christmas and he never stayed long. More times than not, instead of traveling with Kathy, he just called collect. *Merry Christmas!*

Kathy came when she could, but she cut her visits short using the excuse; she didn't want to drive home in the dark. She admitted many times she too had cried all the way home from something Mom had said to her, or for the sadness she felt in their house. My family kept going, but it was taking a toll on my marriage. Lee grew more agitated, and we'd argue driving home over how upset I would get after each visit. I vowed to make other plans for the upcoming holiday. But time and again I felt an ingrained duty to respond to each request, like a marionette jumping each time it's string is pulled, and no inkling how to break free. *You don't turn your back on family.*

Rose divorced her alcoholic husband of fourteen years with the conviction, "I'm not about to live the rest of my damn life mimicking Ma's marriage." So she and her thirteen-year old daughter, Jacqueline, moved back to Augusta. She assumed having their granddaughter around would please them. But coming home turned out to be a huge mistake. She, too, was caught up in our parents' web of guilt driven commands; jumping each time they called. Rose had witnessed chaotic episodes during previous visits, but it didn't compare to being dragged through the drama on a daily basis. It was as if our parents held a spell over us just like when we were kids; we were still trying to please them and win over their approval.

Rose had a hard time finding a job and struggled financially. Until she could get back on her feet, she and Jackie lived with Mom and Dad for two months. However, they begrudged having to again help Rose. They blamed her incessant spending, lazy habits, and failed marriage for her impasse.

Jackie had a difficult time adjusting. She had been pulled away from her father and friends. She craved love and support however, Mom made no attempt to cultivate a relationship with her only granddaughter. Mom criticized Jackie's appearance and disapproved of her boorish behavior, while thoughtlessly taking every opportunity to shame her. I didn't blame Jackie when she stopped coming around, she had enough self-esteem issues without being methodically attacked by her grandmother. Mom's animosity for "her girls" never wavered, not even the shock treatments had softened her nature.

I fostered an unhealthy dread that something horrible might happen, specifically to my boys, like sacrificial lambs, a tragedy to make my parents turn their lives around; shake them into reality, teach them a lesson, make them come to their senses. Why couldn't they see past their self-inflicted misery, or the insight to bring their turmoil to an end? There had been no life-threatening illnesses or untimely deaths to weigh my parents down. They created their own homegrown hell. *Why would anyone deliberately invite heartache into their lives?*

Gail had become fed up with the family, she stopped participating in all family gatherings. Dad wrestled with the reasons for why she stayed away. I watched him agonize over his past mistakes knowing things couldn't be rectified. But the sins passed down have a way of breathing new life into the next generation and each one of us must figure life out for ourselves.

In their later years, birthdays and holidays were treated as just another day. The siblings had scattered in different directions and any momentum to rally as a family grew feeble. No one had the heart to celebrate anything anymore.

Dad loathed shopping so I'd pick up Mom's present for him. I didn't mind; I just wished he wouldn't wait till the last minute to ask for my help. I bought Mom a pair of purple silk pajamas from Dad, but when she opened the gift she sneered, "You know I hate purple." She appeared hurt as if I deliberately chose her least favorite color to ruin her birthday. She imagined anything I did for her was first and foremost a cruel intentional plot against her. I should've known Mom's least favorite color was purple. Stunned by her admission, I realized I didn't know her favorite dessert, book, song, or movie. I only knew her favorite movie star. I had become acutely preoccupied excluding Mom from my life. I'm ashamed I knew so little about my own mother.

My parents were in a quagmire of loneliness and remorse. Added to their misery, the kids were older with a new crop of problems popping up. All the while, Dad had to think that no one appreciated him. His feelings and needs had long been neglected. Just as Mom had no one to turn to, neither did Dad. They both rejected the fundamental essence of needing each other long ago; their marriage was crumbling.

I regretted all Mom had missed out on through the years, but the truth being Dad had been cheated out of happiness also. Some sided with *poor Charlotte* while others sided with *poor Herbert*. It depended on which side of the fence you were standing on. Both were equally pitiful and at fault. Mounting burdens had taken their toll and Dad lost interest in everything that he had worked so hard to achieve.

I imagined if Dad was reincarnated, that his past life had to have been from the Wild West. His colorful character and mannerisms reminded me of a hotheaded, rough-riding, free-as-the-wind cowboy. He loved the outdoors, craved freedom, and loathed being told what to do. He didn't talk much but when he did, people took notice. Drinking whiskey and sweet talkin' the ladies defines a cowboy's persona, and Dad's life had no shortage of either.

I sensed Mom's past life weighed equally as sad as her present fate: poor, jilted, and broken-hearted by her lover. Reliving the exact plot of a bleak romance novel. I couldn't imagine Mom in a happy setting.

HOLD DEAR ALL
THE ONE TIMES

I t was difficult to explain to my sons why my parents behaved as they did. As they listened to what I had to say, they did so with a sad reluctance because each time I revealed a family incident, it exposed their grandparents in a shameful light. It was painful for them to hear, but I believed it was necessary. When you understand the truth about a loved one, you tend to accept their human frailties, you forgive more freely, even if that person at times had disappointed you. I prayed that things they had witnessed hadn't wounded them too deeply, and would hopefully make them stronger adults. The boys knew my parents loved them through all the perplexing times, and I know my boys loved them too. That's what sustained me.

No matter what was going on in Mom's life, she remembered the boys on their birthdays, Easter, and Christmas with a card and *a little something* inside to spend.

When the boys were around five and six, Dad took them for a ride on his train. Dad was a conductor/trainman for the railroad and I'm sure it was against the rules to let a non-employee ride, but when Dad wanted to do something, no one could stop him. He pulled out of the train yard and told us to meet him down the road. He stopped the train and let the boys climb aboard. In the engine's cab, I watched them waving with wide-eyed enthusiasm and Dad grinning from ear to ear as the train rolled down the track. I, on the other hand could only fret, "What if Dad is caught and gets fired?" We picked the boys up in the next town. I hope they each remember that day. Outings shared with Dad were sparse.

Each spring, my sons played baseball for the community. The ball field was three miles away from my parents', but during the five years of games, my parents attended one. Lee's parents never came. If my parents came to the boy's birthday party, it was like prior family gatherings: one would get peeved, sit silently in the background, wouldn't participate, appear bored, annoyed, and inevitably leave early. They didn't filter their comments in public, making it a contest to see who could embarrass the other one first. It was as if they needed a witness, or worse, an audience.

Routinely, the one that showed up had to make an excuse for the other's shortcomings. Dad would utter, "Your Mom's got a headache," which translated to "She's down again," and Mom would reveal, "Your Dad's drunk," which needed no translation. They made no apology for their absence; they simply couldn't muster up enough heart to pull them selves together. Dad kept drinking, Mom stayed in her solitary world; allowing everything to churn into an ordeal. The boys saw my parents in their most vulnerable condition for so long it I wondered had it occurred to them that this way of living was not conventional. Still ill-equipped on how to handle either one of their illnesses, I remained ensnared in a web of tormented loyalty. My parents' morose behavior had to be baffling, but the boys childlike innocence and unconditional love brought a balance to my parents' failings. My sons had no choice but to seize each situation as it unfolded. No matter what was lacking in substance from their grandparents, they accepted them for who they were. I continued to pray the boys could lift my parents' spirits and in turn they would enjoy their grandsons and arrive at a happier mindset in their later years.

Daniel said with all the innocence of a child, "Mom, remember that one time I went fishing with granddaddy?" *That one time.* I held dear to all the one times. They loved their grandkids, just not enough to change, and the years marched on.

Over the years, I tried to hide my disappointment but the shameful truth was, everyone lost out. The kids were getting older so I made the decision to stop exposing them to my parents' habits. I distanced us by using ball practice, church, and weekend camping trips as our excuse to not be able to visit as often. I shielded the boys from as much as I could, but it was inevitable that my parents' problems had already spilled over into our lives; none of us were immune.

Daniel, acted for the Augusta Players at the local community play-house. He had the lead role as Wilbur, the pig from the play *Charlotte's Web.* He had been in many plays but this was the first and only time my parents would see him perform. With no forewarning, Dad got up and left during intermission. Mom was visibly shaken that Dad hadn't stayed until the end. What was his problem? Was he bored, tired, uncomfortable in the seats, needing a drink, or just not interested in his grandson's achievement? That is what I meant by one or the other causing conflict at special times that were intended to be a happy, shared occasions. He not only abandoned Mom, putting the burden on us to get her home, he also let Daniel down- who, by the way, won best actor of the year for his star performance as Wilbur. I could tell by the hurt in Mom's eyes that she had every reason to feel let down and alone. She was finally doing something with her husband like normal couples do, only for him to walk out and humiliate her. Mom longed for Dad's companionship, but he was emotionally absent for her when she needed him, and he had no inkling how much she needed him.

My parents weren't the only ones that instigated discord, Lee's parents also fell short in their role as grandparents. The moment Mr. Skinner's divorce became final, he moved on with his life and married the woman he had been seeing for a long while. He closed the door on his sons and grandchildren. I resented Lee's father and stepmother for their absence in our lives. They proclaimed to be devoted Christians who put family first, which they did, however, it was the step-mother's two daughters they spent all their time with.

We couldn't count on Lee's mother either. She had been diagnosed as narcissistic with a adult/child personality. Between her divorce from Mr. Skinner, (whom she referred to as *that man*), and two additional marriages, she was never in any position to involve herself with her grandsons. She did love them in her own peculiar way.

Raising our children was our responsibility and Lee and I never lost sight of that. I expected the grandparents to act like adults by sharing a slice of their lives, but it was never to be. Grandparents should never disappoint their grandkids with broken promises and neglect. What luck, our family having three sets of dysfunctional grandparents, all living within five miles of each other, yet no meaningful connection.

The grandparents received the short end of the stick by thoughtlessly brushing aside (for their own selfish reasons) two incredible boys that would have brought immense happiness into their lives. They owed my boys nothing except love.

Lee and I did our best to keep the boys busy and fill in the gaps from their grandparents' absents. We devoted ourselves to our boys and supported all their hobbies. We took them somewhere practically every weekend whether it involved a weekend get-away or an outing to get an ice cream. All my whining can't change things, but it pisses me off to think of all the things in life that are ours for the taking with no strings attached. But these are the very things we allow to slip through our fingers like rain drops. I want to shout to the masses, *wake up, open your eyes, we are so blessed!* Happiness doesn't fall into each of our laps at the same exact moment; it enters at different stages of our lives, many times disguised as pain. It's up to us to enjoy our lives and be wise enough not to let any person we care about feel unloved.

TWO WRONGS NEVER MAKE IT RIGHT

It was Mom's perception of people that threw me for a loop, and I never got accustomed to her detached viewpoint. Mom remained true to one piece of her doctor's advice; to not hold anything back, and speak her mind. Mom was known to blurt out loud off-handed remarks about anyone and it didn't matter who she offended. Could she been using her mental illness as a facade to hide behind, making it her weapon of choice? Mom knowingly set out to hurt people. For example: Kathy came home one Christmas and pressed for time, she invited her friend to Mom's house to exchange gifts. One problem; Mom disliked the girl. When Kathy's friend walked in, Mom blurted out, "My God, you've gotten so fat!" Mom's brazen viewpoint and cunning smile possessed the pretense of being innocent of any wrong-doing. I was embarrassed for everyone. I called Mom out on her behavior. She dismissively replied, "You don't know what you're talking about." Do I think Mom was the slightest bit remorseful? *Hell no*. Her defiant stare, transparency, and coy smirk ignored any resemblance of regret.

One particular occasion, Mom went riding with Kathy and her husband, David. Without warning, the truck hit a bumpy patch in the dirt road. Mom thought out loud, "What a good road to ride down if you wanted to terminate a pregnancy." Then she ended with a taunt, "Sorry I didn't ride down a bumpy road years ago." David was taken aback by the bizarre and insensitive remark that flew out of her mouth. As for Mom, this was rational thinking. Each malicious thought was often fired off with a random zinger that left a resonating sting. You see, three months prior, Kathy was two months pregnant when she miscarried. Was that Mom's way of retaliating for all the injustice she felt life had dumped on her? *What made Mom declare war on everyone who loved her?*

Mom's mental illness kept everyone at bay. When someone trampled on Mom's feelings, it devastated her, yet she was radically disconnected with how she treated everyone. It was always about who snubbed her or what someone said behind her back. She couldn't think past her own suffering, therefore she never recognized or took responsibility for her own insensitive actions. She could spew plenty of heartlessness, yet if she felt cornered, would tumble into the pitiful victim's role. I will never know which parts of Mom's mind had been altered or erased. She grew so cunning and selective with her memory, I often questioned how much was sincere and how much was mockery. As time passed, Mom grew set in her ways which sabotaged any happiness and kept her in a dismal state of mental conflict. There would be no changing her. *Why does anyone deliberately bruise another human being?*

Mom had an irrational tendency to hold grudges against anyone that crossed her, real or imagined, especially those who showed Dad any degree of attention. Mom's rancor intensely burned, making it impossible for her to forgive or forget anything that was directed at her, and each episode swirling through her mind took on a bigger persona and twisted each incident into another long, drawn out saga. Her mind worked like a bank computer keeping impeccable records of each infraction she endured, always adding to the list then locking them safely away.

Could I be imagining this? Hell no. I witnessed this counter attack of hers too many times, directed against too many people.

Mom was extremely keen on remembering each wounding event to her, but she couldn't recall anything that might shed blame on her own actions. Her selective memory reawakened each of Dad's indiscretions and his behavior towards her. Mom rehashed a shopping trip to a men's clothing store. She purchased a birthday present for Dad; a tan corduroy sports jacket with dark brown patches on the elbows. She complained how the hanger cut into her middle finger as she carried it four blocks to the car, only to have Dad not appreciate her effort. He voiced his ingratitude, "What in the hell did you go and buy that for Charlotte? I don't need a damn jacket." Dad never wore it. This affirmed Mom's belief, "He doesn't appreciate a goddamn thing I do for him." Her detailed description of the present and of Dad's rejection was uncanny. Just an ordinary observation, except it happened over thirty years ago.

Mom read about a woman arrested for brutally beating her daughter. She reacted in disbelief, "I can't believe a mother would do such a thing." It never occurred to Mom that she repeatedly crossed the line from punishment to abuse with her own girls. I took a deep breath for courage then spoke, "Mom, you don't remember beating us?" Touting her signature smirk she replied, "You girls deserved it." She justified her actions as discipline. She'd never confess any of her short comings to me. I never gave her the satisfaction of mentioning our ill-treatment again. *Don't wallow in self-pity, JoAnn. It's time you found your inner strength to move on.*

Had her behavior towards her kids haunted her as she got older? Had she felt any shame? Why would she? In her younger years, she was too spiteful to have remorse, and later in life she seemed to take her actions against us in stride. Had all memory been erased by the shock treatments or had she simply chosen to place guarded recollections on a shelf to never be thought of again? The truth in the way she treated us was never affirmed. In her mind, she did nothing wrong and acted stunned that I suggested any different. We deserved it, plain and simple. She never make the connection that it could have easily been her that the newspaper had written about.

Mom never identified that she and her father were very much identical. She resented him, and we resented her just as much. Mom despised her father's detestable behavior towards her, nevertheless, she instinctively linked his actions with her own disfavor of her daughters. Mom kept her father's legacy alive every time she showed favoritism toward her son and grandsons, and malice to her girls and grand-daughter. Mom's odious actions were another unceasing heartache we girls endured. Could Mom have conquered her illness by tapping the power within her, therefore making our lives better than hers had been? Had the intimacy not shown for her children been beyond her control? She relentlessly focused on her tormented past and neglected to carve out a meaningful belief in herself.

While studying to become an Episcopalian, I questioned my priest, "If we are forgiven for our sins; why are our sins passed on from genera-tion to generation?" He answered, "Learning from the parents' behavior; such as actions of cruelty, prejudice, indifference, etc., are unintention-ally passed down. Therefore, the cycle continues."

Friends heard my cynical overtones fly out of my mouth each time I criticized my parents. That's how I coped, but watching their facial expressions made me realize how harsh and bizarre I must have sounded. I regretted coming across like an ungrateful daughter exemplifying little respect, but ironically, it was my inherent respect that kept me from turning my back on them. *Or was it loyalty or duty?* I was at my wit's

189

end over ceaseless incidents involving both of them. No one had an inkling of the hell I lived through and I was too ashamed to talk about things that had happened. I lived in an invisible dominion of chaos while trying to grasp what normal life signified. *What's normal? Who's normal? Where do I fit in? Figure it out, JoAnn; accept who you are. Give what you can, change what you have the power to, learn from the past, and be thankful for all you've been blessed with. Keep moving forward, try to enjoy life, and stop with those damn pity parties.*

After years of enduring my parents' disapprovals and demands, my friends couldn't understand why I continued to jump every time they called. "Why do you do this to yourself? Haven't you been through enough? They're never going to change; they only bring you down. Walk away and end this misery." I constantly asked myself the same questions; yet in a naive way, I still hung on to the hope that they would change. I had endured so much for so long that I felt if I walked away now, I would be abandoning them. And it didn't help matters any watching their health begin to falter. Even as my perspective changed, deep rooted in my mind echoed the conviction that I must obey my parents no matter what.

It took a lot for me to talk back to Mom, even though I was grown. I held most things in, but inevitably an argument erupted and I exposed everything that had been eating away at me. I should have known this too would come back to haunt me.

Years passed and once again, Mom and I had bruised each other's feelings to the point of erupting. This time, she threw in my face word for word the argument we had years prior. I'm not exaggerating; she retrieved every word. Her brain worked like a tape recorder. Just hit the rewind button and play. Her accuracy blew me away. *Damn, I must have hurt her deeply.* It wasn't my intention, but what is one blow-up in the heat of an argument compared to everything she said and did to me throughout my life? I recalled the gist of our last quarrel, but it was eerie to hear Mom quote my exact words, turn them around, and throw them back at me. By using my words against me, I had assumed the role of villain again. Unbelievable the depth and intensity her mind could distort events, yet they were vividly real to her. Why was this quarrel different from any of the others she'd been in? Had she filed each tiff with my siblings in her mind too?

I never intentionally meant to hurt Mom or plotted against her for the pleasure of seeing her hurt. That would be crossing a line and any effect would only manifest deep guilt. A deliberate spiteful act against anyone only propagates more problems. Besides, I could never muster up enough malice to give back as nasty as I got. I didn't have it in me. In spite of the misery she imposed, I believed in a fundamental respect for her simply because she gave birth to me. Just to be able to say what was on my mind and get it off my chest would have rendered me some peace, but two wrongs never make a right, and never assume that feelings run parallel. Will she ever respect me or accept me for who I am?

The last time I got pulled into one of their battles was just before Dad quit drinking. Mom called me moments after a hellacious fight, threatening to leave Dad and end it all. Mounting despair and unresolved disputes allowed their threats to escalate. She had reached her breaking point; I naturally feared the worst. Once again, I rushed to her rescue and interjected myself into her destitute arena. I tried to talk to Mom woman-to-woman, hoping I could share some insight on conflicts. I should've remembered my place with them: do not meddle in their business. Yet, once again I became entwined in an endless drama of mayhem. I knew I had walked a thin line; it couldn't appear that I had taken Dad's side. I instinctively wanted to hug her and tell her that if she would stop being so hard-hearted maybe Dad wouldn't be so ill-tempered. In an appeasing tone I suggested, "Maybe Dad would change if you would try and meet him halfway. Try keeping the house picked up and have dinner ready when he comes home from work." I hoped she'd see things differently but her sobbing proved opposite. I had only placed a temporary bandage for a dire wound. Mom's feelings towards Dad were spiteful at best, showing no degree of compassion, compromise, or forgiveness. She had reached the end of her rope; she wanted out. I'm scared of what she might do. After the pep talk, I fixed lunch and made a feeble gesture to straighten up the house; giving me an excuse to keep an eye on her a little longer. Later that afternoon, I called to check on her. She said Dad had returned home.

The next day, we were invited for dinner. I was apprehensive about going, but assumed they had settled their quarrel. Caught off guard at the dinner table, Dad pointed his finger in my face and bellowed, "Who in the hell told you to come into my house and throw away things that belonged to your mother? From now on, keep your nose out of our goddamn business." All his anger had been thrust on me. I about fell out of my chair with shock and humiliation. The smirk on Mom's face let me know that she had taken delight in Dad chastising me in front of my family. *Poor Charlotte*, the one that's always trampled upon, however, she neglected to mention to Dad that she had been the one that called me crying hysterically and begging me to come over. The things I threw away were food coupons I had found stuffed in a drawer that expired five years prior, a ton of disposable take-out food packets, and straws. Once again, Mom had dismissed my advice and turned on me. Damn her! Dragging me away from my family and pleading for my help–and like a fool I rushed to her side only to be manipulated again, just like a dog that gets kicked time and time again but keeps coming back. Why had Mom gone psycho on me? All I tried to do was make her realize that if things were going to change, she had to play a part in the change. Had I said anything that remotely sounded like I was taking up for Dad? If so, then (in her mind) I must hate her. They both confirmed my theory; that I can't help them, or change them, yet I don't seem to have enough sense to stay away. Am I as insane as she is? I remained on edge that I could fall into Mom's world of crazy; she broke my heart; my nerves are shot!

Finally, Dad had paid her a little attention and she devoured every morsel. Believe me, I was glad Dad came to her rescue and elated they again patched things up, but not at my expense. I wanted to scream, "If you showed Mom some meaningful affection and spent more time with her, she might not have so many meltdowns!" I sat at the table wanting to bolt and never return, but instead I swallowed hard and fought back my tears. I robbed them of any victory; determined neither one of them would make me cry. But it remained a catch-22.

Whatever Mom told Dad pissed him off good. I wished I had heard the embellished rant she related to Dad. Had it occurred to Dad that she had twisted her story for sympathy? Of all people, he knew how she could manipulate; he bitched about her enough. So what made Dad defend her and turn on me? Did he think I had encouraged Mom to leave him?

Dad left me too stunned and hurt to come back with any defense of my own. How could I set the record straight? Damn, JoAnn, when will you ever take up for yourself? It's their problem, they're the problem. My part in their epic quarrel was after the fact, and minimal at that. I had reached my limit with both of them. I'm sick of being their whipping post. *Their betrayal stung.*

Respect, duty, and fear had been instilled in me so early in life that I obeyed my parents with no questions asked, at whatever the cost to my sanity. After all the years you'd think I could stop putting so much intensity on everything they said or did. I had to let things go if I was going to survive their ongoing mini-dramas. Remember your place with your parents. What actually happened that day was never mentioned again...ever.

Nothing ever changes in their house: same dance, different song. What in the hell did the shock treatments actually do for her? She wasn't a bit better, still crazy, just on a different level. She still exhaled distorted versions of the truth. He's drinking more. I don't know how he's able to function. That's the kind of insanity that constantly went on between them, with one disheartening episode following another; as one cooled down, another bubbled to the surface. What satisfaction comes from stirring the stink while involving others? All their chaos and drama caused me enormous anguish; the mental strain had surpassed burdensome.

I tried to move on with my life but I couldn't get over the resentment that lingered because understanding something and feeling something is comparable to north (being my mind) and south (being my heart) on a compass. No matter how many self help books I read or how many life lessons I learned, each memory unearthed a wave of sorrow, bringing me back full circle to depression. I must put my past behind me, but scars don't go away. They fade a little and shrink a tad, but they're always there, especially the ones hidden deep inside. I grappled with the magnitude Mom's sickness and Dad's drinking had on my adolescence, while simultaneously staying entangled in their never ending dramas.

It had been thirty years since Mom's nervous breakdown and Dad's drinking ran parallel with her illness. That's an enormous span of years to let slip away and a hell of a lot of living to regret. As Dad got older, his job demanded more with longer hours and more responsibility. He exhibited a sad and faraway look in his eyes as if he was riding the train and yearning the next horizon held the answers to all his troubles. I hoped he found a sliver of peace when he was away from the never ending drama at home. Mom's illness was too overwhelming and his personal burdens had taken their toll. I could see Dad's momentum slipping. In spite of his many faults, he strived to keep the family together.

Mom realized if she was going to enjoy life, it would not include Dad's companionship. She signed up for a china painting class held at the instructor's home. Mom later told me the women acted snooty and made her feel like she was beneath them. Mom often felt insecure around others as she constantly battled with her identity, never feeling comfortable in her own skin. Had they made Mom feel unwelcome, or did Mom imagine this due to her paranoia? Whatever the reason, she never went back. My heart broke to see her not have any self-confidence. Her father had beaten her down emotionally, followed by her husband. The stigma of mental illness stripped away the last bit of her sense of worth.

Dad did all the cooking when Mom was down, and this is when he desperately needed to have his family around. He would call you early morning and invite you for dinner. Dad's intentions were straightforward but somewhere in-between the invitation and arrival, he got plastered. Dinner would either be overcooked or raw. It was left up to me to pick up the pieces, finish cooking, or salvage what was left of the meal. He'd beg his mother to dinner, then get so drunk one of us would have to drive her home.

What a pathetic humiliating evening, watching a grown man make a fool of himself in front of his family and mother. I ached for my grandma as her eyes helplessly watched her son self-destruct. Grandma had lived through a mountain of sorrow; this was just another upsetting outburst to endure. My granddad and several of their kids were heavy drinkers; alcohol being no stranger to her life. At eighty-years old, she didn't deserve the burden of worry from her adult children's actions. She had to feel powerless and ashamed; I know I did.

Dad's boisterous, overbearing voice commanded everyone to enjoy dinner. We acted like robots as we dined and endured his outrages as customary behavior. He couldn't be controlled. As the tension welled up, my appetite faded. It sickened me to watch him try to eat while he swayed, cursed, and belched through the entire meal. Mom was the only one that didn't seem to be affected by his conduct. Oblivious to her surroundings and immune to her condition she would come to the table on command, eat, and immediately go lie back down without any exchange of conversation with her family or mother-in-law. The peculiar fact was no matter how bitter the memories of the night before were, I never had the courage to confront either of them about what had taken place; therefore, their conduct was never challenged. With no one rehashing his humiliating behavior, there wasn't a reason for him to apologize or no need to promise it would never happen again. Did Dad remember being drunk in front of his mother? Did Mom have a clue how creepy her zombie-like demeanor made others feel when they were around her? With the previous day gone by the wayside, the next day was just that. Justification for their actions was forfeited long ago; We tolerated their behavior; that's how we coped. I was thankful no one was killed or the house didn't burn down. Yesterday is behind me, and everyone's safe for another day. *Maybe it won't happen again.*

Dad couldn't harness his demons, permitting his inebriated state to mask his misery. It's cowardly to run from your problems by turning to alcohol, especially when you involve others. I despised his actions, so why did I feel pity for him, and why did I defend him? I believed Dad never stopped trying to make things right but he used drinking as his escape and his downfall. If his drinking binges were an indication of loneliness, why didn't he realize it was his indecent conduct that pushed everyone away?

DAD'S TURNING POINT

One evening, Dad answered the phone and fell to his knees, letting out a wail of anguish I had never heard before. His older brother, Robert, who was also a railroad man, dropped dead of a massive heart attack right in the train yard at the age of fifty-six. Dad and Robert's life appeared identical and the reality of Robert's premature death left Dad fixated his own mortality. Heart problems ran in Dad's family so every time Dad got drunk, he rehashed Robert's passing with a wailing committal, "I'll be the next one to drop dead, just like Robert." I've never condoned Dad's drinking, but I understood that he was saddled with immense burdens and stress. He deserved more out of life; *most people do.* I'd witnessed Dad's inner strength before; why can't he harness it now? Instead he chose a lonesome and remorseful mindset. Mom clung to her pills, and Dad leaned on his booze.

Twenty years later the inevitable happened, Dad had a heart attack. We rallied and kept vigil at the hospital. Mom endured the ordeal by blabbing all the stormy details of her life to any stranger that would lend an ear. Whatever rolled off her tongue could not be censored. She shared sordid episodes of why she hated her mother-in-law, the numerous times she caught Dad cheating, and how badly he drank. She confessed how her kids let her down with all their life blunders. She rehashed all the misery she endured from her father, and that's when she pulled in sympathy by divulging details of her nervous breakdown. By then, the tears were flowing. There she goes again, spilling her guts to strangers. You see, when an outsider is cornered in a peculiar situation, they can't pass judgment; they can only give an unbiased attentive ear, thus giving Mom the solicited attention she constantly craved.

Will Dad have the strength to pull through? Being the fighter that he was, his time wasn't up yet; the heart attack only slowed him down. I reminded Dad, we are not masters of our fate. He went back to work and back to drinking; letting it consume a majority of his years as well as well as his wallet and liver. It would be ten years before his heart gave him any more problems.

As the years rolled on, Dad bucked his new bosses and the ever-changing procedures that the railroad implemented. Dad maintained a healthy dose of common sense, loyalty, as well as being a quick learner. He made a damn good living in spite of his ninth-grade education. He worked his way up to conductor and this alone should have made him proud. A co-worker of Dad's told me, "Your Pap is one of the hardest workin' men I've ever met." As a child I sat in amazement watching him utilize a #2 lead pencil and figuring in his head the mileage of the train's trip, tonnage in each railroad car, and the estimated time of arrival to and from each destination.

I'll never know how Dad managed to hold on to his job with his temper and drinking so out of control. It didn't take much for anything involving the railroad to send him into a rage. Truthfully, Dad felt insecure and worried about losing his job. Dad's rants were endless, "Those young know-it-all (son-of-a-bitch) bosses with their goddamn college degrees make my blood boil." His drinking while off duty made matters worse. He'd phone a lead-boss late at night drunk, and curse him out. It might be over working conditions or a new rule that had been implemented. Railroad life had always brought challenges so eventually his mindset split from a blessing to a burden. Whichever it was, it was definitely his escape–that and the booze.

Twenty years passed and I was still praying he would make it home safely and not to harm anyone in his path. The railroad ordered Dad to get help for his drinking problem or be fired. He felt incensed and shamed being ordered to rehab, but he had no choice. He alone had allowed alcohol to dictate his fate. If he lost his job, he would lose his salary, medical benefits, retirement, and everything he had worked his entire life for. How could a worn out, fifty-year-old alcoholic get back on his feet? Who would take care of Mom? I finally understood the enormous pain he must have been in, only I was too immersed with Mom's illness to realize that he hurt too, just in a different kind of conflict. If he was going to salvage any part of his life or if he craved any quality of life, he must stop drinking.

The first time Dad went to rehab, he checked himself out before he finished the program and he went right back to drinking. Dad didn't see himself as a drunk. After all, he held down a very demanding job, always paid his bills on time, and provided for his family. He wasn't starving, homeless, or unemployed. He was just an angry, aging drunk, and a pitiful one at that.

It became hopeless and unbearably shameful to be around Dad. Once again, his bosses were breathing down his neck. Liquor served as the cornerstone of his despair, but he wouldn't own up to it. Not his wife, mother, family, friends, bosses, the one heart attack under his belt, or rehab could persuade him to stop drinking. His driver's license had been suspended from a previous violation, but he kept driving while intoxicated. Pulling-in favors from the *good old boys* had worn thin. If he got caught again, he would be looking at jail time. How many more wrecks can Dad live through? How many more times will Dad pass out and forget to put his cigarette out, or turn off the stove? Dad used up his nine lives long ago.

Dad was ordered into rehab for the second time with a new condition: he had to complete an eight week program. With his job in jeopardy and his options running out, he left for rehab. But in his usual stubborn rebellion, he fought it all the way. I sent "get well" and "miss you" cards once a week to let him know how much the boys and I loved him. He wrote back but his letters carried an air of defiance, indignation and denial. He wasn't ready to own up to the true reason for being there. Dad confessed, "I do nothing but eat, sleep, attend meetings, and tolerate them damn druggy's." Each letter spoke of boredom. "Nothing exciting ever happens here, so there is nothing to write about, Love Dad, Love Granddad, or Love Pat," depending on to whom the letter was addressed. He wished us well and instructed us to look after Mom and each other. I sensed an undercurrent of worry in each letter. No doubt, he had to question how effective his concerns would influence us, or how well we would implement them. Knowing he couldn't leave left an additional layer of anxiety to endured. Gradually, his mood changed to acceptance. Near the end of his stay, his letters read of anticipation about coming home.

During each escalated drunken episode, Dad boasted, "No goddamn person on this earth is gonna' tell me how to live my life. And I'm not gonna' stop drinking 'til I'm goddamn good and ready." This made the third time an outsider intervened on behalf of Dad's life. His naval commander, the divorce judge, and now his railroad boss. They all played a huge part in how he would "live his life," and each decision brought him anguish. Simply put, each time Dad felt cornered, he couldn't understand that he needed to be saved from himself.

Dad returned from rehab but continued to drink. Within two months, his mother died, then, unexpectedly his nephew died in an electrical accident. Mom went to Kathy's house unannounced, and supposedly, had left Dad for good. Within six weeks, (out of the blue), Dad conceded, "I'm done with liquor." Mom came home.

It is said you have to hit rock bottom before you turn your life around. Dad's stubbornness stood in the way of him resolving his own dilemma. But stubbornness is a two-way street, and the vice that kept him drinking, would now become the virtue that would keep him sober. Once he made his mind up to stop drinking, he never looked back. I wish his mother could have witnessed his triumph over the bottle.

Dad started going to AA and embraced it with all the conviction of a changed man. He faithfully attended the meetings, and when he couldn't due to his work schedule, he listened to taped testimonies of recovering alcoholics. He traded the liquor bottle for a new companion: earned AA chips. His thirst to defeat his addiction was supported by people just like him, all sharing a humbling yet sobering message: their war with alcohol.

In the beginning, Mom accompanied Dad to each AA meeting. She stood by his side for the most part, but soon the novelty wore off; she stopped going, though she wouldn't divulge why. Had Dad's pledge come too late or perhaps she reached her point-of-no-return. For all the years Mom begged Dad to quit, when he finally did, she couldn't adapt. Mom didn't have it in her to forgive and she resented him even more for his past screw-ups and of how much of their past he'd squandered with drink. She begrudged all the praise Dad got for beating his addiction. She felt he didn't deserve any respect from us; after all, the entire family had suffered under his decades of consumption. Was AA stirring up too much of the past? Had someone alluded to the fact that Dad's drinking was partly her fault? *Who knows?*

I supported Dad by attending numerous AA meetings, especially his milestones like the one month, ninety days, one year, etc. I was proud of him for ultimately turning his life around and for his ongoing commitment to sobriety, but this too turned bittersweet. I was equally disheartened for all the sullied memories and empty years that he lamely discarded like his empty vodka bottles.

As different speakers (mostly men) shared their sagas about their long and difficult journey through hell with drugs and/or alcohol, I found myself resenting them and conveying all my compassion to their (neglected) families. I couldn't muster any pity for their plight. The endless heap of pain and destruction left by their selfish actions was pathetic; I felt only shame for them. I struggle with the notion of alcoholism being a disease. These people quit when they were damn good and ready to quit, but not until. You don't quit a disease and it seldom quits you. I saw alcoholism as a crutch, and a selfish one at that. But I must give credit; the support the AA members gave each other was noble and I held no ill will to any of them that were trying to turn their lives around, but it sickened me just the same. Perhaps I was too close to the predicament because the more I listened, the more their stories all sounded identical. Time and again they exposed their multitude of lost jobs, crumbled marriages, scattered and neglected children, wasted dreams, and woes of bankruptcy and being penniless. They typically ended with, "But I've got me a good one (spouse) now; one that understands me and accepts me for who I am." They each sounded like so many country (cry in their beer) songs; same dance, different song. *Whatever.*

Dad's sobriety thrust Mom into a new facet of life, but she never adapted to his new allegiance. All the attention had shifted to Dad giving Mom's paranoia the green light to again rear its ugly head. Wounded by resentment, she felt abandoned by anyone who supported Dad. Not only did Mom stop going to the AA meetings with Dad, she wouldn't go to Al-Anon meetings for the spouses. She defiantly retorted, "I'm not the damn one with the drinking problem. Why in the hell do I need to go?"

She then took it one step further and began baking (eighty proof) rum cakes. That's right. She had never baked a rum cake in her life until Dad stopped drinking. She made a big production out of going to the liquor store to buy a bottle of rum. When I asked, "Mom, why do you want to bring liquor into the house?" With her usual quip she replied, "I'll do as I damn well please. I shouldn't have to give up liquor; he's the one with the problem." Just another disturbing jab with no logical outcome. Truth: Mom didn't drink, ever, until we were grown. When we went for dinner, on occasion, she would order a glass of wine with her meal, but she never finished it. Was her mental illness working overtime? Mom, what were you thinking? Was this a spiteful act to get back at Dad or hoping Dad will deliberately fall off the wagon so you can rub his nose in it? Is it your mission to prove that if he is the weak one, it makes you the strong one? Now that he has cleaned up his act, are you scared that you would have to try harder and make some changes too? If he succeeds, are you afraid he'll realize he doesn't love you anymore and will find the strength, where you hadn't, to leave for good? If he wins, you will lose.

It felt good to know Dad had put most of his demons to rest and he wasn't at war with himself any longer. For the most part Dad was a pretty straightforward person when he was sober. I could breathe a sigh of relief that he was no longer jeopardizing anyone's life with his drinking. Still, it was hard for me to shift gears, even though I, too, had prayed for a breakthrough. I despised his drunkenness and I hated her coldhearted ways. Dad's drinking had generated chaos, making Mom the heavy in many situations. Could she have been the one in the right all along trying to protect us and save her marriage, especially when he got stinking drunk? Deep inside, I empathized with both.

It is naive to think someone's bad habits will magically disappear, only to be replaced by a new persona when the bottle is laid down. Dad stopped drinking, though he was still the same man with the same regrets from his past. They hadn't melted away like the ice in his glass. I assumed when he stopped drinking he would emerge back to his old witty self, but he didn't. Dad was tormented with burdens and struggled in his later years that he couldn't bring his family together. The absence of alcohol changed nothing, and hoping things would be different was an empty prayer. Much like the wagon Dad wanted as a child, his remorse came too little too late.

Now the real test, to find within himself the determination to move forward with his life from something other than liquor. His uphill battle would be solo because he wasn't going to get any support from Charlotte. Mom wasn't about to let him forget anything he ever said or did to her or the family. Each day he struggled to not pick up a drink, and who would blame Dad if he threw in the towel, because nothing in his life had given him peace. Mom's sickness lingered, his job was more demanding, his parents were dead, his children were creating new dilemmas of their own and sadly his health began to falter. But through all of his trials, an inner strength emerged. I never witnessed him take another drink, and I never heard anyone else say they did either. When Dad made up his mind to stop drinking, by God, he kept his word.

Dad's burden to grasp the depth of Mom's mental illness had been clouded by his past infidelity and by the denial of alcoholism. Five years had passed since his last drink, yet he stayed at a loss as to why Mom couldn't conquer her illness. Dad's determination couldn't hide the sadness in his eyes. It had been an enormous sacrifice taking care of his mentally ill wife with no end in sight. How he kept pushing himself, I'll never know. Perhaps it was the guilt he felt for being a huge part in her plight or his belief in duty. When all was said and done, he was ultimately responsible for Mom. Many men have walked away from lesser turmoil; so why stay? Could it be his resolve, or did he realize he loved her after all?

It was a defining moment in Dad's life when he stopped drinking. He made it a priority to bring his family together. He tried to keep peace in the family, especially around the holidays. He made it his duty to never forget anyone's birthday, especially Mom's. I hoped for happier times together, but this expectation proved unrealistic and short-lived. We simply picked up where we left off. Gatherings were like all past events; we couldn't undo the void of past heartaches or change our old habits of dealing with each other.

Just as the shock treatments caused Mom to lose parts of her memory, the booze had killed off a fair amount of his brain cells; they each remained in limbo. Their quarreling intensified, prolonging their oldest pastime: playing the blame game. They had no clue or desire on how to change course. Lost years, damaging accusations, shameful threats, endless grudges, wasted holidays, hollow visits, and empty conversations devoid of affection had been the bane of our family's existence.

Dad's kids had long since scattered and the grandchildren were teenagers with lives that didn't include him. That's a given with kids; as they try to achieve independence, they fall short in sharing themselves with their elders. Dad had gained much insight into "life's lessons" from the *pitfalls of the bottle*. He wanted to keep his kids and grandkids from repeating his mistakes. But the next generations didn't heed his words of caution. Each must find their our own way. It's only when you look back that it's all so perfectly clear; hindsight is 20/20.

ONE MORE BUMP
IN THE ROAD

B y the time Dad retired and stopped drinking, I had hoped their
fevered lives would finally settle down, but sooner or later life will
throw even the strongest of families a curve, and so it was with my parents. They were hit with a new dilemma. They received a letter from the
Department of Transportation stating the county would purchase (take)
their property to make way for a four-lane highway, expanding straight
through their front yard. At this stage of their lives, being uprooted
was one more traumatic event they didn't need. The move proved difficult for them to *have* to give up their home and *have* to resettle. It took
an immense toll on them, considering they were in their sixties with
health problems.

Dad had already endured one heart attack while fighting his personal battle to stay sober. Mom was still locked in a perpetual sway of
ups and downs. Her illness for the most part had settled down. She
could cope as long as her daily routine didn't deviate beyond her comfort zone. We still had no clue how long either mood would last, but at
least she was manageable. Its been said that death, divorce, and moving
are the three most stressful events people go through in life, and once

again, Mom and Dad would be put to the test. It is also said, *that which does not kill you will make you stronger. We'll see.*

Mom never cleaned and she wouldn't throw anything away so packing turned into a huge undertaking. I don't know how any of us survived the move. First, they quarreled over the location. Mom instantly found a house she loved, but Dad concluded, "It's too far out." It weighed heavily on Dad's mind that he would suffer another heart attack and just like his brother, not make it to the hospital in time. Truth was, Robert died instantly; nothing could have saved him. Still, this fear haunted Dad.

Dad found a house in the same vicinity of their previous one. It's give and take with floor plans. Some things were nicer than what Mom had and some things weren't. Mom hated the house Dad picked. Mom was too weak-minded to handle change so within no time, her paranoia resurfaced, feeding her inability to cope. There were too many unaccustomed decisions that needed to be made. What little optimism Mom had was depleted during her breakdown, leaving no reserve to pull from.

Wanting to move and *having* to move evoke two distinct emotions with opposite outcomes. Moving day took its toll sending Mom into a tailspin. She resisted every aspect of change and whatever suggestions to make things easier only sparked agitation making her hell-bent to do the opposite. We couldn't calm her. She fell back into her familiar fixation of believing her family was plotting against her; I helplessly watched her lose ground.

My sisters and I had taken several loads to the new house and were cleaning out the last closet when Mom began crying, cursing, and accusing us of taking her things. All of her belongings stayed tucked away with her obscure memories, and we had no desire to intrude on either. We tried to console her but she demanded, "Get the hell out of my house and leave my goddamn things alone. I didn't ask for your god-damn help." I wanted to scream back that we were there to help Dad. I knew to kept my wounded feelings to myself. We left.

While unloading the car, we told Dad how she went psycho on us and how she only wanted him touching her things. He shook his head in dismay. My heart ached watching as the sweat pour from Dad's forehead. He pushed himself to the point of exhaustion. I was afraid he would drop dead of a heart attack. Once again, I felt ashamed that I had let Dad down. Mom didn't seem concerned by what she had put everyone through and she was no help. I resented giving up another weekend from my life to help the woman who never appreciated anything I did for her. She could be as nasty as she wanted to be but knew I wouldn't abandon Dad. She made me sick, still lashing at us for all her frustra-tions. You won again Mom; I'm still around doing your heavy lifting while you ridicule and degrade me.

Mom didn't enjoy the new house, and every chance she got, she threw in Dad's face what a dump he'd chosen. Her scrambled brain couldn't grasp that the old house was no longer their home; that nei-ther one of them had a choice. It now belongs to the county. Why she acted irrational about leaving that house puzzled me. It held mostly twenty years of sorrowful memories.

Mom and Dad hadn't been in their new home long when Lee and I attended a company Christmas party. My (soon to be) manager came up to me and said, "Your parents are our next door neighbors. *Ah shit; son of a bitch! Oh hell no!* A wave of panic went through me and I sensed my knees buckle. I felt obligated to give her a heads up so I responded with a feeble quip, "Well, they ain't no Ozzie and Harriet." I had been too freshly sideswiped to go into detail about my comment. Besides, that wasn't the time or place to spill displeasing news. Afterward, I felt embarrassed by my saucy remark. But this was how I dealt with my anxiety. If they were smart, they would keep their distance, and not get drawn into my parents' web of drama like so many had been in the past. *I warned them.*

Mom and Dad lived in the new house about ten years and Mom wouldn't unpack her box of knick-knacks, leaving her curio cabinet empty. I offered to help her unpack, but she insisted, "I don't feel good today, we'll do it some other day." Mom put everything off to "some other day." This was her way of coping with any situation she didn't want to face. Mom didn't own anything of monetary value, just a few sentimental pieces. Did her knick-knacks evoke morose memories since some pieces had belonged to her mother?

Some mothers allocate which possessions they want each child to have after their passing. It would have meant a great deal if Mom had delegated certain keepsakes to each of us. But her endearing mementos came after her death. It was up to each of us to select a piece and recall our own nostalgia.

YOU CAN'T
LIVE BACKWARDS

Thinking back, I can't recall if anything in her life made Mom truly happy. She created her own hell and never unearthed a reason to turn her life around; her illness simply would not allow it. Dad, on the other hand, tried hard to make the best of things. He continued to garden, but as his health declined, the only remnants were a few tomato and varied pepper plants. He kept going to his AA meetings, took care of the house, and worked in the yard until his illness forced him to be house-bound. Dad's resolve is what kept me moving forward.

As each holiday and birthday rolled around, my parents' eagerness for celebrating quietly waned in sentiment, teetering between lackluster enthusiasm and anxious dread. Mom and Dad exchanged money and a card and told each other to go buy what they wanted. As you get older, you find there is nothing you need or want, nothing that is except the gift of security, health, peace of mind, and love if you're lucky. You realize you have already accumulated all the material things needed and can live without any more meaningless gadgets and collectibles that do nothing but promote a dusty clutter. Mom would plan a get-together for Dad's birthday, retirement, or another AA milestone. The irony was, even when they tried to get us all together, it was still more of a duty than a festivity.

Yes, Dad quit drinking, but he grew raw and grouchy. Although he had sobered up his mind kept replaying all his screw-ups. He couldn't distinguish between how many of his memories were distorted and which ones were painfully accurate. The haunting realization that he couldn't retrieve or undo past mistakes must have smothered him with mounting regrets.

My grandma had a picture that hung over her sofa of an angel protecting a boy and girl as they crossed over a bridge. I found that exact print in a gift store and gave it to Dad for Father's Day. I thought it would remind him of his childhood. To my shock, he didn't remember the picture. When I tried to jog his memory, he got very irritated and thrust his anger at me. How could you not remember a ten-by-twelve picture hanging in the house you grew up in? Maybe Grandma didn't have it when Dad was a boy, but it hung in the exact spot my entire life. Did the picture have a sad connotation? Was his memory that far depleted? Realizing there were things he couldn't recall reduced him into a quiet shame.

Rick took Mom to see Robert Goulet in, *South Pacific,* at the Fox Theater in Atlanta for her birthday. A few years later, I took her to see him in, *Camelot.* She was thrilled to see her idol in person. When the play ended, we walked to the theater's side to wait for him to address the crowd, and if she was lucky, get his autograph. Instead, a spokesman walked out and announced, "Mr. Goulet won't be signing autographs." I felt like the pompous ass could at least acknowledge his loyal fans (excluding me), but what did he care. Oh well, that was a small disappointment in comparison to what life had already thrown her way. I wished we had shared more outings together but they were few and far between. Catching Mom when her mind had any clarity was hit-or-miss. We were both adults, but we still behaved nervous around each other, like strangers with nothing in common except the love of the arts.

I had given my husband a 50th surprise birthday party but only Dad came. Mom was down again. Dad began using a cane to get around. He didn't go many places, especially at night. He didn't like parties, but the effort he made in coming showed he was trying to make up for lost time. He didn't stay long but we were happy he came.

There were a slew of events they both let slip away. When my oldest son, Matthew, graduated from college with an art degree, Mom proudly attended his graduation, but Dad did not. That summer, Matt put on an art exhibit at Barnes & Noble; this time Dad came, but Mom did not. Matt took their behavior in stride. He was proud that Dad cared enough to attend, especially in his declining condition. It was comical watching Dad try to grasp the meaning of Matt's contemporary art. I believe he felt sorry for Matt so in a show of support he offered, "Matt, tell me what that drawing is supposed to be of. I'll buy it. Is ten dollars enough?" Matt reluctantly said, "Granddaddy, they sell for $250 a piece." Dad's stunned reaction over the price caused an uproar from us. It reminded me of his unique sense of humor that for so long had been soundless in his liquid world.

All through life, Dad expressed himself using peppered phrases and old-time sayings that he plucked from his relatives and railroad buddies. They fit the mindset of his upbringing. But Dad's dark side spoke in a negative connotation about black folk. However, over the years there had been many instances where a black man proved to be his trusted friend. This was another example of Dad's conflict with the changing world. In spite of Dad's preconceived ideas, he primarily judged a man by his work ethic, and as long as any man, black or white, pulled his weight and took care of his family, Dad respected him. He despised the Big Man trampling over the Little Man, and believed every person should be given a second chance and not be kicked when he was down. He took up for the less experienced men on the job every chance he could. Dad believed in fairness.

Dad was a man of simple means and never wanted much. Example: Don't give him a belt as a gift if the belt he wore was still in good condition. You'd have to return the new one. He considered it wasteful.

DAD IS DYING

There was a short time after Dad retired and prior to his illness that he and Mom found a pond where they started fishing together. They loaded up his pick-up truck with tons of fishing gear, minnows, red worms, fishing license, bug repellant, hats, chairs, cups, paper towels, water jug, lunch, and midday snacks. They couldn't leave behind their medications, radio, flashlight, or umbrella. God only knows what else Mom had stockpiled in her purse. Their fishing excursion lasted no longer than six hours at the most, but they never left home without a week's supply of cigarettes. They hardly caught enough fish to brag about but they seemed to enjoy themselves just the same. It may have been short-lived, but this was the closest they came to mutual contentment. As time crept on, most of their hurt feelings faded, allowing their battles to draw to a hush. The irony was Dad's health began to fail the moment he turned his life around. He's say, "It's getting harder to get movin'. These damn legs of mine...I just can't go like I used to." They had to give up fishing, and in no time at all Mom began harping about how much she missed going. She knew he enjoyed fishing above all else. Much like the rum cake incident, she maliciously used this opportunity to render him sorrow and rub his nose in the fact, well Pat, "If you hadn't stayed drunk all the damn time, we could've enjoyed more things together." I remember their early years when he begged her to go fishing with him and she wouldn't. As always, they were both out of step with each other's desires.

You rock along and think your family's behavior isn't as strange as you perceived, that is until a pivotal event happens, then you realize how disconnected your lives have been. Four years before Dad died, he was rushed to the hospital with his second heart attack. That same week, Mom caught the flu. She was rundown and rapidly losing weight to the point of needing to be hospitalized. Rose, Gail, and I were running back and forth between work, checking on Dad at the hospital, and taking care of Mom. Dad had worked himself into a tizzy worrying about Mom and he didn't need this added stress while trying to recover.

Dad made arrangements with his doctor for Mom to be admitted into the same hospital. This would have taken the burden off Dad and us if she would agree to go, but she was adamant; she wouldn't leave the house. She never forgot it was Dad that had her admitted into the psychiatric ward thirty years prior, and she couldn't make the distinction between being hospitalized for mental illness versus physical illness. She believed Dad was having her "committed" all over again. The paranoia re-emerged and Mom became frantic; no amount of reassurance could change her mind. Would she flip out again? I've witnessed her outlandish behavior for so long I forgot this is normal behavior for her. Even after thirty years, her mind was still trapped by illness. *She will never be cured.* Stupid me, I thought perhaps her mental illness had melted away with time. In reality, she was just wearing down with age. *Will she ever have peace?* Dad had no choice but to give in to her, "Just leave her be." I realized then what hell we all had endured, coping with mental illness.

A few weeks passed and Mom recovered from the flu; she gained most of her strength back but she lost precious body weight that she never recouped. That was the first visible sign her physical health was declining. She was sicker than any of us realized. She began to hold onto pieces of furniture as she walked through the house; equally, her breathing became shallow when she got excited. Concerned, we suggested she needed to see a doctor, but she alluded that her problems were the beginning of a chest cold or allergies from the pollen in the air.

Dad came home from the hospital only to have their lives take a different turn. You get to a stage in your life and think, where did all the years go? Time really is a thief and we seldom get second chances. They both equally had a choice to have a fulfilling life but they exhausted their younger years with bitterness and spitefulness; their later years were squandered on apathy and blame. Their future time would be divided between sickness and regrets. Now the real test for living would begin.

It didn't take long before another setback involving Dad's health emerged; he needed a defibrillator to regulate his heart. The doctor predicted it would last a year, but Dad was a fighter and it lasted three years, thank God, but not without a glitch. When he tried to lie down, it felt like his breathing was being cut off. So the last years of his life, he slept in his chair in a semi-reclined position.

Another oddity that elevated our family's dysfunction came one year later. Dad was in the hospital having the battery in his defibrillator changed. He had a few zaps from the defibrillator, but for the most part, seemed to be doing fine. It was considered a routine procedure but Mom and I stayed with him while my sisters went for lunch. Within an instant, Dad went into cardiac arrest. The nurses whisked Mom and me out of his room as they rushed to save him. I burst into tears, tugging on Mom's arm, and needing her to somehow be my strength. We both thought Dad had died, but within minutes, his doctor had stabilized him and he was back among the living.

It had been years since Mom had seen me upset about anything, and she was taken aback by my outburst. She made more of a production over my behavior than she did about Dad's close call. She told everyone she had never seen me cry before. *Isn't crying as natural as laughing?* The fact that Mom never witnessed me crying shows the division that had been forged between us for most of my life. To admit to never seeing her child's tears hit hard. I guess the tears I cast off as a child when I was being demoralized and beaten held no merit, or all the times I felt alone and cried myself to sleep were too muffled in my pillow for her to hear. Stunned, I realized it wasn't just distance I put between our relationship. I kept the promise I had made to myself long ago. I deliberately hadn't shared my feelings with the very person who gave me life. I still had painful memories smoldering inside and I, too, had grown selfish with my affection.

Next, an oxygen tank emerged. Dad had smoked all his life, and the smoking had taken its toll. Dad tried to quit smoking when he first became ill, but everyone around him smoked. Mom and my siblings wouldn't give up their habit, so I suggested they smoke on the screened porch to keep the house air clean. If Dad didn't see them smoke, he might be less tempted to start back. Besides, no one should be smoking around an oxygen tank. This plan lasted less than a week. Rose convinced Mom that any change in the weather could make her sick, so with Mom's best interest at heart, Rose and Mom turned the sun room into their smoking parlor. They each smoked three packs of cigarettes a day so, truthfully, they both resented having to jump up each time they wanted to light up. They sat smoking and watching TV like content little mice in a science experiment while thousands of carcinogens swirled around their happy, clueless heads. It never occurred to either of them that each time they opened the door to the den, their smoke infiltrated where Dad sat confined.

Heart attacks, emphysema, defibrillator; I'm afraid of what's next. Dad had been having trouble urinating but his stubbornness kept him from seeing a doctor. None of us knew how long he had this problem. He reluctantly gave in and made an appointment with an urologist. I saw a worrisome look on his face. He'd been comparing notes with other railroad men who had the same ailment and had a fairly accurate perception of what the outcome would be.

The day of his appointment, I mustered up the courage and showed up unannounced at the doctor's office. I'm thankful I did. If I had asked Dad if he needed me to go with him, he would've bucked, "Ain't no need in you comin; stay home."

Then came the doctor's diagnosis, the biggest blow of all: prostate cancer. Dad was taken aback; the expression on his face is one I'll never forget. A death sentence for sure. My heart broke. I don't know how any of us kept from breaking down. Perhaps we were trying to be strong for each other. Dad quickly rebounded and for the sake of Mom and me, he stoically sucked up the devastating news and took it like a man. Mom, well, she was just Mom. I asked the doctor on a scale of one to ten how he would rate the cancer's aggressiveness. He said in the range of seven to eight. Dad wasn't a candidate for chemotherapy because of his heart condition, but the doctor gave us hope by explaining if Dad had his testicles removed, it would be like taking away the gas that fueled the engine (the cancer).

We left the doctor's office and went to eat at the S&S Cafeteria. Dad didn't miss a beat as he ate a hearty lunch. Not a word was spoken, especially about the doctor's findings. I could hardly sit still and I was choking on every bite of my food. I couldn't get out of the restaurant fast enough and call each sibling with the news. I sobbed the entire way home.

At first, Dad said he would not have the operation. I knew it was a man thing with him, so I tried to make light of the operation by asking, "Dad, are you planning to father any more children? If not, you need to think about your health. It's no different than a woman having a hysterectomy." He didn't answer; instead he rolled his eyes as if I was crazy for even asking such an absurd question. Maybe this fresh comparison helped put things into perspective for him; I don't know. We didn't mentioned the cancer, but subsequently he agreed to the surgery. The operation would buy him a little time even though it was risky due to his heart and lungs. True to form, the cancer came back in one year.

When I realized his cancer was winning the battle, I became panic-stricken, not only about him dying, but also for the fate of his soul. God had a hand in helping Dad and me. While at the mall, I bumped into Alan Faulkner, an old classmate of mine who happened to be the chaplain at a local hospital. I couldn't control my tears as I explained my father's illness and my concern for his salvation. I told him I knew about things Dad had done in his life, and that was probably the tip of the iceberg. Alan suggested, "Go to your dad and tell him how you feel." In a burst of admission I confessed, "I can't do that. My dad has never seen me cry; I'll get too emotional if I try to talk to him." That was something I couldn't do around my parents. In an insightful tone Alan said, "They taught you well." He then told me, not to worry, that God knew Dad better than Dad knew himself. With Alan's words, I felt a calm come over me. I honestly believe all things fall into place for a reason. I left the mall with every intention of talking to Dad about God's love and forgiveness.

I called Mom and told her about my talk with Alan and that I was on my way over. When I arrived, I sensed by her sheepish grin that she had blabbed to Dad my reason for the visit. Damn, I should have known she couldn't keep her mouth shut. Needless to say, each time I tried to bring the subject up, Dad would change the subject. We never made eye contact; as I fumbled with my intent, he fumbled with the TV remote. All I could share that afternoon was an expression of help-lessness. Inescapably, I couldn't stop the tears from rolling down my cheeks. I left feeling that I had failed him. I couldn't break the barrier of silence between us, even in the extreme situation that he faced. But two have to go down the road together, and if we never shared intimate conversations before, now was the worst time to start. Remember he is the parent, larger than life in my eyes, and I am his child who he feels he must protect and spare pain. I had to respect my dad's privacy. I prayed, "Please, dear God, help him find his way."

Dad's next step was sixteen radiation treatments. He balked at first, then conceded to have the procedure. I didn't have the courage to watch Dad struggle or the physical strength to help him, so I made arrange-ments with Uncle Bevel, Lee, and my sons to get him to his appoint-ments. As much as he hated relying on us, he couldn't do this on his own. The effects of the treatments left Dad weak. Dad had said numerous times, "I never want to be a burden to nobody."

Dad had appointed me as Executor for their affairs several years prior. Once again, the dysfunctional Hoovers raised their opinions, causing more chaos. Rose would call to see if he needed a ride to the hospital, knowing I'd already made arrangements. Dad worried who would give him a ride, would they forget, would we get him there on time, was he putting us out, and so on. I had to keep reassuring him, "Don't listen to Rose, one of the guys will drive you." Dad didn't have any confidence in what I said I would do. If I was five minutes late, he would be backing down the driveway, heading out on his own. If I said I would be there, then I would be there. *He doesn't know me at all.*

Dad didn't need this extra aggravation at this stage of his illness and I didn't need the turmoil in mine. I told Rose time and again that neither she nor I were physically capable of handling Dad, so why she kept offering her assistance baffled me. We never were on the same page when it came to what was best for Dad. Why didn't she respect my decision and support him instead of causing havoc? Was she trying to win his approval or was it a control thing? She loved being bossy. Whatever her reason, it caused Dad added anxiety that he didn't need.

Dad saw himself as the breadwinner with a duty to care for his family. He couldn't bear the thought of looking helpless in our eyes. He was too proud to ask for help and he tried his damnedest to keep it that way. He wasn't accustomed to depending on anyone so when he did need help, he had a hurtful way about asking or accepting help from us. He grew impatient and angry, realizing he could no longer do for himself. Watching Dad's health decline was excruciating. This man, who took care of so many for so long, now needed our help.

It became extremely difficult for Dad to get around. He didn't have many options so he immerse himself into TV. He enjoyed wrestling, Bonanza, championship bull riding, and old westerns. He also watched the Atlanta Braves; however, he did more cursing the players than enjoying the games. I wanted to treat him to a Braves game in Atlanta so he could experience the action first hand, but by the time he quit drinking he was too worn out to make the five hour round trip, and sit three hours on hard bleachers. It bothered me more than it did him. Dad said, "I can enjoy the game on TV and follow the instant replays better than I can see way up in the stands." He was right.

Dad couldn't count on Mom for comfort and he needed someone stronger than me to lean on for what he was about to face. Thank God, our prayers were answered; Hospice stepped in. The support given by Hospice was the bridge that Dad needed to make peace with himself and God as he faced his own mortality. How exceptional for strangers to help a stranger (Dad) helping them come to grips with death. I believe things in our lives come together at the right moment, and maybe this death sentence forced Dad to stop rebelling at life and start embracing it. The Hospice volunteers were the driving forces that brought him full circle. They were amazing; they were his strength and his liberator.

Dad viewed life with a different perspective as most people do when they get older or sick. He would grumble each time I mentioned taking a trip. His gruff disapproving voice would bellow, "Why in the hell do you wanna' go there for? You're just throwing away your damn money. Travelins' dangerous; stay home, save your money, and rest." all the while shaking his head in skepticism. I'd fire back, "I'll be resting (dead) soon enough." Toward the end if his illness, I had the opportunity to go to Maui, but I was torn about whether or not to go. What if something happened to Dad while I was away? In his drinking years, I would tell my siblings, "If something happens to Dad while I'm gone, put him on ice until I get back." That was my cynical response for coping with his drunken occurrences. He had ruined so much of my life, I'll be dammed if I'm going to let him ruin my trip. But I mellowed, and Hospice walked me through my guilt and told me not to put my life on hold. Dad would not want it that way, and besides, life has a way of falling into place, allowing things to work out. So it did. Hospice gave me the courage to move on just as they did for Dad. I went on my trip, and this time, instead of fussing at me for going, Dad said, "Go have a good time." *Thanks Daddy.*

It sickened me to think of what went through Dad's mind in the long, drawn out hours of the nights when he couldn't sleep: regretting things he said and did to his family and friends, having remorse for things he can't remember he said and did, and knowing nothing could make it right. But the saddest of all was his wish for things he never got to do. Dad blamed his body for betraying him by tolerating a disease to invade his body. He wouldn't admit that it was his years of smoking and drinking that had created a large amount of damage. Had he realized how much money he wasted on cigarettes and liquor and the costly debt of paying off "the good old boys" for getting him out of one scrape (jail) after another? As most people do when looking back on their lives, he regretted his recklessness and wastefulness and it hit him like a ton of bricks what he could have attained.

Each of us has a dream and I remember Dad always wanted a place in the country with an ample sized pond. He drank enough liquor to fill a pond, and don't think it didn't haunt him. Maybe he felt he didn't deserve happiness, but he did; we all do. The hardest realization is that happiness is within our reach. I guess no one ever told him he was worth anything either. He said to me, "I've worked hard my whole goddamn life and now that I'm retired and could enjoy myself a bit, it's bein' taken from me." That was the only time I witnessed Dad questioning his fate, yet it was more bewilderment than anger for the hand he was dealt. I had no answer for him. I felt powerless knowing I couldn't fix his pain. What good was I? I had let him down at his darkest hour. True to form, he sucked it up and was careful never to complain around me again. Dad wasn't about to saddle anyone with his troubles.

Even though Hospice was a godsend for both of them, Mom retained her jealousy for Dad, especially when the nurses fussed over him. Mom admitted to me, "Your Dad won't tell me nothing. He only wants to talk to the Hospice women." Her feelings were crushed. After fifty-three years of marriage, she was still being shut out of his life. But answer this, how can you confide in someone at the most harrowing moment of your life when they have never been there for you? But she had been there for him; through all his years of unfaithfulness and drunken stunts, she had stood by him. Didn't that count for anything? But human presence carries little weight when emotional abandonment dominates the relationship. Mom didn't realize that each act invokes a distinct consequence. She felt he didn't need her, though he may have been trying to shield her from worry until he could come to terms with his own fate. Perhaps he wanted to spare Mom any additional suffering since he had contributed to a substantial part of her misery.

Dad had been Mom's protector after her breakdown, but he now realized that both of their lives were about to change. Dad skirted around the issue of what needed to be done for Mom "if" he died. But he divulged to me a larger concern: that one of the siblings would move in and take over. Knowing how vulnerable she was, Dad tried to prepare Mom for his absence in her life, but how much of his advice could she absorb? Mom's childlike behavior and looming paranoia rendered her incapable of making any rational decisions on her own. Adding to her dilemma, Mom hadn't taken care of herself or the house for thirty plus years.

As Dad got weaker; the pain increased. He had difficulty standing and it took all his strength to take care of himself. But I knew Dad wouldn't sit still; that meant giving up, and Dad was no quitter. If Dad didn't kept busy he would go stir-crazy. Cooking and laundry was all he could manage. Hospice sent over a hospital bed, but Dad sent it back. He wouldn't even try it for one night. You don't give in; you fight.

Mom on the other hand had given up years ago with no will left, not even for her own survival. It didn't seem to faze Mom that his health was spent. Mom still expected him to cater to her every whim. For all the hell he put her through in the early years of marriage, this must have been his atonement to her, inversely, her lack of attention to him had to be her revenge. *But when is a debt paid up? When do you break even, or at best, call a truce? Will the give and take ever balance out? Remember, for better or worse?* It sickened me to watch a grown woman "not" do for herself or her ailing spouse. For this reason, my resentment for Mom welled up inside, once more.

As Dad's life was coming to an end, he worried incessantly about Mom's fate. He leaned on me to carry out his wishes. He voiced quite often, "She's a damn handful." He resigned himself to the fact that he helped create her problem, and if she hadn't changed by now, this was as good as it would ever get. Dad wouldn't talk about his illness. His resolve was fueled by his perpetual worrying about Mom should he die.

At this point in my life, I had no tolerance for Mom's behavior, past or present. I had been obedient to her every rule, chore, and demand since childhood. Mom expected to be waited on from sunup to sundown and it didn't matter who she inconvenienced. Mom's care had been Dad's burden and if he should die first, she expected her girls to pick up where he left off. I put my conflicts aside and promised Dad that I would make sure she was taken care of in every way after his passing. Hopefully, this would give him some peace at night with one less worry. They both cringed at the mention of a nursing home, so we did everything we could to keep them comfortable in their house. A nursing home would be our last resort. Dad put his trust in me, and although I didn't agree with all his requests, my promise to him was enough to honor his wishes. *Not all your worries went unnoticed, Dad. I did as you asked: I did the best I could.*

Dad's mobility was diminishing so he basically lived in his recliner for the duration. He still refused the hospital bed. Mom couldn't comprehend that Dad needed help. She wouldn't go out of her way to do the simplest task. For example: his catheter leaked so he needed a clean towel to sit on but it was an uphill battle for Mom to provide him with that simple comfort. Added to his humiliation, were frequent emergencies to urinate, so he kept a bucket beside his chair for his catheter to drain. Regardless of whether she was being lazy, spiteful, or obtuse, she never emptied his pee bucket. When I stopped by the house, I tried not to embarrass Dad (any more than possible), but first and foremost, his bucket had to be emptied. Without making a big production I simply picked up the bucket and flushed the urine down the toilet. He'd say, "Leave it be, Jo. I'll get to it later." But I knew he couldn't, and Mom wouldn't. His medications and urine caused a strong odor and the bucket needed to be disinfected after each use. The combination of the three smells left a lingering reminder that death was looming. Dad had always been a clean person. He had to be humiliated to not be able to care for himself.

The last months of Dad's life, they bickered about his pain patches, where to place them, when was the last time they had been changed, and had Mom forgot to re-order more. All Mom had to do was one simple thing, change the damn pain patch once every three days. Why can't she remember? Write yourself a note, put it on the calendar; but for God's sake, don't let them run out! Damn it, Charlotte, make a humane effort! Several times I witnessed Dad sitting on the edge of the recliner rocking back and forth with no one to allay his pain. As his illness intensified, so did his frustration with Mom. She was useless. She was empty. Mom had nothing to give. Her neglect and lack of compassion for Dad proved shameful. Was she in denial and refusing to believe that he was dying, or was her malice against Dad still playing out?

We will all regret things we should've done for someone, especially in their final days. It Was a Sunday, and I offered to cook them dinner. I delivered their food about six o'clock. Dad was irritated at me for being late. He snapped and hurt my feelings. Didn't he understand I worked all week and I had to take care of my own family and home? I tried to help them but each misstep, like forgetting an item on the grocery list, or picking the wrong brand provoked dissatisfaction. I still couldn't measure up. I'm not trying to make excuses for myself, but their obstinate behavior made every errand nerve-racking. The following Sunday, I didn't offer my services but by five o'clock. my conscience got the better of me. So Lee and I drove over to check on them. We weren't in the house five minutes when my Cousin Danny walked in with two Kentucky Fried Chicken dinners. I felt so ashamed. I should've swallowed my pride and understood the depth of Dad's anguish. Why didn't I grasp he wasn't angry with me; he was lashing out at his fate. Dad knew he was dying but it had to be hard to face the truth. We both let our stubbornness get the best of us; what a senseless emotion we let rule our lives. It was too painful to think he didn't have much time left, though all the signs were staring me in the face. It wasn't pride that dominated me; it was fear. If I'm fearful of what's to come, what must Mom be going through?

We'll all face the death of a loved one sooner or later. It was a blessing that as large as our family was, no real tragedy had ever befallen us. Thankfully, Dad's parents died a natural death in their eighties. We, however, stay less in tune with reality. We aren't brave enough to deal with painful situations so we shelter our feelings, squander precious time, and ignore death by not preparing in life. It's easier that way. Out of sight, out of mind. I'll think about that tomorrow. We remain distracted with books, movies, TV, clubs, sports, bars, shopping, computers, and social media. And if that hasn't used every minute of our day, we then numb our senses by self-medicating with booze, pain pills, or mood-enhancing drugs. When forced to face sickness or death, we are ill-equipped and fall apart. No on can escape the inevitable.

Dad had his last radiation treatment in April but due to his weakened body, his large size, being hooked up to oxygen 24/7, and an uncontrollable bladder, he never left the house again until his last trip to the hospital in December.

I had taken a week of vacation to get a head start on my Christmas shopping and baking. First thing that Monday morning, Mom called and said Dad's defibrillator had shocked him several times and he had fallen. Mom weighed ninety-eight pounds; too frail to pick Dad up by herself. I told her I was on my way. Rose also had already been called to help. I walked into the den and saw him sitting on the floor looking at his bloody elbows he scraped from his fall. Together, Rose and I could barely get him back into a chair. He appeared nervously agitated, but stayed in control and ordered me to call 911.

As I gave the paramedics directions to their house, I observed Mom through the French doors to the sun room cutting out pictures of tiny humming birds in a magazine, and gluing them onto a lampshade while smoking. Mom's actions were child-like; oblivious to what was going on in the other room. Had she slipped back into crazy? Why won't she help him? Had he snapped at her before we arrived? Was that why she hadn't cleaned his bleeding arms or called 911? Is this her way of not having to deal with the inevitable? Does she realize this might be the last time she will see him alive? When Mom fought with Dad, her anger always got the best of her, and I wish I had a dime for every time she bellowed, "I wish the hell you were dead." Well, her wish just may come true today. I couldn't count on her for anything but I needed her desperately that day. *Mom get the hell up and help Dad. You can't zone out now, I'm frightened.* I didn't understand (at that time) that maybe she did realize what was happening and it was too painful for her to face. Mom did what she knew best: retreated into her secret world that only her mind could travel to for protection. Ever since her nervous breakdown, evading a crisis came as natural as breathing for Mom, and no matter how the drama played, out she accepted the destiny. It would require on her part an exhausting amount of awareness to question why or help with any problem. She was a broken spirit, swaying like a blade of grass to whichever way the wind blew; this was all she could handle.

The paramedics arrived and immediately began working on Dad. One asked for his ID and insurance card. Mom replied in an odious tone, "Nobody gives a shit what happens to me. I'm sick too you know." The paramedics appeared baffled by her outburst but continued to try to stabilize Dad. Mom wouldn't help me look for his card. I finally found his wallet lying under a chair. It had fallen out of his pants when he fell. As soon as I gave the insurance card to the paramedics, we were off to the hospital. *She's so damn pathetic.*

Rose and Mom didn't arrive at the emergency room until three hours later. Rose said, "Mom had to eat breakfast, drink her coffee, take her medicine, and put on her makeup before she would leave the house. Each time I tried to hurry her up, I only made things worse. Mom insisted that I stop rushing her; I was making her nervous."

Within that time, Dad could have died, but he hung on all day and that night. He lay helpless on the bed as his defibrillator repeatedly zapped him. As each discharge of electricity delivered another excruciating current through his body, His eyes were pleading for help. The doctors had to wait for the defibrillator to stop discharging before he could be moved to ICU. I couldn't do anything but stand there and watch him grow weaker with each zap. Once again, I felt I had let him down.

Dad carried around a burden that he wanted resolved. When we arrived at the emergency room, he pleaded, "Please Jo, make peace with Gail. I know your sister's crazy, but try to get along with her, okay?" She had been keeping her distance from the family for the past three years. Watching his family unravel upset Dad and he was adamant about wanting everyone to get along with each other. Did Gail realize what she had put him through? What had any of us done to her for her to loathe being united with her family? Again, Dad begged me to make amends with her. The urgency in his voice indicated how deeply he wished our family rift to end before his death. It was of the utmost importance for me to not let this family falling-out upset him, but how can I apologize when I didn't know what triggered the disagreement to begin with? With all quarrels, if one person is unwilling to meet you halfway, the relationship will stay broken. But I had to honor his request, so I promised, "Okay Dad. I will. I'd try anything to have him settle down. I don't know if he sided with me, hoping I would relinquish my stubborn pride or if he thought I was the most levelheaded, but he put his trust in me. I also don't know what he said about me to her, but we pulled together for his sake. I hope this brought him a brief moment of contentment knowing that he had finally healed his broken family. Peace and forgiveness at the end is all any of us really desire. *It's the only thing that matters.*

The doctors got him stabilized; the defibrillator stopped shocking him, so they moved him to intensive care around 5 P.M. I prayed this was a sign he might be getting better. My mind told me he was slipping away but my heart said, *not yet, there's still hope.* I looked down at the catheter bag and he had very little output of urine; his kidneys were shutting down. He was still in a lot of pain and extremely fidgety. Looking back, I knew he had suffered longer than he let on.

While Dad was in intensive care, Mom grew agitated in her attempts to pin down Dad's doctor, only it wasn't concerning Dad's fate, but rather about her own. The doctor stopped to give us an update on Dad's condition when Mom blurted, "Dr. Adams, I'm having trouble breathing. Do you think you could examine me too?" The doctor snapped, "Mrs. Hoover, I'm extremely busy trying to save your husband! If you're sick, please call your own physician or my office and make an appointment." His curt remark sent her on a crying marathon. She adding the doctor to her ever-growing, "I'll never forgive you or forget this incident" list.

By night's arrival, there wasn't much change in Dad's condition. Mom was exhausted and had had enough of the hospital for one day so Rose took her home. I offered to stay the night. "I'll call there's any change in his condition." He was thrashing around in pain as if he were literally doing battle with death, and that if he could just get out of the bed, he would somehow cheat death one more time. He kept asking for a wet cloth for his head and a sip of ice water, all the while apologizing, "I'm sorry, Jo, for havin' to bother you." I gave a meager response, "You're not bothering me Dad; just tell me what you need."

The following morning, his nephew, Ronnie, visited Dad and assured him he would be back the next day. Dad submissively replied, "If I make it through the night." I was scared; there had been no reports of progress. His body was shutting down. I knew he was slipping away, but I couldn't face losing him. I played a mental game of denial. He is dying-no he's not. Should I call my sister and brother in Savannah and tell them to rush home? If I call, then I am admitting to myself there is no hope? He's getting better because the defibrillator stopped zapping him. No, his heart is weakened and his kidneys are shutting down. I could not make the call, but thank God Gail did. I functioned on autopilot and tried not to think past ten minutes at a time. I was afraid to ask questions; afraid I might hear the unavoidable. A nurse kept telling the doctor he was dying, but the doctor wouldn't give up on Dad...*neither will I.* I knew his time was imminent but I couldn't accept losing him even when death is staring down at you.

The next morning, Dad ate a large breakfast and his defibrillator hadn't kicked back in. That gave me false hope. Mom and Rose came midday and by then, Kathy arrived from Savannah. Dad's family is large and many relatives were visiting including LeeEllen, who stayed with him for the afternoon. A nurse came to check on Dad and he proudly introduced his sister to the nurse. I saw the adoration they had for each other by the way they were holding each other's hands. As loving and supportive as my aunt was to Dad, I couldn't help but think that Mom was the one who should be by his side. I later learned Mom remained in the waiting room telling dirty blond jokes.

Late that afternoon, Mom informed Dad, "I'm going home." Dad snapped back, "Why are you leaving; it's early?" Her reply was equally snippy, "I've been at the hospital all damn day; I'm tired; I need to rest." Even on his deathbed, Mom felt slighted, and she resented the empathy that was shown to Dad, however, it was only toward the end of Dad's life that he received the attention and respect that had eluded him. They were out of step with their intuitive feelings for each other, even in his final days.

Once again, Rose took Mom home. Kathy and I stayed the second night with Dad. I They knew I would call if there was any change. When Dad settled down, Lee and I left to get something to eat. When we returned, he was asleep. As the night progressed, he started thrashing around again. The nurse gave him a shot around 11 P.M. He shot straight up in the bed and then laid back down. Kathy and I fell asleep not realizing he had drifted into a coma. When we awoke at 5 A.M., a nurse informed us that he was leaving us and to call the rest of the family. He never regained consciousness and died about 11:30 A.M.

Before Dad died, all the family except my brother, Ricky, en route from Savannah, and my son, Daniel, en route from Atlanta, were at his side. Aunt LeeEllen returned that morning and stayed till the end. Could Mom realize that her husband was dying? Dad wasn't suffering any longer, but it took a while for his heart to stop beating; the defibrillator was still trying to keep him alive. We each had enough time to say goodbye but I found myself lost for words. I was running on empty. My sorrow left me emotionally drained as I tried to bundle my lifetime of feelings into one last unshielded I love you and I will miss you. *Oh Daddy, what a heartbreaking, yet joyous relief. You've begun a new journey and I hope you find peace.*

I stayed back and made all the arrangements and Rose took Mom home. A new chapter in our never-ending family drama would emerge as this one ended. We feebly began positioning for our new role in Mom's life. However, we too, were in mourning and needed to be comforted by our mother, while simultaneously having to comfort her. It was now Mom's turn to soak up all the attention she felt she had been cheated out of.

A funeral director came to the house requesting a picture of Dad for the obituaries. I found a framed picture of Robert Redford stashed in Mom's photo box. Who holds on to a picture of a movie star? A teenager perhaps, but not a woman in her seventies. Is this the man that comes into her dreams? She certainly adored him. For a split second I contemplated handing him the picture and saying this was Dad. I was making a joke, but I had let my emotions make a foolish choice, especially under the circumstances.

I was surprised at how well Mom held up at the funeral service. Rev. Faulkner presided over Dad's funeral with unconditional kindness. He talked about Dad's commitment to his family, the temptations in his life, and his battle to overcome his addiction to alcohol. His message of struggle and forgiveness put Dad's life into perspective.

All the support from Dad's family and friends meant more to me than they will ever know. At the funeral, a co-worker spoke of how Dad enjoyed cooking up many-a-meal for the train's crew. And how he loved to brag about fixin' a pot of catfish stew, homemade waffles and sausage, or barbecue chicken washed in his mystery sauce; served with his home grown sliced tomatoes. Dad was a decent man in spite of his flaws, and I prayed his good deeds outweighed his shortcomings.

You've heard it all before; *I'm so sorry for your loss. At least he's not suffering anymore. He's now in a better place. He sure will be missed. He's at peace at last, blah-blah-blah.* No amount of rhetoric will fill the void.

Mom soaked up all the attention given to her by everyone. Maybe she was relieved it was over, or perhaps she was in denial. I don't think it had sunk in how lonely she would be without him around. Mom could now enjoy her life without Dad cursing or degrading every move. She's free to go anywhere she wants. But her contention was she wished him to be coupled with her and now he can't.

Had she finally forgiven him? I guess she had always loved him. I know they lived a crazy life, but you get accustomed to having someone around, especially when you've been together over fifty years. Would she miss him or be at peace in having him gone (finally) from her life? She told him countless times, "I wish the hell you were dead." But by the time her wish became a reality, it was too late to matter. She had become a prisoner of her own infirmity. Mom's health was rapidly declining and she was just as trapped in her new widow role as he was when he battled cancer.

Mom told me that Dad had been dead for about a week when she woke to find him kneeling at the side of her bed, stroking her hand, and telling her everything would be all right. It gave her immense comfort. I believed her. Providence can be experienced by any of us when we take the time to connect with life's surroundings.

I sense there is a connection with loved ones after death. I had my own insightful moment that gave me assurance that Dad was at peace. A week after Dad's death I went back to work. But this particular morning, my daily routine fell out of sequence. I'd repeatedly heard on the radio a beautiful rendition of "Amazing Grace." That had been one of the songs chosen for Dad's funeral. I'd inevitably be stuck at the back behind a line of vehicles for at lease fifteen minutes at the railroad crossing watching the train as it slowly crawled down the tracks. This morning, I was the first car in line waiting at the crossing. Coincidently, for the first time the train flew through the crossing as Amazing Grace played on the radio. *Could that be Dad signaling me that he was at peace?* I don't expect anyone to appreciate the significance of three irrelevant occurrences coming together at the exact same moment that sparked a personal connection. That one act was more precious to me than anything I could conceive on my own. It gave me peace to move on, just as I believed Dad had.

MOM'S TURNING POINT

Now that Dad was gone, Mom's helplessness was very much a certainty and she knew her daughters were her only link for survival, but could she trust her girls to do right by her? Mom retained enough mental aptitude in maneuvering her daughters to carry out her demands. We each obediently resumed our positions and accepted our task, picking up where Dad left off.

After Dad died, Rose and Gail would not leave Mom's side, day or night. Both echoed, "I'll stay as long as you need me. You can count on me for anything." Mom whined, "JoAnn, I don't need them both hovering over me; I wish they'd leave me alone." However, she wouldn't tell them to leave. Instead, she chose to burden me with this request. I pointed out to my sisters, "You need to work out a schedule where one stays every other night, otherwise, you'll wear yourselves out. Besides, you're defeating the purpose by overlapping visits. Mom will adjust to living alone. She endured when Dad worked out of town. She'll definitely be needing you more down the road." But to no avail, they ignored my advice, and did as they saw fit. Just as I predicted, their boastful pledges to Mom quickly burned out. They mutually reneged on their promises. We had Mom's best interest at heart but we each had a different approach concerning her welfare.

My commitment to take care of Mom was disguised as half duty and half pity. I assumed after Dad's death her reasoning would come back into focus, but there was no compromise, no amount of rational thinking, or any degree of understanding. She remained trapped in this tug-of-war battle for so long that it was inconceivable she could switch gears and think differently about her family.

A week after Dad was buried, we rushed Mom to the emergency room under the pretense of a heart attack. We got the shock of our lives when the emergency room doctor told us the extent of Mom's illness. Basically, her lungs were spent. To our dismay, emergency trips to the hospital would become routine as we helplessly watched her health decline. The emergency room is a place to get patched up, not a place to be cured. There was nothing more they could do for her. Mom's condition was chronic and reduced to the point of needing oxygen 24/7, just like Dad. She was sent home and an oxygen machine became her constant companion.

Mom was seventy and even though her body was frail and her breathing showed sporadic signs of weakening, there was never a clear pattern to piece together. Yes, she was skinny but she ate like a horse, in addition, we were still dealing with her bipolar condition that kept her either hyper or docile. We should have picked up on her declining health sooner but we were so consumed with Dad's cancer that we didn't see she was going downhill. Did Dad know of Mom's illness or had he been left in the dark? Perhaps Mom hid her disease because she didn't want us hounding her to stop smoking or maybe she needed more time to accept her fate.

After several more visits to the emergency room, the staff began losing their patience with Mom. They showed little tolerance for a person who couldn't breathe yet refused to stop smoking. She began smoking at the age of fifteen and her habit increased to three packs of cigarettes a day for most of her adult life, predictably taking its toll on her health. Mom knew each cigarette added one more nail in her coffin, but she loved her smokes. She willfully vowed, "I'll never give em' up. They're my only enjoyment." Ya gotta die of something," became her (dying) motto. She couldn't resign herself to the reality of dying from a choice that had been made when she was a naive teen. The bad habit dispensed nothing more than a minute's pleasure, so with no one to blame but herself, she consciously decided to keep puffing away in spite of the warnings. A smoker knows when they've reached the point of no return. With no cure for her disease; she would progressively get worse.

It was Mom's turn to be pampered and cared for and it didn't come a moment too soon. She kept each one of us girls on our toes with specific demands she wanted carried out. It was expected of us: it was our duty. Rose was in charge of Mom's medication and sat with her at night, Gail cleaned her house, and I took care of her finances. We all cooked and ran errands for her while working and taking care of our own homes. Yet as committed as we were and with all our effort to make her comfortable, she intuitively kept us at a distance.

I made Mom an appointment with her doctor under the guise of learning the truth about her condition. That's when I realized Mom got more than medical treatment from her; she received an attentive ear while being spoon-fed attention without ridicule. The doctor's office had been Mom's sanctuary and the doctor, her confidant. This was Mom's way of escaping from her monstrous girls and getting the attention she craved. Mom introduced her doctor to me and said, "Remember, this is the one I told you about." I was once again humiliated; I felt my face getting hot. God only knew what distorted things she said about her family. Mom could tell her anything and everything and, believe me, she did.

Soon after Dad died, Mom asked me in a meek, pitiful voice, "Are you going to put me away?" She feared being committed, whether it was a nursing home or a psychiatric ward. Her query startled me, so I delicately tried to ease her mind, "No Mom, a nursing home is not in our plan. We promised Dad we would always take care of you. We want you to be safe and comfortable at home." It never sank in that she had always been taken care of. She agonized each time we took her somewhere, wondering if we were lying to her and if so, would the trip be her demise. She distressed over routine doctor visits, sheepishly asking, "Where are we going again? You sure you're not dropping me off at a home?" I tried to make light of her comments by laughing them off, but our loyalty held no merit, she believed we were conspiring against her. However, she had no choice but to lean on us for her care. *What in the hell was churning through that mind of hers?*

Mom wouldn't do the simplest task I asked of her, even though it was for her own good. I'd ask, "Please place all the mail in one spot. Use the basket on the kitchen counter." I explained, "I don't care if you open the mail, it's yours to open. I just don't want any important papers to get misplaced." This was a logical request, yet each time I would find the mail in a different place, any spot except where I asked her to put it. She was deliberately being uncooperative, but why? She was the one that asked me to help her with all the legal business.

Her paranoia had reawakened, nudging her to do the opposite of everything we asked while her mind increasingly distorted the truth. It became arduous trying to help her, especially when she fought you every step of the way. With Dad gone, she must have felt like the wolves were closing in, and her mind worked overtime to try and keep us at bay. It had to be exhausting, her broken mind doing battle against her daughter's advice. The more we tried to reassure Mom by telling her we loved her, the more guarded she became.

Nine months after Dad's death, my son Matthew got married. Mom was frail but promised Matt she wouldn't miss his big day. She seemed happy for both of them and excited to be a part of their celebration. I couldn't spend much time with Mom because I was running around like a chicken with my head cut off making sure things ran smoothly. Later I learned that Mom's feelings were hurt; she told everyone I had ignored her. But I hadn't left her alone; she had my other sisters to jump at her every whim. I could never please her.

Then I was told Mom had filled the ears of everyone around her with family smut. Here Mom sits at her grandson's wedding, surrounded by people she doesn't know and all she can talk about is her cruel father and her husband's infidelity. *My God, it's a celebration, not a damn therapy session. Why can't she enjoy the moment? For once, can you stop focusing on yourself and shut the hell up? Today isn't about poor Charlotte.* Shit. Another humiliating moment to try to explain away.

SHAME ON ME

After Dad's death, my resentment of having to take care of Mom consumed me. But I promised Dad I would take care of her, and my word was all I had left. I too, (like Dad) have resolve. My promise seemed so inadequate as pay back for all he sacrificed for us. I was mentally exhausted from Dad's lengthy illness. The burden of Mom's lifelong sickness and my conduct became spiteful at best. After all, I felt she hated me my whole life, only to endure an additional layer of misery (she) created after her mental breakdown. I loathed her vulgar comments and resented her vengeful disposition. I despised all the years of unpredictable moods, apathy, and her ungratefulness. I hadn't gotten over how she beat and belittled me or her abandonment at each milestone of my life. But most of all, I hated her unwillingness to try to get better. I finally came to the realization that if she hadn't changed by now, she never would, but it didn't stop me from worrying about her. This was when my anger intensified. I was just sick and tired of her crap!

Our relationship continued to be dysfunctional. It didn't matter if I tried to connect daughter to mother or woman to woman; it simply wasn't happening. I had the added burden of having to own up to being part of the problem. I had become skillful at finding fault with her. This was how I kept my sanity.

I hoped after all the years that something would snap her back into reason. Who in their right mind would want to live in constant bitterness, torment, and isolation? How naive of me to think Mom would magically change after Dad's death; after all, she had blamed him for all her misery. But not even Dad's death brought her out of her rut, from under a cloud, the ups, the downs, her illness, her depression, her hell, however you wanted to label it. No pills, prayers, therapy, or willpower could transform her mind into normal thinking. Decades of living with mental illness had nudged her into a fractured realm that fit like an old, comfortable, worn-out bathrobe that she had no intention of removing.

Mom was a pack rat, and she made matters worse by not picking up after herself. I walked in on Mom throwing her nightgown on the floor. I confronted her, "The hamper is right by your side; why don't you use it?" She retorted, "That's what I've got you girls for." It made no difference who she imposed on. I resented being used. She expected to be taken care of by Dad or us girls, and she was.

Again, the haunting belief that I might go crazy like her plagued me. My lowest feelings of Mom came to a head on the day Kathy came from Savannah to visit. I wasn't going to Moms'; I had spent so much time with her already, plus I felt she and Kathy needed some time alone. I definitely needed a break from the insanity, but Kathy begged me to come, saying she missed me, so I reluctantly drove over. Kathy's relationship with Mom wasn't much better than mine. She felt equally uncomfortable being alone with Mom. She had her share of horror stories about how Mom treated her. I kept Kathy abreast of Mom's physical and mental condition, as well as her unwillingness to cooperate. Kathy dreaded the three hour drive to Augusta. That's a long time to relive hurtful memories while not knowing what you will walk into.

Kathy hadn't been there long when Mom began showing signs of tension. She couldn't handle more than one person around her. I sensed her anger swelling as I tried to explain how to properly use her breathing equipment. With her deep cold stare penetrating right through me; her hostility spewed, "You think you know every goddamn thing; you're Hitler's preacher." She threw in my face, "I didn't ask for your help, so leave me the hell alone." No, she didn't ask me to help; she demanded my help. She's too spiteful to admit it. Bruised by another verbal attack, I realized our bond was never to be. Everything I had done for her since Dad's death meant nothing. I could never please her no matter how much support I demonstrated. It's time to concede; you and your Mom never got along to begin with. Nothing about me had changed in Mom's mind except that I grew from a filthy little ragamuffin into a self-righteous, know-it-all bitch. Damn, how much venom can one woman spew out of her frail, sick body?

It is a gut-wrenching feeling to do your best for someone, only to be ridiculed and looked down on with disdain. Did Mom resent my cutting in on her time with Kathy? Was she envious of the bond Kathy and I shared? Did she think we were about to gang up on her? Who knows what swims through her muddled mind and what in the hell does "Hitler's preacher" mean anyway? *When is her hating me going to end?* Every good intention I tried was met with contempt and resistance. In her mind, any deed appeared as if I was plotting against her and every suggestion implied I was putting her in harm's way. Nothing had changed except the passing of time. She still used her girls to lash out at for all her insecurities and misery.

Once again, I failed to stand up for myself. I began feeling physically sick, and I felt myself losing control, but I wasn't about to stay and give her another opportunity to verbally demoralize me. I'd be damned if she would see me cry. *Suck it up, JoAnn, they are only words. You're an adult. Why do you let her get to you? She doesn't have any power over you anymore. Don't forget you must respect your parents. Remember, she's crazy.*

I left abruptly with Kathy running behind. I was too mentally drained to pull myself together and only when I was out of Mom's sight did I burst into tears. I confided in Kathy, "I hate her. I understand she's ill, but I hate her." We both knew she wouldn't be on this earth much longer, but it would not be her death that saddened me; it would be my fear of reuniting with her after my own passing. As a Christian, I believe you reunite with loved ones after death, except how could that be if they despised you in this life? A lifetime of pain and rejection on earth was enough to endure, but to have to deal with her in the afterlife sent me into a tailspin of unimaginable despair. Through my sobbing, I reconciled that I couldn't sink any lower. *Am I going crazy too?*

I was suffocating in the promise I had made to Dad. I had long passed the call of duty with her. I wanted to scream, "You're sucking the life out of me!" It felt as if pieces of me were snapping off like over-burdened limbs, leaving piles of dead fragmented failures. My attitude toward Mom had grown disgraceful at best. Admitting how I felt about her was so unnatural that it made me sick with shame. *I'm going to implode with failure and guilt.* If I didn't get a grip, I feared I would loose my mind. With all the sincerity I could muster, I prayed to God for guidance and forgiveness. *Please God, don't let hate win. Let this nightmare end.* Soon after that incident, my prayer was answered.

A friend, Harriet Scarborough, shared two movie tickets with me for helping her raise money during a March of Dimes campaign. Her kind gesture in itself was a small miracle because I refuse to pay full price to see any movie. It was a cold Sunday in January and Lee was watching the Super Bowl so I invited my daughter-in-law, Cheryl, to the movies. *A Beautiful Mind* was playing and I knew by the previews that it was a true story about a man that had been diagnosed and treated for schizophrenia. I hoped to gain some insight about the disease, plus I applaud any movie based on someone's experiences. As I watched this man struggle with his inner demons, I realized this was what my mother must have gone through throughout her nervous breakdown. The scene where they administered the shock treatment brought back a ghastly feeling that had been buried deep inside since I was a teen. Mental illness in its perplexing form must be the most excruciating hell anyone experiences. The degree of torment suffered within a damaged mind cannot be measured; I've been told it's limitless. My hostility towards Mom had been crippling for so long that I had never thought about the emotional pain she endured. It was impossible for me to wrap my brain around her sickness. All those years she journeyed alone; she had to be terrified.

For years, my ignorance left me frightened that I would fall into the same world of insanity. What triggered her downfall? Was she ill before she married? Is her condition mostly her fault, Dad's fault, our fault? Could it happen to me? How much hell must you endure before you crack? Do I have the same gene? Will it attack me when I go through menopause? I can't explain how I held my composure, but as soon as the movie was over I bolted out the theater's side exit. I slid down the outside wall and sobbed uncontrollably with a pain so deep I couldn't speak. Cheryl, stunned by my emotional outburst ran to get the car, leaving me alone with my anguish. God took me in his mercy, and in a split moment, I felt the hate release from my body as understanding filled inside. Still sobbing, I thanked God for this moment of glorious sadness. *Grace comes into one's life as rarely and instantaneously as witnessing a falling star; both are equally spectacular.*

This was the saving grace I desperately needed to keep my promise to Dad. I finally had a clearer insight into why my mother acted the way she did. I lived too closely to the pain and hadn't stepped back far enough to understand the bigger picture. When I couldn't stand my behavior any longer, I prayed for God's mercy. How simple a process, and yet I spent so much time and energy fighting the enemy that I lost a large piece of myself along the way. If Mom had died before my prayer was answered, my life would have been forever altered. Would I have found the courage to come to terms with myself, the grace to forgive her, or the strength to move forward? I'll never know because I know I too have short comings.

MOM IS DYING

The tension between us had eased and I now had a calmer attitude when it came to helping Mom, but she still remained a handful. I eventually accepted that this had become Mom's way of life. And when I did, her behavior became less oppressive.

Her breathing had become more labored, but she still refused to use the breathing equipment properly. Trying to make her understand she shouldn't turn the oxygen any higher than three turned into a battle. The doctor made clear that higher did not imply healthier, and if she continued upping the oxygen level, her lungs would convert the oxygen into carbon monoxide and she would simply go to sleep and not wake up. I also called the technician in hopes his instructions would drive home the importance of not adjusting the settings. I went one step further and called Rose, who'd later be staying with Mom, and repeated the technician's instruction, "Rose, I didn't make the rule; please don't adjust the oxygen setting." I left Mom that Friday afternoon reassuring her, "Rose will be here soon, and Kathy is driving in from Savannah and will stay with you tomorrow." I had no intention of returning until Sunday; I needed a break.

When Kathy arrived, she called and mentioned that Mom seemed extremely groggy. Once again, Kathy asked me to drop by. She said she missed me and I missed her too, so I reluctantly made my way over about eleven-thirty. When I arrived, Mom wasn't alert, but I didn't think her behavior gave cause for alarm. After all, she had numerous days of lying down and not responding. I assumed she had a rough night and needed rest.

Kathy cooked lunch, but Mom was too weak to walk to the table, so I brought her a plate. She ate the entire hamburger and then fell back on the sofa. When I tried to raise her arm it fell limp to her side. Kathy's visit, the time of day, and lunch should have been enough to stimulate her. She didn't act overly medicated, more like being in a deep sleep. Only then did my instincts prompt me to check the setting on the oxygen machine. Someone had turned the control to its highest level. I immediately turned it down and called the technician. He cautioned, "Watch her, but since you caught it in time, her drowsiness will probably wear off by late afternoon; she should be okay."

Mom's paranoia would lead her to do the exact opposite of what she was told not to do, but this went beyond explanation. Had Mom tried to take her life again? Grieving Dad's death and dealing with her declining health made it understandable to want to give up. Mom didn't have anyone to confide in like Dad had with Hospice. Her only companion was her inner voice coaxing her to retreat to her safe place. Mom wouldn't admit to changing the controls.

I called Rose around 3:00 P.M. and told her what had happened. I asked if she had adjusted the setting. Rose insisted she hadn't. She said she left early that morning allowing Mom to sleep. I was curious why Rose hadn't phoned to check on Mom. They talked multiple times each day. Perhaps she also needed a break. Another baffling incident that we never mentioned again.

Winter was ending and the fear of Mom catching the flu had waned but she wasn't totally out of the woods. She was still losing weight and didn't have the strength to fight off as much as a cold. Her oxygen needed to be increased. The mere tempo of her breathing consumed the largest part of her energy. The doctor suggested the breathing machine be moved from the living room into her bedroom. Since each treatment had to be taken first thing in the morning and last thing at night. Having the machine close by would make her routine easier. All she had to do was roll over and place the damn mask on. It made perfect sense but Mom wouldn't hear of it, again, anything you suggested would be misconstrued by her distorted mind.

The tension between us girls began to mount. We each had our own perceptions of what was best for Mom while continuously at odds concerning her care. Mom was being coddled by one, scolded by another, leaving the third daughter caught in the middle. Mom's unwillingness to take her medicine properly prompted arguments between us: who would monitor her daily dosage and oversee her refills, what she should and shouldn't eat, did she really need to bathe each day? Should she be left alone? We stayed divided on issues concerning her overall welfare: should we hide her car keys or sell her car? Should she change doctors? Yes, she should stop driving at this stage of her life, and no to changing doctors. How can we get her to stop smoking? She should stop smoking, at least when using the oxygen. Rose's soft heart and shared addiction assured Mom that she would never run out of smokes. Rose rationalized, "It would be so cruel to take away her only pleasure."

Mom became so frail that her doctor suggested she take a nutrient enriched drink to build her strength back, but his concerns were refused. In brash defiance Mom insisted, "It tastes like shit." When it came to Mom's well-being; the more we disagreed and the more we turned on one another, the more Mom lapped up all the misguided attention. Clearly we were all out of sync. As frail as Mom was, she still kept conflicts brewing.

There were endless toss-ups trying to decide if someone needed to spend the night, and if so, which one stayed last. We each worked and had an excuse for not staying. Kathy and Ricky lived three hours away. I lived and worked across town with a family to look after. But to be honest, I couldn't tolerate the smoke that inundated my lungs. Gail lived and worked across town with two dogs to care for. Rose lived three miles from Mom, but needed to focus on her teenage daughter.

Rose complained, "I can't sleep on Dad's old mattress; it hurts my back. You'll have to buy a new mattress if you expect me to sleep over." Rose then suggested, "Move in with me during the week and let JoAnn and Gail take care of you on the weekends." That's when I stepped in, "Rose, Mom's too ill to bounce between houses. It'll wear her out shuffling back and forth, packing her medicines, breathing equipment, and clothes for each stay. Exactly how would this benefit Mom? She'll still be alone during the day while you're at work. "I brought to Mom's attention, "You'll be at Rose's mercy for your every need." What irony. I knew they could only tolerate each other's peculiarities in small doses until one would inevitably grate on the other's nerves.

Rose repeatedly planted grandiose ideas into Mom's head by persistently reciting, "Mom, let's take one last vacation. You love the beach and it would do you good to get away. I'll drive; we'll take your car." She also tried to convince Mom to sell her home and move to an apartment. Again I held strong in my pledge to Dad and put my foot down on her half-baked plan. It was maddening trying to keep both of them focused; they were like two peas in a pod. I'd read that after a spouse's death, you shouldn't tackle any life-changing decisions for at least one year. It made no sense to leave a home that was paid for. Besides, Mom was too frail to withstand a vacation or be uprooted from her familiar setting. *Were we each doing what seemed best for Mom or what was best for ourselves?*

Another layer of disease surfaced: senile dementia. She was getting harder to handle. The time had come; leaving two choices: be admitted to a nursing home or hire a lady to sit with her during the day. Agonizing over my promise to Dad, I would try to keep her in her own home where she would be more content. We were calling Mom several times during the day and were taking turns caring for her nights and weekends. Between delivering her medicine, dropping off food, and sitting with her, she wasn't left alone for very long. She wore the three of us out with unbending demands, false alarms in the middle of the night, calling our workplaces with nit-picky requests, not following the doctor's orders, refusing to use her breathing equipment properly, not taking her meds accurately, and wetting the bed. She exhibited no effort to help herself.

Reluctantly, Mom agreed I could hire a sitter. She fixed Mom's breakfast and lunch, and since Mom loved to be waited on, you would think having someone to keep her company would be right up her alley. Only it didn't work out, possibly because it was my idea or because Mom resented having to pay for the sitter out of her pension check, but it was a lot cheaper than a nursing home. True to her nature, Mom turned this arrangement into a fiasco. She wouldn't eat the meals the sitter prepared and would insist, "You can leave early today; I'm doing fine." It came as no shock that Mom didn't want her. She remained belligerent at every turn. I couldn't make Mom understand that if she didn't let the lady stay and help, then her worst fear would come to pass. So we dismissed the sitter. Mom's doctor mentioned, "Mrs. Hoover couldn't survive in a nursing home given her unique personality." I knew what she was alluding to. Together with the doctor's remark and my promise to Dad; I delayed thinking about her dilemma for the moment.

A neighbor asked if her ladies' church group could visit Mom. Any visitors by this time made Mom happy. They shared cookies and prayer and in return, Mom shared an earful of her lifelong heartaches.

Mom received meals-on-wheels five days a week, but other than drinking the half pint of milk, most of the food went to waste. I begged Mom to cancel the service but she wouldn't. She looked forward to the volunteer's visits. Otherwise, it would be just another boring day. It's a superb organization that depends heavily on volunteers and runs on a shoestring budget. But honestly, with so many shut-ins on restricted diets and multiple medications, they have no choice but to serve bland food from a limited menu.

Another insane habit Mom had was smoking while wearing the oxygen tube in her nose. She would light up with no worries. Time and again I tried to explain, "When you light a cigarette, the oxygen could ignite and catch your tube, face, hair, or clothes on fire." It was hurtful to have someone you love respond with an illogical sarcastic reply, "Well, I haven't blown myself up yet." I mockingly replied, "No, not yet, and I hope I'm not around when you do." I knew Mom had been smoking in bed. The ashtray on the nightstand overflowed with cigarette butts. Her bed was littered with empty cigarette packs, used tissues, and candy wrappers.

Toward the end, I didn't have the heart to scold her. It was her only pleasure left and the damage had been done; no amount of concern could stop or save her. She was only going to do as she pleased anyway. Mom's behavior had been childlike for so long, but after Dad's death, she quickly went downhill. Remember the old saying, "Once an adult; twice a child."

As her disease intensified, her living space in the den was reduced to an thirty foot circumference. The clutter consisted of Dad's recliner, two chairs, an ottoman, a coffee table, two end tables, and a sofa that frequently doubled as her bed. She had at her disposal the phone, phone book, and her personal address book. One end table held a lamp, medicine, a coffee cup that stayed half full, a watered-down glass of tea, various pieces of jewelry, a hairbrush, ink pens, stamps, eyeglasses, and makeup. Her purse was nestled on the side of the sofa where she sat. She kept at least three pairs of bedroom slippers and two pairs of loafers under the end table. There was at least two weeks' worth of newspapers surrounding her feet. I'd fuss, "Mom, if you don't pick these papers up, you're going to fall and break your neck." It made no impact.

The sofa had throw pillows, a blanket, sweater, two bed pillows, socks, the TV remote, VCR remote, VHS movies, and a large box of tissues with a cluster of used ones that were scattered haphazardly. Placed within arm's reach were half-empty boxes of snacks, candy, cookies, and a salt shaker. Ignored piles of unopened junk mail, store fliers, rubber bands, plus numerous insignificant items all distributed arbitrarily on the chairs and sofa. Mom guarded at her side three cartons of cigarettes and disposable lighters. Each ashtray overflowed with cigarette butts that emitted a stale oppressive odor. This reaffirmed Mom could never give up her smokes. Scattered around were takeout bags from dozens of fast food restaurants that Rose had dropped off containing packets of sugar, salt, pepper, condiments, straws, and plastic utensils. She wouldn't pick up or throw anything away, even though a trash can occupied a space by her feet.

Easter came early that year and Mom kept asking me what we were planning for the occasion. I agonized over how I could get out of spending another holiday with her, so I kept putting her off. I was ashamed of myself once again and struggled with the promise I made to take care of her. I had come a long way with my perspective towards Mom, though I still had a lot of healing ahead of me. With a better understanding of her mental state, I honestly forgave her for the most part, but I still struggled with the "why" of it all. Now wasn't the time to be selfish.

There wasn't much cause for celebration. I dreaded having to drag my family to her dismal house, but my inner conflict screamed 'duty' and I couldn't disappoint her. I knew this could be her last Easter so at the last minute I put a dinner together. But for now, I had to focus on another crisis. Once more, Mom had to be rushed to the emergency room, only this time by ambulance.

They went through the usual checklist. They took x-rays of her lungs, started an IV drip, followed with a breathing treatment. I stepped into the hall and I saw an intern showing Mom's lung x-ray to who I assumed was his son. In a superior tone he explained, "This is what your lungs will look like if you take up the nasty habit of smoking." How dare he use my mother's x-ray as a scare tactic for his own crusade. Yes, he deals with illness every day but where was his compassion? This was my mom, and as a human being she deserved more respect than was given to her. It was a Catholic hospital for Christ's sake. I wanted to report him for breach in ethics and nail him to the wall for violation of the privacy act. But truthfully it hit hard, knowing she had damaged her body and there would be no cure. In Mom's era it was *oh so glamorous* to smoke. All her movie star idols lit up, so why not her? No one knew then the hidden dangers in tobacco. Too expect Mom to give up the (addictive) habit after fifty-plus years was improbable. The dangers of smoking held little consequence at this point. Her life as she knew it was over; she had long passed the point of no return.

The doctor asked, "Mrs. Hoover, how often do you use the inhaler?" She timidly answered, "Three times a day." His voice turned curt, "You should only be using the inhaler sparingly. You're too dependent on it." As he walked out the room, he instructed us to take her home. I thought Mom needed to spend the night in the hospital for observation but the doctor seemed more irritated at Mom than worried. Why didn't Mom's excessive use of the inhaler or her physical frailty sound an alarm? *I think she's dying.*

I caught her doctor in the hall and asked, "How much time do you think Mom has?" I had to know; my head was telling me she wouldn't make it through the night, that is, until the doctor relayed his apathetic prognosis, "She could live at least two years." I was stunned.

Each return visit from the hospital left Mom weaker. We had no choice but to spend more time with her leaving us drained. That Saturday, Gail stayed with Mom, changed her bedding, and thoroughly cleaned the house. I stayed the next day. When I entered her house, it looked like a bomb had exploded in the den. I knew Gail had just cleaned so I scolded her, "Mom if you've got the strength to mess up, you've got the strength to straighten up. What happened?" She meekly replied, "I can't find my inhaler." Had it been accidentally thrown out when Gail cleaned yesterday? Mom was panicky; she relied heavily on it to breathe and she couldn't get another one until the doctor's office opened on Monday. I wish I hadn't yelled at her, but she acted like a child, so I treated her like one.

I cooked a hearty dinner and had enough food for lunch the next day, except Mom wouldn't eat leftovers. This blew my mind. Mom was too sick to cook, yet refused to eat anything leftover, not even the meals brought over by Aunt LeeEllen. She only ate what you cooked that day. The remainder went to waste. How can you be that picky when you are dependent on someone to bring your meals? Was that her way of having control and insuring one of us would have to drop by each day? She gobbled down dinner and her appetite gave me hope. I washed dishes, straightened up the mess she made, but I still hadn't found her inhaler.

I convinced Mom she needed a bath. As I washed her hair, I couldn't hold back my tears. Seeing her bones protruding beneath her skin thrust a jolt of panic through me that took my breath away. She looked so used up; betrayed by her body. By late afternoon, she had tired out and her only concern was, "Did you call Rose? Are you sure she's coming? When?" I knew she had enough of me for one day so I reluctantly decided to leave. I reassured her that Rose was on her way. I had an ominous feeling she was slipping away and honestly I didn't want to leave, but the day had worn both of us out. She needed to rest. I pulled out the drive as Rose pulled in.

My nerves were wearing thin and I was running out of ideas on how to care for her. Yes, her health was declining; still I couldn't shake the doctor's disturbing prognosis of her living two years. None of us wished Mom dead, but it didn't seem possible she would make it six months.

I still have a mental picture of Mom reaching for a tissue to wipe her runny nose, fumbling to keep the oxygen tube from falling out of her nostrils, and simultaneously puffing on a cigarette. This in turn triggered a coughing spell from choking on the smoke that had made its way down the wrong pipe. Just as her living space was shrinking, so was each breath of air she tried to claim. She had difficulty trying to carry on a conversation. Helpless and heartbroken, I knew I couldn't make it through two more years the way she demanded attention. I might have to go back on my promise and place her in a nursing home. I couldn't think beyond a day at a time.

By Monday, Mom hadn't improved, so Rose took her to her primary doctor for a second opinion and I assumed to get another inhaler. Again, Mom's cry for help was brushed off and her doctor did nothing except send her home without an inhaler. Why didn't the doctor see she desperately needed it? Rose should've demanded Mom be given one. Rose asked the doctor how long she thought Mom had and her doctor said she could live two more years. Damn, two doctors within three days of each other echoed the same prognosis. Perhaps the emergency room doctor's report had something to do with her decision. They didn't prescribe any new medication or change her previous medicine. They didn't write a prescription for an inhaler, nor would they concede that her time was limited. *Were we overreacting?*

That night, Mom was getting more agitated and things were beginning to spin out of control. Convinced her doctor was neglecting her, and if she didn't feel any better by the next day, she would change doctors. I promised Mom I would make an appointment on that Tuesday, but until I could talk to the doctor, all I could do was try to reassure Mom things would be okay, but my sincerity held no merit. Mom was furious at Rose for not getting her another inhaler. But the insanity being, Rose had tried to give Mom one of her own new inhalers with the understanding that Mom could replace it when she got a new prescription. The exchanging of inhalers didn't make sense to Mom. She couldn't think straight. Adamantly she lashed out, "Rosemary, you're not taking my new inhaler." Rose was caught in the crossfire.

I regretted letting Rose take Mom to her appointment. I should have taken her myself. Tuesday arrived; I called the doctor's office and was told she was off for the day. She would be in Wednesday, so I made the appointment for Wednesday at 9 A.M. This made the fourth day Mom had been without an inhaler. I called Mom back at 10:30 A.M.

and gave her the new appointment time. By now she was livid with the doctor and Rose. Mom couldn't be consoled. I believed we'd be taking another trip to the emergency room. I called back around noon but she didn't answer. I wasn't concerned at that point. I thought she might be in the bathroom or just not answering to spite Rose. As sick as she was, there was still enough hell in her to cause clashes. I got busy at work and it wasn't until 3:00 P.M. that I tried again, still no answer. Now, I'm worried.

Lee was about to get off work so I asked him to drive by and check on her. Lee called me back. "Jo, something terribly bad has happened; you need to get here quick." Paralyzed with fear, I needed a co-worker to drive me to Mom's house. I walked into the den and immediately saw Mom lying dead on the floor in a flimsy dirty cotton nightgown. Her eyes were open and her mouth held a yawning pose as if she was gasping for air. By her position on the floor, it seemed she tried to get up and instantly collapsed, perhaps from a heart attack. I thought, "It must have happened in an instant." I don't think she suffered. I can take comfort in that, but it broke my heart that she had died alone. I took a blanket and covered her up. Rose had already arrived; sobbing and telling me how their last conversation erupted in a quarrel over the inhaler, and how much she regretted being curt to Mom. I snapped, "Stop right now Rose; it's over! Don't go there." You have to understand, Mom was always at odds with one of us. It just happened that Rose was her last target. Rose didn't need to be saddled with any guilt. The madness had to end.

Dad's family was very supportive in spite of all Mom had put them through over the years. People began coming into the house, and I was embarrassed at the mess the house was in. I couldn't straighten up until the coroner arrived and pronounced Mom (officially) dead. From an outsider's eye, the home would appear to have been ransacked; only that was how Mom lived. I'd like to say she was eccentric, that would sound more mystifying, but she lived like a hoarder; that was her normal order.

Lee silently stood with the policeman in the kitchen. My heart broke knowing he was the one who found Mom. The policeman had no expression, just another day on the job. It felt like déjà vu, having to make funeral arrangements all over again.

Looking back on her behavior, this is what I believe happened. Mom had been in a down mood for months and hadn't exerted much energy therefore utilizing minimal breaths. Five days prior, her bipolar condition changed; causing her opposite mood to kick in. If she hadn't gone into her up swing, she might have lingered six more months. But her frail lungs couldn't keep up with the demand for oxygen that her hyper body needed, and without the assistance of an inhaler, her lungs simply gave out. I realized I'm not qualified to give a medical opinion, but it makes more sense than what the emergency room physician or her primary doctor assessed. I found where she had written down her doctor's appointment for the next day. I can only guess she died between after we talked and the first time she didn't answer the phone. She weighed eighty-seven pounds.

Mom died Easter week and was buried on Good Friday. Easter Sunday was spent at her house with my siblings dividing her personal belongings and eating takeout from Burger King. How ironic. My dreaded duty was never to be. I didn't have to cook a big meal or spend the day with Mom, but I was still tied to her life and my heartache was far from over.

Once again I asked Rev. Faulkner, for his services. He delivered Mom's eulogy with the same sincerity and respect that he had delivered at Dad's funeral. Alan expressed empathy for Mom's battle with her illness and demons, and shared a belief that Mom had now found peace.

I previously had asked Alan to please not portray either parent as a saint at their funerals. I carried guilt for Dad's past behavior and I felt a deep shame concerning Mom's mental illness. I've attended many funerals where it was apparent the person officiating the service had never met the deceased, yet it didn't stop them from portraying admiration, making the connection of eulogy and the deceased an awkward encounter. I knew differently; their lives were just as flawed as my parents' were, and the artificial praise concerning the deceased's life fell on deaf ears. Maybe it's stated out of respect, or denial, or as a final act of love for the departed. Perhaps it's a way to bury the person's shortcomings with their body. *Who knows?* I couldn't condone that type of rhetoric; It would be hypocritical, and who was I trying to fool? The relatives and friends who attended my parents' funerals, probably knew more about their turbulent lives than I did. My parents were human, they stumbled many times and now they are both dead. I could do nothing more for them except try to validate their lives with an honest admission of their struggles and triumphs. I felt the power of God's love and forgiveness at both funerals.

I'm sorry, Mama, one of us wasn't with you in the last moments of your life. I'm so sorry you died alone. How eerie, how ironic, so many times you wished the hell you were never born, and many times you wished the hell we had never been born. Maybe it was better this way. But you deserved more from life than you received, you just never believed you did. I hope you now realize you were loved. I pray you, too, have found peace.

SHUG' IT
AIN'T OVER YET

I began the wearisome task of sorting through all of my parents' legal papers, personal possessions, and all the nonsensical clutter that goes with cleaning out a home. I grappled with how drawn out a lifetime of imprints can be; accumulating pictures, knickknacks, furniture, dishes, tools, and everything else along the way, only for death to mercilessly dismantle their existence in the course of a few months. The house is now emptied yet the interior appears smaller in size, but that damn smell of smoke still lingers. I walked through the bleak rooms and try to envision them sitting in their favorite chairs but their images are beginning to weaken. I sense a wave of dread; if I were to blink, they would disappear right before my eyes. I search each room needing a voice to speak out and assure me they are together, but each room remains silent. Instead, unwanted memories diligently nudge from every corner they had once loitered in. It's time to put their struggle to rest. Whatever I am longing for will never be found here. Face facts JoAnn; it's over. I can't correct mistakes, speak any last words, or cry out about anything that had been eating away at me. Wishing I had been there for both of them more at the end saddens me still. I saw them going downhill, but I battled with the mental angst; maybe it wouldn't come to pass, it can't be happening now. I have no strength to cope with the unknown; How stupid of me to believe their time wouldn't run out until they got their life in order. They slipped away; all is final for everyone involved, not just for the departed. Thinking about death is too painful, too final, too obscure. I didn't have the heart to imagine life without them, even though there were many times I tried.

I must apologize to my siblings for the times I lashed out, especially when they didn't agree with my way of thinking or how I did things that concerned my parents. I tried to do right for our parents while nursing my own wounds. I now realize caring for someone doesn't automatically make you absolute in your judgment or excuse various decisions. I regret some choices that involved my parents, but in the end, I was able to embrace my promises, and when night came, I could lay my head down with a clear conscience. My burden and conflict had ended. My siblings must take their own journey in their own time.

Odd how recollections of little significance will cross your mind. One thing that struck me about Mom's softer side was that she never threw away a single card that had been given to her. I filled three trash bags full of cards from everyone and every occasion. Like her life, they weren't in any order; just cluttered and ignored. I found her school autograph keepsake and inside she had written that her favorite book was Anne of Green Gables. She never shared this nugget of pleasure with her girls, weaving another emotional divide between us. She didn't know I loved that book too. And Dad, I remember how he refused to look at anyone lying in a coffin. He'd say, "I'd rather remember em' how I knew them."

While cleaning out, I ran across five baby books tucked away in a drawer. The hospitals gave each new mom a book to record their baby's legal name, date of birth, height, weight, and the progress made during each milestone. The printed birth announcement, along with keepsakes of the lock of hair and the first tooth were safely tucked within a small envelope to be forever cherished. I found my older sister, Rosemary's book and one for each of my younger sisters, Kathy and Gail. There were two for my brother, Ricky; *weird*. Mine should have been included but it was missing.

I know I had one; I had often looked at them when I was young. Mine was made of soft pink pastel leather, and on the front was etched a chubby, pink-cheeked baby wearing a cloth diaper, and an oversized white lace bonnet and holding a pink rattler. My birth picture was glued to the first page. All I can conclude is in a fit of rage over something I said or did, Mom must have thrown it away. Mom could be very vengeful if she thought she could hurt you. I found my birth certificate, so at least I know I was born. That's all I have from my childhood. *This will be the last time you hurt me Mom, but not the last time I will cry.*

After Mom's death, her cousin Margie confirmed that Mom had been truthful in describing her dad's brutality. Margie recalled her uncle's temper and admitted she wasn't allowed to visit Mom when he was home. Given that it was extremely harrowing for Mom growing up, why did she allow her children to be subject to the same misery? Instead of Mom emulating her mother's tenderness, she gravitated to her dad's cold-heartedness, only to repeat his unfeeling deeds. Each decision regarding her kids was channeled through her perverse state of mind with no replica of the suffering we endured or the consequences her actions created. Behavior is learned at a very early age but we have a deep perceptive in the difference between right and wrong. Ultimately, we are solely accountable for each decision we make. *Or are we?*

It's a jolt to think, just because they're gone from this life doesn't mean you won't be upset by them any longer. That's simply not true.

Death doesn't erase past behavior. In fact, incidents will surface long after their body has been lowered into the ground. Months after their passing, I was still finding out things that left me mortified. My parents' boorish conduct was influenced by liquor and mental illness. I knew I couldn't clean up their mistakes but I was sick of being humiliated by their conduct.

A relative rushed over as soon as they heard about Mom's death. With a room full of people and Mom dead on the floor she blurted out, "Did you know Charlotte had my husband arrested?" Wow, I knew Mom was vindictive, but that news flash took me aback. Shocked and embarrassed by her outburst, all I could muster was a weak submission, "No, I never knew that." I quickly turned away thinking to myself, "Could you shout any louder? Why in the hell are you telling me about this now? When did Mom do it? Why did Mom do it? What do you think Mom can do about it now? What was I supposed to do about it? *It's not my problem, but you just made it my shame.*"

A short time after Dad's death, I was helping a new customer with his banking. I asked his employment, and he stated that he worked for the railroad. I reiterated that my dad retired from there after forty-two years of service. For a brief moment, I felt proud, then he asked Dad's name. I told him. He didn't acknowledge knowing Dad; in fact, he gave no response whatsoever. I was waiting for, "Oh yes, I knew him, he was a hard working man," or, "Yes, I'm sorry for your loss; he will be missed." Nothing but his deep callous stare united with dead silence left me feeling chastised and humiliated. Could he be one of the bosses Dad had harassed beyond annoyance late at night when he was drunk?

Another shocking moment came when a black couple entered my office. I had been their personal banker for twenty-plus years. We developed a connection and shared a mutual fondness for fishing. In the course of our conversation I mentioned my dad had recently died and they reverently asked his name. When I told them, the expression on both of their faces coupled with their knee-jerk response of leaning back and almost falling out of their chairs, sent me once again into an instant state of shame. They acknowledged they knew Dad, and that many times he had gotten drunk and passed out at their house. Why they thought I needed to know that tidbit of information went beyond discreet. What did they expect me to say? How could I respond to something that I knew nothing about or had any control over? My mind was racing with so many questions, but I couldn't bring myself to ask a single one. I was taken aback to have heard what I did, and horrified what more they might reveal. I bet they witnessed plenty of Dad's crude behavior. How long had they known each other? They seemed to be kind, normal folks to me, so what tied them to my rowdy father? It was too raw in my mind; I couldn't connect the dots.

The couple quickly collected themselves and left in a rush. I don't know which one of us was more stunned; me for learning about Dad's shenanigans or them realizing I was his daughter. I guess they figured they had spilled enough dirt for one day. For the first time in my life, I was speechless. Damn, I probably won't see them again; I've lost two good friends. Who else is out there privy to smut about my parents that's going to catch me off guard and leave me frozen in my tracks? Stop apologizing for their stumbles and feeling guilty for their behavior. The majority of us have plenty we wish we could erase from our past.

It is not normal to be ashamed of your parents' behavior, but I was. Even after their deaths, I was embarrassed by the lingering stigma of Mom's mental illness, and I detested Dad's weakness for being a womanizer and a drunk. I concealed my sorrow while I navigated through life, but it was only after my parents' deaths that I could absorb the perplexity of my family's convoluted threads. There are no flawless people.

A TAPESTRY OF TRUTH

Carrying emotional pain throughout one's life is vastly exhausting, yet there are plenty of lessons to be learned if you don't let hate, malice, or ignorance destroy you. The past doesn't transcend into an excuse for you to repeat the same behavior; it can only change through recognition. I must be willing to accept why things fell into place as they did if I expect peace in my life. If not, I risk drowning in an abyss of melancholy. I must keep striving to learn, forgive, love, and appreciate life, but these are challenging sentiments to conform to if your spirit has been wounded. I cope by clinging to the theory *things could always be worse.* It is my constant battle, but one I do not intend to lose.

Why my parents remained together was a mystery in itself. Their bickering got on each other's nerves up until the end. Was it out of love or duty that they stayed together? Had they grown too tired and sick to make a change so late in their lives? How do you stay with someone that long and not have some kind of connection? I assume many reasons. For all the years my parents quarreled and all the hell they put each other through, they unknowingly accumulated fragments from life that cemented a bond felt only by them, a smile, a look, or a memory from out of the blue that held their marriage together. Masked with secrets, their commitment to each other proved just as strong as love. *Isn't caring for someone and loving someone the same?*

If I told you my parents loved each other, you would think I was delusional or in denial. It was only after they both died that I read Dad's memorial book from his funeral. I was taken aback by what Mom had written on the first page: a love letter to Pat: "God gave us both a gift when we met each other. When you died, Pat, I lost a friend, my lover, my husband, and the father of our children. I look forward to being with you and God, Jesus, and the Holy Ghost whenever my time comes. I love you and always will, God bless you, dear one," signed, Charlotte. Dad had been her only love. This was her way of connecting from deep within her heart. So why did she hurt him so? Were all the contemptible things she said to him her wounded heart fighting back? I was lost for words as I read her sincere devotion to him, when in reality their marriage played out so differently.

There wasn't a fairy-tale ending for Charlotte or Herbert; their life read more like a tragic 1930's romance novel. Mom poured her soul out to Dad on a piece of paper that he would never read, but these are her words and I can't begin to interpret her inner self. I had observed a hint of Dad's affection each time he signed an anniversary or birthday card: To Charlotte, Love always, Pat. It's true, a relationship between a man and a woman is just that, between the two of them.

There are just as many secrets as there are souls taken to the grave and for whatever reason, the ones left behind assume a vexing obligation to unravel their past, yearning for truth, and peace of mind. It helps you get on with living instead of being stagnated with unanswered questions or burdened guilt. But many times, the answers are forever lost, like drops of rain that dissipate into the earth. Mustn't let the unknown consume you. It's how you adapt to the past that will open your eyes into a clearer logic. *Is this where forgiveness begins to take over?*

If I am going to ponder the impact my childhood had on my life, then I must accept responsibility for my own actions as well. I can't sling arrows at others if I can't acknowledge my own shortcomings. The fundamental reason for forgiving my parents meant, above anything else, I could move forward without acrimony. I had to understand where their behavior came from...*sounds simple.* The more I learned, the more I understood. The more I understood, the more I forgave. The more I forgave, the less the pain was for me, and the more my heart ached for them. It was not until I put myself in their shoes and tried to understand the motives behind their actions that I came to terms with why I felt and reacted the way I did. By the time I learned the bits and pieces about their upbringing, I realized they weren't shown any outwardly form of affection either.

What I salvaged from my past was a deep consciousness that I was loved, though time and again it was disguised as duty. There is no earth-shattering reasoning to this thought, it's more about leaning on my understanding of how they took care of us. They did their best to provided us with the basics in life and protect us from the outside world, until their own world fell apart. Their journey began out of step and they never achieved a natural rhythm.

One ill-fated reality remains; I wish I had found the courage to let them know in spite of their secret marriage date, it wouldn't have altered my love for them. We've all been bruised at one time or another by the very ones we love. Did they realize that I never abandoned them, especially when they needed help? I hope so.

You believe life will get easier, and hope it does but, I understand there are things I will never have the answers to, some things I must let go of, things I needed to come to terms with, and hurtful things I will never forget, while gratefully embracing the life that is uniquely my own.

I try to make the best of my life by reading self-help books. The ones that help me are, *Believing In Myself* and *Days of Healing* by both Earnie Larsen and Carol Hegarty. They are written for the masses recovering from alcohol and drug abuse, but for me, their messages hit home, helping me to move forward. Mom and Dad did their best, and for this, I am sad and grateful.

When I feel overwhelmed by the perplexity of life, I step back and draw on the image of a tapestry prompting my uncertainties to be put into perspective. The back reveals a quagmire of multicolored strings that are tangled, crisscrossed, knotted, cut, worn, split, and frayed with various lengths curving in every direction that form an utter mess. However, the flawless, colorful, exquisite front of a tapestry symbolizes the essence of humanity exhibiting purpose, strength, love, beauty, and unity representing each individual's random purpose in life. In spite of our imperfections, we mesh into a world full of caring, lively, proud, complicated, determined, and forgiving people. I realize the years ahead will hold many unforeseen struggles. I pray this lesson will carry me through because there is no escape from heartache.

My quest initially was for the *truth*, and truthfulness isn't mysterious or sensational. It's more of a noble and satisfying achievement. It led me to understanding. I had to keep moving forward, and that's when I stumbled onto forgiveness that took me beyond my goal, I found peace. Think about it, truth goes hand in hand with forgiveness and peace. With a clearer mind, I strive for closure.

I won't dance around my past any longer. I have chosen to embrace my life and learn from each experience. As I come full circle with my feelings, I realize the adversities throughout my journey have truly made me a stronger person. I found within me the courage to break the cycle of abuse. In retrospect, perhaps the greatest obstacle I had to overcome was finding love for my mother. THANKS BE TO GOD!

ACKNOWLEDGMENTS

There are many people who, over the years, have been my saving grace. Thanks to my sisters, Rose and Kathy, who continually give me support and unconditional love, when all the while grappling with their own private hell. Our common thread: not to wallow in self-pity or let our past destroy us. I love them so. I wish them peace.

I am grateful for my friends, Nancy Dansby and Lorraine Jensen, for putting up with me for so long. They kept me on track as I struggled through each drama.

Thank you, Jesse, for being a true friend to Mom.

To Rev. Alan Faulkner, a friend in Christ. You have my heartfelt appreciation for the kindness and candor you showed my family. I value the generous support given to me from Mrs. Elizabeth Estes and her writing group. Thank you, to my friends Drew Davis and Sharon Schroeder for their unselfish encouragement and help.

To Sandra Skinner, my sister-in-law, who helped me get through many rough episodes by listening to my endless cries for help, knowing at different times I was hanging on to my sanity by a thread.

I deeply appreciate everyone's encouragement when I felt like giving up on this book.

Thanks, Daniel, you done good...

Thanks Matthew, I've always believed in your art...

CPSIA information can be obtained
at www.ICGtesting.com
Printed in the USA
LVHW021501300720
661941LV00015B/528